1895

CARNEGIE LIBRARY

PITTSBURGH

PRESENTED BY

ANONYMOUS

Values in t

WITHDRAWN
FROM THE COLLECTION
CARNEGIE LIBRARY OF PITTSBURGH

| CLP-Main | |

THE CARNEGIE
LIBRARY OF
PITTSBURGH

Social Sciences Department

DEMCO

Sociology and Economics
Controversy and Integration

AN ALDINE DE GRUYTER SERIES OF TEXTS AND MONOGRAPHS

SERIES EDITORS
PAULA ENGLAND, *University of Arizona*
GEORGE FARKAS, *University of Texas, Dallas*
KEVIN LANG, *Boston University*

James Burk

Values in the Marketplace

The American Stock Market
Under Federal Securities Law

JUL 10 1992

KF
1070
·B87
1992

Aldine de Gruyter • New York

SOCIAL SCIENCES
THE CARNEGIE LIBRARY OF PITTSBURGH

About the Author

JAMES BURK is Associate Professor, Department of Sociology, Texas A&M University. Dr. Burk serves as Consulting Editor for the *American Journal of Sociology,* and is a frequent referee and contributor for major journals. He is author of *Morris Janowitz on Social Organization and Social Control.*

Copyright © 1988 by Walter de Gruyter & Co., Berlin.
All rights reserved, including those of translation into foreign languages. No part of this book may be reproduced in any form—by photoprint, microfilm, or any other means— nor transmitted or translated into a machine language without written permission from the publisher.

First paperbound edition: 1992

published by

ALDINE DE GRUYTER
A division of Walter de Gruyter, Inc.
200 Saw Mill River Road
Hawthorne, New York 10532

LIBRARY OF CONGRESS CATALOGING-IN-PUBLICATION DATA

Burk, James, 1948–
    Values in the marketplace : the American stock market under
federal securities law / James Burk.
        p.   cm. — (Sociology and economics)
    Originally published: Berlin ; New York : W de Gruyter, 1988.
    Includes bibliographical references (p.   ) and indexes.
    ISBN 0-202-30397-7 (paper)
    1. Stock-exchange—Law and legislation—United States.
2. Securities—United States.   3. Stock-exchange—United States.
I. Title.   II. Series.
KF1070.B87   1992
346.73'092—dc20
[347.30692]   91-28533
                                                         CIP

Printed on acid-free paper.

10   9   8   7   6   5   4   3   2   1

Acknowledgments

Even small books, as this one, require material resources to complete. I am grateful to the National Science Foundation for awarding a doctoral dissertation grant in 1980 which enabled me to begin collecting data for the study reported on here. McGill University and Texas A&M University supplied additional funds permitting me to gather more data and to present preliminary reports of my findings at numerous conferences. I am grateful for their support as well. For material aid of another kind, but no less valued, I thank Jaime Vinas for his help in preparing the index and Connie Alexander, Lori Cheatham, and Melonie Hopkins, who typed, in a hurry and without complaint, the tables and appendices which appear at the end of the book.

Other kinds of support have been important for me as well. My children, Jacqualine and Theodore, grew to maturity listening patiently to their father's stories about the stock market – not the usual children's fare. Their good will (and that of their mother) has been a blessing on this work.

I am indebted also to those who read the manuscript in its several versions in whole or in part. Here I name only those who read the work in its entirety (some more than once) and who tried by various means to improve what I had to say: Benigno Aguirre, Connie Arnold, Patricia Burk, Ernest Q. Campbell, Ben Crouch, Carl-Ludwig Holtfrerich, Morris Janowitz, Edward O. Laumann, Donald N. McCloskey, Michael Schudson, Richard Sylla and Mayer Zald. To this list I must add my good colleagues at Texas A&M University whose strong support of my research has made writing this book a pleasant task.

I owe special debts to Edward Laumann, who first encouraged me to undertake this project, to Edward Shils, whose seminar on traditions led me to think seriously about various beliefs concerning stock prices, and to Morris Janowitz, who introduced me to the problems of social control and the methods of institutional analysis. I am indebted also to Bianka Ralle for her prompt, professional (and always helpful) work as editor.

Chapter Two, on "The Origins of Federal Securities Regulation," is a revised version of an article published earlier in *Social Forces* 63, 2 (June, 1985): 1010 – 1029. It appears here with their permission.

There is, finally, another, whose name I need not mention, but without whom this book would never have been completed: whatever good this book might do is done for him.

Table of Contents

Part III: Unintended Consequences for Market Control

Part IV: Conclusions

Appendices

List of Tables

Part I

Introduction

Chapter 1

Markets, Moral Order, and Regulation

Stock market averages are broadcast every day over the television and radio, and detailed information about stock trading activity is published in our daily press. This is not done only for the wealthy. Whether we own stock or not, we attend to the movement of stock prices, feeling good about ourselves and our society when stock prices rise — unless they rise too suddenly — and worrying about our well-being and the well-being of our society when stock prices fall — especially when they fall suddenly and far and over long periods of time. Why should we do so?

The stock market of course is an important economic institution which facilitates the raising of capital funds for business and permits the rapid transfer and dispersion of corporate ownership. But our fascination with its daily work is not narrowly economic. It is more profound than that. The stock market occupies a unique place in American culture. It stands as a symbol which in condensed form signifies our common life within a market-based, capitalist economic organization and within the moral culture which supports and sustains that organization.

We are in many respects positive in our attitude toward the market and what we think it represents. Its strength and capacity to generate wealth (so it seems) out of nothing is our strength as well. The material prosperity of our society we believe depends on the institutions of private ownership and aggressive trade in "free" markets, both of which are pillars of the stock market. And we elevate to the role of "hero" those who are able to master the uncertainties of trading to create huge fortunes for themselves.

Still we are not only positive toward the market. We are rather ambivalent about a style of life which appears at best to be amoral, in which individuals are guided (again, so it seems) only by the norms of acquisitiveness and are willing to utilize any means to increase their wealth even if it results in doing harm to others. And we castigate those who we think try unfairly to advance themselves by selling worthless securities, by spreading false rumors, by trading on "insider" information or by any other similar means. We quickly judge these acts to be morally reprehensible and condemn them in a way that we cannot so easily do to our entire way of life. Perhaps the occasional ferocity with which we attack "high finance" and "Wall Street" is, in part at least, a way of purging our uneasiness about the goodness of that way of life.

Sociologists know that markets are a source of moral controversy in modern society. Many of the longest traditions in the discipline and, to be inclusive, in all of social science have as one purpose to figure out what difference it makes to base so much of our social life on the mode of association which flourishes in markets. Not the least important questions which have been raised by these traditions ask: How might we resolve our ambivalence toward the market? What is the relation between markets and moral order? And if they are somehow opposed to one another, is there any way by regulation we might be able to enjoy the material benefits which markets bring without sacrificing a morally satisfying way of life?

These are the questions which animate this study of the stock market. They are too broadly put perhaps to expect a final answer to them here. Yet some progress with them might be made. The aim of this study is to trace the effects of federal securities regulation on the moral order of the stock market and on the market's subsequent institutional development. The argument shall be that our ambivalence toward the stock market cannot be resolved by regulation. Regulation may lead to a substantial modification of the market's moral order. As we shall see, beliefs about how one ought to trade stocks and who ought to be allowed to trade stocks underwent important changes as a consequence of federal securities law, and these changes altered substantially the organization of the market. But they did not, in the end, clearly strengthen the market's capacity for social control. This argument is not a call for deregulation. Effective market regulation is a necessary "guarantor of trust" that encourages us to face the contradictions and uncertainties of a market-based society.[1] Nevertheless, it is no sure technique to fix the operation of the market according to plan.

The place of the stock market in American society has been dynamic, changing and adapting to the growth and development of the larger societal order of which it is a part. It entered this century as a series of local, private markets which actively involved a relatively small number of individuals trading for their own account. But it was rapidly expanded through the first third of the century into a national mass market for the securities of industrial corporations. Shareownership became very widespread to include nearly ten

---

1 Susan P. Shapiro, *Wayward Capitalists* (New Haven: Yale University Press, 1984), pp. 190 – 192.

percent of the population by 1930 a proportion not very far from what it is today.[2]

Throughout most of this period the market was unregulated by any government and so it approximated the ideals, and displayed the difficulties, of a laissez-faire economic organization. During the thirties, the attitude of laissez-faire was replaced by a more proactive regulatory approach which made the stock market an object of federal securities control. In part because of federal regulation, over the middle third of the century individual investors were replaced in importance by the dramatic rise of institutional investors who entered the stock market for the first time. That transformation precipitated a crisis which nearly caused the market (in the form we know it) to collapse in the late 1960s, a crisis the causes of which are not yet entirely resolved. Since then, changes in the market have been shaped and are still being shaped by the pressures of an internationalizing economic organization. Of course, our economy and especially our capital markets have never been hermetically sealed within national boundaries. But, relatively speaking, they were more dominated by a domestic orientation before the 1970s than they can now afford to be. Adapting to this fact is the primary challenge for the stock market in the last third of this century.

This book focuses on the events of the second third of the century, of the period after laissez-faire and before internationalization, which extends, roughly, from the 1930s through the 1970s. It is a critical period sociologically. Its beginning was characterized by the emergence of a political outlook in which social progress and welfare were believed to derive rather more from rational planning and control than from the inevitable forces of progress "at work" in history.[3] Large-scale industrial and urban development, immigration, and the challenge to religious sensibilities posed by science were among the forces which forged this outlook. They defined what was modern and were recognized to be the basis of prosperous society. Yet they were also recognized as forces which were (at least potentially) powerfully corrosive of social stability. They made it difficult to form and to maintain a moral consensus able to regulate the exercise of private power and the pursuit of private

2 N. R. Danielian, "Ownership of Securities in the United States," *The Securities Markets*, ed. Alfred Bernheim and Margaret G. Schneider (New York: Twentieth Century Fund, 1935), pp. 35–62, 723–737. In 1985, the New York Stock Exchange estimated that 20.2% of the population owned stock; but as recently as 1980 only 13.5% of the population were supposed to do so. See Table B.1.

3 See Edward Purcell's *The Crisis of Democratic Theory* (Lexington, Ky.: University Press of Kentucky, 1973) and Michael S. Schudson, *Discovering the News* (New York: Basic Books, 1978), pp. 121–134.

interests. If nothing else, then the experience of world war and economic depression finally taught the poverty of that simple faith in laissez-faire which believed history would automatically work out for the best. To achieve human welfare, social control would have to be actively asserted, guided in democratic society by the reason of experts accountable to the people through the agencies of government. It was in this context that the initial attempt was made to reconstruct the normative order of the market by means of federal securities control.

In the fifty years since then, we have entered a new period of doubt, of self-doubt. The efficacy of human beings to control social organization through the reason of experts has been challenged in theory and experience. Students of complex organization over the last forty years have been busy pointing out that rationality is bounded and that organization is an emergent product of internal negotiations and compromises undertaken in confrontation with "environments" which are characteristically uncertain. In this conception, the efficiency of bureaucracy is no matter to take for granted.[4] And in practice, the burgeoning of governmental regulations in the period following the Second World War, especially since the late 1960s, did not lead to any obvious improvement either in economic development or in the quality of life. Government regulation, it began to be argued, more often hindered than helped to promote public welfare. As a consequence, there was through the 1970s and early 1980s a notable movement toward deregulation, beginning dramatically with the end of the draft in 1973 and extending from there more directly into the economic realms of finance, transportation, communication, and elsewhere.[5]

It is within this context that we shall examine the origins of federal securities regulation and trace its long-term effects for market organization. Doing so will involve us in, what Anthony Giddens has called, "the analysis of strategic conduct."[6] It is a mode of analysis informed by two assumptions. First, it takes seriously that market participants act purposively in the pursuit of their own interests, but that they do so on the basis of limited knowledge. Second, it assumes that the stock market is a complex institution the parts of which are imperfectly integrated. Limited integration, of course, implies limited consensus which hinders system-wide efforts at social control. In com-

4 Terry M. Moe, "The New Economics of Organization," *American Journal of Political Science*, 28 (1984), 739–777.
5 Robert B. Horwitz, "Understanding Deregulation," *Theory and Society*, 15 (1986), 139–174.
6 Anthony Giddens, *The Constitution of Society* (Berkeley and Los Angeles: University of California Press, 1986), pp. 288–293.

bination, these two assumptions lead us to consider the unintended consequences of the action of market participants for the stock market's institutional development. Adopting this analytical strategy will, I hope, shed light on the process by which we actually construct a moral order in markets. If so, it may be of some use to us as we think about the prospects for market regulation in the future. If that hope is to be realized, however, we have first to locate this general analytical strategy within the traditional theoretical debate about markets, moral order, and regulation.

Markets and Moral Order

Markets are social institutions characterized ideal-typically by what Michael Oakeshott calls a transactional mode of association.[7] In this mode of association, two or more actors are related solely by a desire to satisfy their own wants. The association, in principle, is not permanent but terminates when either actor obtains the satisfaction which was sought or concludes that the satisfaction desired cannot be obtained through continuing the relationship. It may involve cooperation, as actors join forces to construct a more efficient means for achieving their end, but this in no way alters the character of the relationship. It is intermittent association driven by each actor's pursuit of his or her own interests. Sociologists are familiar with Talcott Parsons's description of this kind of purposive social action as understood, in his terms, by utilitarian social theory. It is atomistic, with individuals calculating about means and ends, but with no necessarily common orientation to a collective purpose which organizes the whole "system of action."[8] His is an important image to keep in mind because it conveys precisely what Oakeshott and we think about markets in pure form: They are amoral institutions in which actors gather and exchange with one another (that is to say they exercise power over one another) in a solipsistic pursuit of their advantage.

Of course no market is like this. When we say that markets are social institutions, what we mean, in part, is that they, like all social institutions, are constituted by a moral order. The term "moral order" (or what in this study shall be an equivalent term, "normative order") refers to the conditions

7 Michael Oakeshott, "The Rule of Law," *On History and Other Essays* (Totowa, N. J.: Barnes & Noble, 1983), pp. 121 – 125.
8 Talcott Parsons, *The Structure of Social Action* (Glencoe, Ill.: Free Press, 1968, orig. 1937), pp. 51 – 60.

of action which specify how people ought to behave. I include within this order both cultural elements (i. e., beliefs about what one ought to do and how one ought to do it) as well as social structures of authority organized to establish, maintain, or change institutional rules (or norms) to express and support these beliefs.[9] The moral order of a market, then, establishes rules about how one ought to trade, who is allowed to trade, what are acceptable terms of trade, etc. and it includes some kind of structural apparatus charged with the duty of enforcing market rules. That all markets are constituted by a moral order of this kind is no news to sociologists. It has been an important contention within the discipline since Emile Durkheim formulated his theory of the noncontractual bases of contract. But how this moral order is (or ought to be) established is a matter of serious contention within the social sciences and a serious policy question.

One argument we have to consider, perhaps the best known one, is the view I will call the neoclassical economic perspective. This perspective has its roots in the economic theory of Adam Smith and the private property theory of John Locke. Its essential claim is that markets create their own moral order, that moral order emerges naturally from transactions of exchange among market participants. If that is true, then markets truly are self-regulating, as this view also holds. But I wish to put this last claim on one side until we treat regulation per se. Now it is crucial to understand how markets are supposed to create their own moral order.

Two different arguments are offered. First, because people participate in markets to satisfy some want or desire, they will be attentive to the wants and desires of others; they will search for some way to supply another's wants in order to have their own desires met. The idea is simple, yet important. It is the motor driving the notion of "market discipline." Only to think of oneself in markets is, by this account, to risk that no one will wish to trade with you. While there may be short-term rewards to dishonest, avaricious, or other exploitative or entirely self-regarding behaviors, in time people will learn they can get a better deal by trading with someone else; the rewards to vice will necessarily dry up. Competitiveness, in short, is supposed to be a builder of "good" character. It may be genuinely "good" character or crafted

9 The term "moral order" is not very commonly used by sociologists today, though it is a perfectly good term. The term "normative order" is perhaps more common. I take my meaning for the term from Robert Cooley Angell who in his book on *Free Society and Moral Crisis* (Ann Arbor: University of Michigan Press, 1965), p. 16 refers in slogan form to moral order as "how oughtness is organized." See also Robert Wuthnow, *Meaning and Moral Order* (Berkeley and Los Angeles: University of California Press, 1987).

for display, as Erving Goffman would suspect, to advance one's self-interest. In either case, it is the apparent "good" character of market participants on which exchange depends and which establishes the market's moral order. Notice that the moral order which is created is a minimal one in this specific sense: It includes beliefs about how one ought to behave in markets (beliefs which are internalized). But it provides for no more elaborate enforcement machinery than is provided by the cumulative consequences of trading as measured (say) by profit.[10]

The second argument depends on a comparative analysis and runs, briefly, as follows. The market supplies a kind of social organization in which people can cooperate with one another to achieve desired goals, and so the market is better than the proverbial state of nature in which there is no cooperation among individuals. And the market is superior to alternative kinds of social organization, which usually rely on hierarchical or coercive controls, because it respects important civil and political rights and the liberties of individuals. As a result the social order which markets create are morally preferable to other social orders.[11]

Of the two arguments, it is the first which holds the greatest interest for us. While the second has a formidable intellectual machinery behind it, it addresses a different issue than we have before us. Its essential claim is that markets create a social order which is good and, therefore, that markets create a moral − i.e., a good social − order. We are not concerned, however, with all of society and the broad question how to create a good social order, important though that question is. Our concern is about the relative autonomy of particular market institutions within society to establish and maintain beliefs about how market participants ought to behave. It is to that concern which the first argument speaks, although not entirely persuasively.

10 The argument is based on the famous passage in Adam Smith's *The Wealth of Nations*, ed. Edwin Cannan (Chicago: University of Chicago Press, 1976), Bk. I, ch. II about the origin of the division of labor. A recent statement of it with the aim of making a moral defense of the market is made by Thomas Wilson, "Sympathy and Self-Interest," *The Market and the State*, ed. Thomas Wilson and Andrew S. Skinner (Oxford: Clarendon Press, 1976), pp. 73−99. A more general sociological variant of the argument can be found, I believe, in the emergent norm theory of Ralph Turner and Lewis Killian, *Collective Behavior*, 2nd ed. (Englewood Cliffs, N. J.: Prentice-Hall, 1972), pp. 21−25.

11 Robert Nozick, *Anarchy, State, and Utopia* (New York: Basic Books, 1974) and F. A. Hayek, *Law, Legislation, and Liberty*, 3 vols. (Chicago: University of Chicago Press, 1973−1979). Criticisms of this argument are nicely summarized by Allen Buchanan, *Ethics, Efficiency, and the Market* (Totowa, N. J.: Rowman & Allanheld, 1985), pp. 64−81.

Even before discussing the alternative perspective, we can notice certain weaknesses in the neoclassicist position. It assumes that markets are relatively simple institutions in which the same norms of trading will be shared and observed by all market participants. Empirically, we know that is not true. Wayne Baker's network analysis of trading crowds in a modern options market supplies convincing evidence that these crowds are not all alike but are socially structured in ways that substantially affect with whom and how one trades (as measured by price behavior).[12] And it ignores, as Oliver Williamson has pointed out, that economic actors may not only seek their self-interest, but they may do so opportunistically, seeking it with "guile" and dissembling to realize "transactional advantages."[13] That such strategies might have long-term payoffs, as Williamson suggests they can, is an important departure from the idea that markets create their own moral order thought of as a positive good.

Opposed to the neoclassical perspective is the view I will call the structuralist perspective. This perspective has its roots in sociology, especially in the theory of Max Weber. Its essential claim is that markets do not and cannot create their own moral order; whatever moral order markets exhibit is derived from the moral order of the larger society in which the market is found. As Mark Granovetter has recently put it, institutions, even market institutions, "are so constrained by ongoing social relations that to construe them as independent is a grievous misunderstanding."[14] People organize politically and deploy group power to modify the operation of markets to obtain goals (e .g., through affirmative action or "buy American" programs) not obviously contemplated by any particular exchange relation. Their doing so helps to explain fundamental differences in the workings of various national economies.[15] The influence of government to shape the moral order of markets is more extensive, in other words, than suggested by the more or less neutral role it plays upholding contracts and punishing the use of force and fraud in markets.[16] It is the critical authority charged with the duty of establishing and maintaining the moral rules which market participants must follow.

12 Wayne E. Baker, "The Social Structure of a National Securities Market," *American Journal of Sociology*, 89 (January, 1984), 775 – 811.

13 Oliver Williamson, *Markets and Hierarchies* (New York: Free Press, 1975), p. 255.

14 Mark Granovetter, "Economic Action and Social Structure: The Problem of Embeddedness," *American Journal of Sociology*, 91 (November, 1985) 482.

15 John Zysman, *Governments, Markets, and Growth* (Ithaca, N. Y.: Cornell University Press, 1983).

16 Amitai Etzioni, "Encapsulated Competition," *Journal of Post-Keynesian Economics*, 7 (Spring, 1985), 296 – 300.

We must be careful not to read too much into this argument, to suppose that it requires authoritarian structures to exist which by command and fiat determine what the internal organization of the market should be.[17] That may happen in some cases, as it does when governments regulate markets for consumer goods in wartime. But there are more subtle processes at work as well. Beliefs about how to trade and with whom to trade are affected by other social institutions and sometimes only informally enforced. At the heart of Max Weber's argument concerning the Protestant ethic and the "spirit of capitalism" lies the idea that religious beliefs which are not directly economic or market oriented may nevertheless have important consequences affecting market structures.[18] And Granovetter emphasizes the importance of actors being embedded in social relations for creating trust and controlling malfeasance within markets.[19] Still, the thrust of the argument is unchanged: The moral order of markets is no independent creation but is constrained and must reflect the operation of larger social forces.

Made to choose between these two perspectives we should, in my view, reject the neoclassical in favor of the structural one. The structural perspective offers a richer and more complete (though less parsimonious) accounting for the various mechanisms at work in the construction of moral order. And it avoids the weaknesses which we associated with the neoclassical approach. Nevertheless, we should be wary of adopting a perspective which is overdeterministic. There is no need in social science to substitute sociologistic for economistic analysis.[20]

I would add this qualification to the structural argument. The behavior of market participants is not shaped entirely by immediate considerations of transactional prudence or by a willingness to conform to regulatory norms enforced by extra-market institutions. Market participants use the order which their transactions and larger social forces help create as a resource to aid them in the pursuit of their own ends. They may do so acting as individuals or, perhaps more likely, acting collectively in the interest of social relationships

---

17 This is one of Granovetter's main points.

18 Max Weber, *The Protestant Ethic and the Spirit of Capitalism*, trans. Talcott Parsons (New York: Charles Scribner's, 1958). Etzioni makes a similar point in "Encapsulated Competition," pp. 290–293.

19 Granovetter, "Economic Action and Social Structure," pp. 487–493. See also Etzioni, "Encapsulated Competition," pp. 293–296.

20 This is not the same point that Granovetter makes, that we need to steer between an "under-socialized" and an "over-socialized" view of social actors. My point is not as broad. It argues against two different conceptions of "over-socialization," the economic and sociological.

formed within the market. How effective they are in their pursuits will vary widely, of course. What we cannot do is ignore their potential influence, ruling out in advance of empirical analysis that their pursuits may be a source of moral order in markets which works at odds to any discernible extra-market influence. The moral order of markets is affected by larger social forces, but it is certainly no simple reflection of them. On the contrary, actors in markets have some freedom to determine the shape their moral order assumes. Indeed, I shall argue that the moral order of markets, though constrained by larger social forces, is in large part created by social actors *within* the market.

Here then are three positions about the nature of the process relating markets and moral order. The neoclassical one argues that markets create their own moral order and it takes little or no consideration of outside social forces. The structural one argues that the moral order of markets is substantially determined by myriad social and political influences operating outside the market. Last, the modified structural view, which I advocate, recognizes that larger social forces are an important constraint on the market's construction of its own moral order, but argues nevertheless that that moral order is an internal, institutional construction. Let's turn now to see how these different positions affect our views about regulation as a means of control.

Regulation as a Means of Control

Whether regulation is an effective means of market control is a long-debated question in American history, especially over the last century. The debate centers on the role government, usually the role federal government, should play in trying to ensure that markets achieve particular goals of economic efficiency, distributive justice, or moral ecology (i.e., a safe workplace, clean environment, etc.).[21]

That debate, of course, is not irrelevant here. But its framework for our purposes is both too narrow and too broad. It is too narrow because it focuses on government as the primary agent of regulation as though markets will be unregulated if government fails to create an agency for the purpose. Because

21 See Theodore Lowi, *The End of Liberalism,* 2nd ed. (New York: Norton, 1979); Stephen Skowronek, *Building a New American State* (Cambridge: Cambridge University Press, 1982); James O. Freedman, *Crisis and Legitimacy: The Administrative Process and American Government* (Cambridge: Cambridge University Press, 1978).

we hold, however, that markets always possess a moral order of some kind and, within it, a structural apparatus of enforcement, then any exclusive focus on government becomes confining and may beg interesting questions. It is too broad because it is concerned to know how market regulation will affect the prosperity, justness, and moral ecology of the whole society. That concern is laudable, but beyond our scope in this work. Here we are concerned with the capacity of regulation to establish and maintain a particular moral order.

Our concern is actually two-fold. It points first of all, as we just suggested, to the structural apparatus which is supposed to establish and maintain moral order and asks whether that apparatus is an effective means to accomplish the purpose. It points also to the recurrent need of all social institutions for vertical integration, to link the pursuit of the private interests of their members to some larger public interest, and asks how well any regulatory system meets that need. These two formulations are formally similar. They both have to do with assessing the capacity of institutions to regulate themselves to achieve their goals.[22] They are substantively related as well. Usually claims about the capacity of a regulatory system to link the pursuit of private and public interests hinge on arguments over how well the apparatus of control establishes and maintains particular moral beliefs. These are claims which neoclassicists and structuralists have hotly disputed.

Stated in its strong form, the neoclassic perspective denies that markets require any external means of regulation to link the pursuit of private and public interests. The argument is not a simple extension of the idea we noticed above, that market discipline forms good character, which asserts an identity between individual and public interests. It is rather that an "invisible hand" operates within the market to assure linkage between the two. In fact, Smith's formulation of this idea in *The Wealth of Nations* is more circumspect than mine. A market participant "led by an invisible hand," he writes, "by pursuing his own interest ... frequently promotes that of the society more effectually than when he really intends to promote it."[23] The assurance, in other words, is relative. Markets are supposed to link the pursuit of private and social interests better than any other institution might do, and especially better than one that intends to promote the linkage. Why might this be true?

The current explanation is epistemological. Our knowledge is bounded; usually it is confined to knowledge of particular circumstances of time and place; and we act based on the knowledge we have. In so doing, we contribute

---

22 This formulation of the problem of social control is taken from the work of Morris Janowitz, *The Last Half-Century* (Chicago: University of Chicago Press, 1978).

23 Adam Smith, *The Wealth of Nations*, Bk. IV, ch. II, p. 477.

to the forces of supply and demand and influence market prices, however slightly. Thus prices condense into a single symbol everyone's knowledge about local conditions across the market. They broadcast (or signal) what is relevant for all market participants to know to adjust their local activities — i. e., their buying and selling — so as to promote the most efficient deployment of their resources. And that promotes the public interest. Because no agency can hope to gather, consolidate, analyze, and distribute as much local knowledge as prices naturally convey, any attempt to control market behavior by extra-market means is bound to produce a less satisfactory result.[24]

The argument is persuasive, but not conclusive. It fails, for example, to deal with the important matter of externalities, that social costs of market transactions may never appear in the market price. It simply is not true, and Smith never argued, that the pursuit of private interests will invariably lead to some public good. "A group of actions," Allen Buchanan writes, "none of which is criticizable in isolation, may collectively or cumulatively have unacceptable results."[25] Worse, it ignores the problem of public goods and free-riding behavior.[26] Given our concept of markets as institutions, there is always at least the public good of the moral order on which market operations depend. Yet compliance with it is not cost free, and in certain cases substantial benefits may be gained from noncompliance. Failure to deal with these kinds of issues, historically, underlies the structuralist response and opposition toward the neoclassical theory of "self-regulating" markets.

Stated in its strong form, the structuralist argument is that linkage of the pursuit of private interests to larger public interests does not occur automatically, but requires political action undertaken on behalf of a larger public. Market regulation by government is supposed to be a collective exercise of instrumental reason employed to overcome the problems of the price system. As Samuel Bowles, David M. Gordon, and Thomas E. Weisskopf put it, "a well-conceived system of regulation would help make more sensible use of our human and natural resources than would result from the simple and unregulated pursuit of profits."[27] It was in such terms that market regulation

---

24 Friedrich A. Hayek, "The Use of Knowledge in Society," *Individualiam and Economic Order* (Chicago: University of Chicago Press, 1948), pp. 77 – 91.

25 *Ethics, Efficiency, and the Market*, p. 68.

26 Mancur Olson, *The Logic of Collective Action* (Cambridge, Mass.: Harvard University Press, 1965).

27 *Beyond the Waste Land: A Democratic Alternative to Economic Decline* (Garden City, N. Y.: Anchor Books, 1984), p. 193. For a similar view see Susan J. Tolchin and Martin Tolchin, *Dismantling America: The Rush to Deregulate* (Boston: Houghton Mifflin, 1983).

by the federal government has been justified in the past: in the Progressive Era, to curb the economic and social instability which resulted from the rapid growth of large-scale enterprise, monopoly, and competition; in the New Deal, "to respond to the anarchy of the market during the Depression;" and in the late 1960 s and early 1970 s, to extend the Great Society programs to deal with the social and environmental impact of business activity.[28] We must be careful not to read too much into a historical gloss. The logic of the argument depends on a relatively high degree of consensus about how people ought to behave in markets and about what means are appropriate to promote that behavior. On the basis of that consensus, regulation is supposed to serve broad societal interests. But such a consensus is unlikely to exist.

Weaker forms of both the neoclassical and structuralist arguments, curiously enough, reach similar conclusions about market regulation, albeit for different reasons.[29] Both agree that market regulation by government serves, or is meant to serve, the particular interests of those who occupy positions of power. Regulation, in other words, exploits the pursuit of private interest to serve special interests. A neoclassicist such as George Stigler is likely to emphasize the material benefits regulated industries gain from their regulation, usually he argues at the expense of consumers.[30] This argument is not unlike that of an instrumentalist Marxist who holds generally that the capitalist class has captured the state apparatus to advance its own interests.[31] More recent, structural Marxist theory has emphasized the relative autonomy of the state which uses regulation as an instrument to balance contradictory demands to accumulate capital and to retain political legitimacy. In this capacity the state may act against the particular interests of some segment of the capitalist class (to ensure legitimacy) while nevertheless operating to preserve the system of capitalist domination (to promote accumulation).[32]

How does this debate inform our concern about the capacity of regulation to establish and maintain a market's moral order? There are two issues at

28 Robert B. Horwitz, "Understanding Deregulation," *Theory and Society*, 15 (1986), 143.
29 *Ibid.*, pp. 140 – 141.
30 George J. Stigler, *The Citizen and the State* (Chicago: University of Chicago Press, 1975).
31 Ralph Miliband, *The State in Capitalist Society* (London: Weidenfeld and Nicholson, 1969); G. William Domhoff, *The Powers That Be* (New York: Vintage Press, 1978).
32 James O'Connor, *The Fiscal Crisis of the State* (New York: St. Martin's Press, 1973); Nicos Poulantzas, *Political Power and Social Classes*, trans. Timothy O'Hagen (New York: New Left Books, 1973); Alan Wolfe, *The Limits of Legitimacy* (New York: Free Press, 1977). Fred Block has recently criticized this argument on the ground that it assumes too much about the autonomous character of economic institutions in society; see his "Political Choice and the Multiple 'Logics' of Capital," *Theory and Society*, 15 (1986), 175 – 192.

stake. The first one is whether deliberate regulation can be an effective means of control at all, linking the pursuit of private to larger interests. The strong form of the neoclassicist argument answers clearly "no" and is, mistakenly in my view, content to rely on the price system to secure this linkage. The weaker form of the neoclassical perspective, however, joins with the structuralist perspective in its strong and weak forms to argue the other way. The second issue is over the content of the larger interests. In their strong forms, both the neoclassical and structural accounts suppose that the pursuit of private interests in markets will be linked to broad societal interests. In their weaker version, both accounts suppose regulation will benefit primarily special interests. Which view should we prefer?

Neither argument in its strong form is particularly persuasive. Their current use is more often to provide a framework for polemical political debate than to sustain serious social science. They are too one-sided in the positions they adopt. Both weaker forms of these perspectives are more realistic. Their evidence favors the general view that the moral order of markets is established and maintained as a consequence of political struggle for some market advantage. It is an argument which fits nicely with the modified structural position I argued for in the previous section. Yet here too we must withhold uncritical endorsement, especially concerning claims about the efficacy of regulatory structures to enforce market rules to the benefit even of special interests. Analyses of political contests among competing special interests must always be alert to the possibility of pyrrhic victories.

It is reasonable to argue, as structuralists and neoclassicists both do in their weak forms, that people try to use regulatory structures to secure their own ends. Resources are mobilized to assure that beliefs about how one ought to trade or with whom one ought to trade favor particular group interests. From the point of view of those group interests, that assurance is a battle won.

It is not reasonable to assume that people can foresee the longer-term consequences of their victory and especially not to assume that unforeseen consequences will work to their advantage. In winning their battle to reconstruct normative order, group interests redefine the context in which market rules are applied. But the meanings and consequences of rules can be very different when rules are applied in a new social setting. Not infrequently, they supply opportunities for other groups effectively to mobilize resources to promote their interests in ways previously contemplated by no one. The result may be unsettling. No matter whether the regulatory apparatus is a government agency or an internal market structure, the result may undermine its capacity to maintain market order. We should not presume a static structure or even dynamic equilibrium in the service of special interests. Nor can we ignore that we are largely blind to the long-run consequences of even our most rational actions.

In taking this position, my argument accepts the idea that knowledge is bounded, an idea that was advanced by the neoclassical perspective to justify its strong argument against regulation. Still our arguments are different. Mine is more realistic. It does not expect the price system to assure the linkage of private and public interests. In fact, given the dynamic pursuit of market advantage by various market interests, it argues that that linkage cannot be assured by any given regulatory structure.

In sum, neither the neoclassical economic or the structural perspective on regulation supplies a competely satisfactory theory of how the moral order of markets is established or maintained. We shall have in this study, therefore, to weave carefully between the two while avoiding their weaknesses. We shall adopt a modified structuralist position to argue that moral order is constructed by social actors organized within the market as they adapt to the constraints of larger social forces. And we shall adopt a modified weak form of the neoclassical (or structural) position to argue that groups attempt to use regulation instrumentally to secure their special interests, but with unintended and sometimes undesired consequences. Now we must test the power of these qualified propositions by seeing how they inform our study of the stock market and its response to the New Deal program of federal securities control.

Plan of the Work

Methodologically, the work I propose — to illustrate the usefulness of these theoretical contentions by a single case study — has an inherent difficulty, pointed out by Theda Skocpol, that it may appear arbitrary.[33] In the first place, a theoretical argument, given in advance of evidence, may be unpersuasive and so may seem arbitrary because it is lacking in its logical or substantive development. Of course, I have tried already to avoid this difficulty by stating my argument as simply as possible and indicating its plausibility by locating it in the context of an ongoing theoretical debate to which I took exception.

33 Theda Skocpol, "Emerging Agendas and Recurrent Strategies in Historical Sociology," *Vision and Method in Historical Sociology* (Cambridge: Cambridge University Press, 1984), pp. 362–368.

Another threat of arbitrariness arises with the application of the theory to the case. The problem is to assure that the evidence is not arbitrarily selected only to favor the theory. To guard against this possibility, I selected three different areas of stock market organization to focus on: the organization of trading (the stock market's core activity), the boundaries which regulate access to the market, and the process and structure of regulatory authority. Focus on these parts of the market and not others is suggested independently of my theory by the work of Karl Polanyi which defines what market institutions are in essentially these three terms.[34] If the theory aids our understanding of the effects of federal securities regulation in all three areas of stock market "reality," then we may have confidence that the results are not arbitrary.

Here is how we shall proceed. The first part of the argument considers how passage of federal securities laws in 1933 and 1934 led to a reconstruction of the market's normative order. Chapter 2 begins with an explanation of the origins of federal securities law. At issue is whether the laws were passed with clear intentions about what regulation was to accomplish. I argue they were not, casting doubt on the proposition that federal market regulation must be seen as a strong form of instrumental reason. Chapters 3 and 4 show the ways groups organized within the market to use federal regulation as a resource, first, to replace beliefs about how one ought to be allowed to trade stocks and, then, to replace beliefs about who ought to be allowed to trade stocks. By altering the moral order of the market in these two fundamental areas, new competitive forces were unleashed which put great strain on the capacity of the market's regulatory system.

The second part of the argument examines the effects of the reconstructed normative order on market control. Chapter 5 considers how the new normative context altered the application of other moral rules — indeed, how it made their application impossible with the result that the market itself nearly collapsed. And then Chapter 6 studies the inadequacies of the governance structure created by federal securities law to aggregate private interests in a way that would lead to market control. The concluding Chapter 7 restates the argument analytically to specify conditions market regulation must meet to strengthen market control and to identify prospective challenges for market regulation.

---

34 He refers to these as market elements and describes them in different but, I think, equivalent meaning words. See his, "The Economy as an Instituted Process," *Trade and Market in the Early Empires*, ed. Karl Polanyi, Conrad Arensberg, and Harry W. Pearson (Chicago: Gateway Books, 1971), pp. 266–270, esp. 267.

The main theme is simply summarized: Federal regulation of the stock market certainly altered the market's moral order and its future course of institutional development. But it has been no effective means to strengthen market control, whether by linking the pursuit of private interests to the public good or by serving some dominant market interest.

Part II

Reconstructing Normative Order

Chapter 2

The Origins of Federal Securities Regulation

Thirty-five years after the fact, Walter Sachs of Goldman Sachs & Company was asked what led him and his partners to increase the speculative fever of 1929 by selling stocks in a dazzling (but tottering) pyramid of investment companies. They were sparked, he responded, by a desire "to conquer the world!" It was "not only greed for money, but [for] power. ... and that was the great mistake."[1] To many, this confession is a tragic understatement of the facts of the matter. Investment bankers in the 1920s were driven by a desire to gain influence over others and to make huge fortunes off their influence. All of them were not, of course, but enough were to set the tone. They took advantage of the mass market for securities, created to sell war bonds during the First World War, by peddling corporate securities of questionable value at artifically high prices. The result was not a permanent prosperity, as some predicted, but a crash, which saw stock prices lose ninety percent of their value over the course of three years, and an economic depression, which lasted for the better part of a decade.

In our popular cultural history, the speculative abuses, the stock market crash, and the depression are forged into a single causal chain to explain the origins of federal securities regulation. If there had been adequate regulation, abuses might have been contained; not the greed, of course, but the acting on greed. Stock prices might not have been driven up so high to fall so low. And the depression might have been less severe. Regulation was the necessary thing. The argument was strongly stated in the Securities Exchange Act of 1934. Manipulation of securities prices and excess speculation "precipitated, intensified, and prolonged" national emergencies which produced widespread unemployment, burdened commerce, and adversely affected the general welfare.[2]

---

1 *Reminiscences of Walter Sachs*, Part II (New York, Oral History Collection, Columbia University, 1972), p. 22.
2 The actual language (sect. 2(4)) is somewhat more cumbersome: "National emergencies, which produce widespread unemployment and the dislocation of trade, transportation,

The argument is hardly unfamiliar. Market failures, like the stock market crash, are often supposed to create economic distress. If the economic distress is grave enough, it threatens the legitimacy of the political elite, who attempt some reform to protect their power. Indeed, even without Marxist assumptions regarding capital market crises, as Dietrich Rueschemeyer and Peter Evans observe, we may believe that state intervention is necessary to maintain capitalist accumulation and high levels of productivity.[3] If that is so, how much more necessary must state intervention be in the wake of a market crash?

Nevertheless, the argument, at least in this simple form, may not be right. Large empirical leaps must be taken before we can say that speculative abuses caused the crash of stock prices which caused the depression which caused Congress to enact the federal securities law. These leaps, I shall argue, are not justified. They exaggerate the determination of political events in response to particular institutional failures.

How, then, can we explain the passage of three major federal securities laws in 1933 and 1934? There is no doubt that moral failures — the greed for money and power — of key financial leaders are necessary for us to consider and that the severity and depth of the depression created electoral pressures favoring reform. But we cannot easily link these factors together, through the crash in stock prices, to form a single casual chain to explain the motives for, substance, and successful enactment of the federal securities acts. A close examination of the evidence suggests a more subtle convergence of events and an element of contingency that left the outcome in doubt until the very end. Before turning to it, it will be helpful to begin with a summary of the main provisions of the laws with which we are concerned and to say something about their place within Franklin Roosevelt's first New Deal.

---

and industry, and which burden interstate commerce and adversely affect the general welfare, are precipitated, intensified, and prolonged by manipulation and sudden and unreasonable fluctuations of security prices and by excessive speculation on such exchanges and markets, and to meet such emergencies the Federal Government is put to such great expense as to burden the national credit." Here is one reason for exercising federal power to insure a "fair" and "honest" stock market.

3 Dietrich Rueschemeyer and Peter B. Evans, "The State and Economic Transformations," *Bringing the State Back In*, ed. Peter B. Evans, Dietrich Rueschemeyer, and Theda Skocpol (Cambridge: Cambridge University Press, 1985), pp. 45–46. See also Max Weber's *General Economic History* (New York: Collier-Macmillan, 1961), pp. 217–218.

Federal Securities Legislation and the First New Deal

Three acts supplied the basis for federal securities regulation. They are the Securities Act, signed 27 May 1933, the Glass-Steagall Act, signed 16 June 1933, and the Securities Exchange Act, signed 6 June 1934. Passed within fifteen months of one another, the first two of these were enacted by the "hundred day" session of Congress with which Franklin Roosevelt began his tenure as President. All three acts document the frustration national leaders felt in trying to face and overcome the challenges posed by the dismal economic depression. Significant in themselves, these acts were also part of Roosevelt's first New Deal recovery program. What were their main provisions? How did they relate to other New Deal measures?

The purpose of the Securities Act, known colloquially as the "truth-in-securities" act, was to put the burden of telling the "whole truth" about new securities offerings on those who offered them for sale. It was, as Roosevelt asked it to be, an act to defeat the customary warning, caveat emptor, by a statutory requirement making "sellers beware."[4] The purpose was accomplished through two means, public disclosure of information about new securities issues and the imposition of stiff penalties for failure to obey the law. New securities offerings were to be registered with the Federal Trade Commission, and, when sold, to be accompanied by a prospectus providing sufficient information to permit investors to judge the security's worth. To assure adequate time to study this information, registry of the issue with all relevant disclosures, was to be completed twenty days before the security could be sold. If the commission believed the filing was incomplete or erroneous, it could prevent the securities sale and launch its own investigation. Failure to comply entailed extensive civil liability. Everyone responsible for information disclosed in the prospectus was liable, jointly and severally, for the entire amount of the offering. Moreover, in any suit, the burden was on the issuers and their agents to prove their innocence. The only acceptable defense, if misleading statements had been made, was proof that they acted to the standards of behavior required of fiduciaries, a very high standard indeed.[5]

---

4 Frank Freidel, *Franklin D. Roosevelt: Launching the New Deal* (Boston: Little, Brown, 1973), pp. 343–344.

5 Arthur H. Dean, "The Federal Securities Act," *Fortune*, (August, 1933); *Federal Securities Laws* (New York: Commerce Clearing House, 1940), pp. 21–36; Michael E. Parrish, *Securities Regulation and the New Deal* (New Haven, Conn.: Yale University Press, 1970).

The Glass-Steagall Act was less concerned with securities markets than with the structure and function of banking. Its primary aim was to assure the solvency of banks and the safety of bank deposits.[6] To do this, the Federal Reserve Board was empowered to limit the amount of credit bankers made available for speculative purposes and to reduce the banker's incentive to make risky loans by limiting the payment of interest on deposits. The act also created the Federal Deposit Insurance Corporation protecting small deposits ($15,000 or less) kept in member banks against loss in the event of banking failure. Our primary interest, however, lies with the last measure taken: Banks were barred from taking deposits and offering new securities for sale or distributing securities to the public. Bankers would have to choose whether they wished to do commercial deposit banking business or investment banking. They could not do both.[7]

Having thus reduced the resources available to support speculation, Congress turned in the Securities Exchange Act to regulate the conduct of speculative trading. This regulation was to be achieved by three means. First, many practices – wash sales, matched orders,[8] dissemination of false or misleading information to raise or lower stock prices – were simply barred outright, while others – notably short selling – were subject to closer supervision and rule. Second, on the theory that price manipulation was facilitated by ignorance, registry and disclosure requirements applied to new securites offered under the Securities Act were extended to all securities listed on the stock exchanges. And, third, the Securities and Exchange Commission was established to take over the securities registration function from the Federal Trade Commission, to register stock exchanges, to monitor their rules,

---

6 Milton Friedman and Anna Jacobson Schwartz, *A Monetary History of the United States, 1867–1960* (Princeton: Princeton University Press, 1971), pp. 434–443; Helen M. Burns, *The American Banking Community and New Deal Banking Reform* (Westport, Conn.: Greenwood Press, 1974), p. 81.

7 Carosso, *Investment Banking in America*, p. 372.

8 A "wash sale" occurs whenever a person trades in such a way that it involves no change in the beneficial (or actual) ownership of the shares. The purpose of such sales for speculators was to create the appearance of trading activity on the hope of encouraging others to trade as well. "Matched orders" involved a series of transactions placed in concert usually through several sources. Typically, these transactions were meant to be offsetting, balancing each other off, though they might be lagged so there was more buying or selling at one point in time than another. The purpose here was usually to induce others to buy or sell in the same direction, artificially raising or lowering the stock's price. If the maneuver succeeds, then profits should be "earned" when the lagged orders are eventually offset. More technical definitions are found in the text of the Securities Act, sect. 9(a) (1)–(2).

and to guarantee that stock exchanges were operated in compliance with the spirit of the securities acts.[9]

More difficult than describing the main provisions of these acts is to say how they were related to Roosevelt's New Deal recovery program. In part, this is because Roosevelt had no definite program in mind to enact when he took office. Not all acts passed in this period can be related logically by a single consistent policy. At least two themes should be distinguished. One was to aid those in direct material need. As compared with the direct help of loans to banks and business, monetary measures to raise agricultural prices, deliberate creation of public jobs, and refinancing of farm and urban home mortgage debt, action to restructure conduct in the securities industry made an indirect contribution to economic recovery, if it aided economic recovery at all.[10]

A second theme was to revitalize business by raising its ethical standards of practice. Calls under the National Recovery Act for codes committing industrialists to fair labor and fair trading practices met with overwhelming and largely positive response before the act was declared unconstitutional in 1935. This act and the public's response was perhaps the most notable manifestation of the revitalization theme. It is within the context of this revitalization movement that we can more easily locate the securities acts. Roosevelt's message to Congress recommending the Securities Act complains about financial practices that are neither ethical or honest, assumes the obligation of government to "give importance to honest dealing," and promises further legislation − the Securities Exchange Act − to correct unethical and unsafe practices so that we can return "to a clear understanding of the ancient truth" that financiers are "trustees acting for others."[11] It is on moral grounds that securities regulation engages Rossevelt's public support.

We cannot leave the matter there. Skeptical minds might wonder whether public expressions of moral concern only mask the pursuit of material interests by groups strategically located in the power structure. In any case, these moral concerns had been expressed in earlier times, but never acted on. Why were

9 *Federal Securities Laws*, pp. 69−99; Rudolph L. Weissmann, *The New Wall Street* (New York: Harper Brothers, 1939), pp. 128−129.
10 Raymond Moley, *The First New Deal* (New York: Harcourt, Brace & World, 1966), pp. 223, 230−231; Lester V. Chandler, *America's Greatest Depression, 1929−1941* (New York: Harper & Row, 1970), pp. 145−160.
11 *The Public Papers and Addresses of Franklin D. Roosevelt*, ed. Samuel Rosenman, Vol. 2 (New York: Random House, 1938), pp. 93−94.

they effective, whether as a mask or an actual spur, to political action in the 1930 s? To raise this question, of course, is to restate the central problem of this chapter, to explain the beginnings of federal securities regulation.

Limitations of the Market Failures Hypothesis

We must begin by assessing the hypothesis that some kind of market failure caused the stock market crash creating a public clamor for federal securities regulation. To do this requires that we distinguish carefully between behavior we associate with market failures and the downward spiral of prices which we associate with the crash and the depression.

"Market failures" refer to any departure from the standard of "perfect" competition. They encompass such disparate events as the formation of natural monopolies, the maintenance of transaction costs at artificially high levels, the distribution through markets of public goods, and manipulative, fraudulent, or deceptive trading practices.[12] Because departures from the ideal of "perfect" competition mean goods and resources are not allocated as efficiently as possible, market failures are often supposed adversely to affect market prices and to impose social costs. They imply, in other words, that the public's interest is not being well served. For that reason alone, they invite a response by government aiming to eliminate the failures, frequently by monitoring market operations through regulation or, less often, by assuming the market's task as its own.

There is no difficulty applying these ideas to explain the beginnings of federal securities regulation. When the original laws were passed, it was a major argument in their favor that they were a necessary (though perhaps inadequate) response to market failures which preceded the stock market's crash in 1929.[13] The argument is commonly accepted today by historians of securities regulatory

---

12 G. R. Hawke, *Economics for Historians* (Cambridge: Cambridge University Press, 1980), pp. 193 – 200; Oliver P. Williamson, *Markets and Hierarchies* (New York: Free Press, 1975), pp. 211 – 218; Susan M. Phillips and J. Richard Zecher, *The SEC: An Economic Perspective* (Cambridge, Mass.: MIT Press, 1981), pp. 18 – 19.

13 Felix Frankfurter, "The Federal Securities Act," *Fortune*, (August, 1933); William O. Douglas, "Protecting the Investor," *Yale Review*, 23 (1933); Ferdinand Pecora, *Wall Street Under Oath* (New York: Simon and Schuster, 1939); M. Nelson McGeary, *The Development of Congressional Investigatire Power* (New York: Octagon Books, 1966, orig. 1940); Cedric Cowing, *Populists, Plungers, and Progressives* (Princeton: Princeton University Press, 1965), chap. 6.

policy.[14] The task here is to consider whether the failures which occured initiated action by the federal government to regulate the stock market. What kinds of market failure actually occured? What effect, if any, did these failures have on the course of stock prices? Is it reasonable to conclude that their occurrence initiated government action to regulate the market?

Three kinds of stock market failure attracted public notice during the 1930 s. The first, of course, was the perception that there had been an excess of speculation during the 1920 s, that there had been a "speculative orgy."[15] Reviving old populist and progressive fears, this speculation spurred a reaction early in the 1930 s to uncover the human agencies responsible for the extraordinary cycle of economic events stretching from 1928 to 1932. Bankers and the Federal Reserve were blamed by Congressional leaders and others for diverting credit from productive purposes to sustain the stock market boom. After the market collapsed, the depression in stock prices was supposed to be prolonged and intensified by "short sellers," who sold stock they did not own to buy it later at a lower price, profiting from the difference. Stock market leaders tried to defend short selling as a means to stabilize stock prices; short sellers, they said, traded "against the crowd" to contain market booms and created "buying pressure" to slow price declines.[16] But they were not persuasive. Testimony before Senate investigators in 1932 suggested that stock speculators traded with the crowd, aggravating price volatility. Meanwhile continuing declines in stock prices undermined belief in the "buying pressure" hypothesis.

Fraudulent sale of securities was a second kind of market failure, this one disclosed during the Senate's investigation into stock exchange practices during 1933 and 1934.[17] Bankruptcies and defaults made clear that many new securities sold were worthless. Whether a security went into default, however, was not entirely a random event as unpredictable as the vicissitudes of the market. Securities issued by some investment banks only rarely wound up in default, while securities issued by other investment banks turned out invariably

14 Joel Seligman, *The Transformation of Wall Street* (Boston: Houghton Mifflin, 1982); Parrish, *Securities Regulation and the New Deal*; Carosso, *Investment Banking in America*, pp. 332–351; John K. Galbraith, *The Great Crash: 1929* (Boston: Houghton Mifflin, 1972, orig. 1955).

15 Cowing, *Populists, Plungers, and Progressives*, pp. 195–200.

16 See, E. H. H. Simmons, "The Principal Causes of the Stock Market Crisis of 1929," *Commercial and Financial Chronicle*, (22 March 1930), 1941–1943.

17 Pecora, *Wall Street Under Oath*, pp. 99–104; Ilse Mintz, *Deterioration in the Quality of Foreign Bonds Issued in the United States, 1920–1930* (New York: National Bureau of Economic Research, 1951), p. 55; Carosso, *Investment Banking in America*, pp. 317–318.

to be worthless. When leading the Senate's investigation, Ferdinand Pecora was able to document reasons why this should be. Some investment banks, he showed, failed carefully to verify the values underlying securities they underwrote, creating opportunities for unscrupulous issuers to misrepresent (or siphon) their corporate assets. Other investment banks underwrote bonds they knew to be worthless, and they peddled these bonds, using high pressure sales tactics, to their unsuspecting clients.

Due also to Pecora's work was disclosure of a third kind of market failure, the manipulation of stock prices.[18] Manipulative practices were more or less subtle. In some securities a double market was formed, as when J. P. Morgan & Co. "sold" securities below market prices to a "preferred list" of customers. More commonly, trading pools were organized by leading financiers with the aim of influencing short-run stock price movements to the profit of pool members. And, not infrequently, bankers would trade speculatively, sometimes using depositors' money, either selling their own bank's stock short — a practice which netted the chairman of Chase Bank $4 million in the fall of 1929 — or "booming" their stock through purchases to keep its price high for "advertising" or "promotional" purposes.

Without question disclosure of this series of market failures, in particular the disclosures by Pecora's investigation in 1933 and 1934, greatly affected the *content* of the original federal securities laws. Speculation was to be curbed by tightening considerably the conditions under which money could be borrowed to finance market transactions. In addition, the Securities and Exchange Commission was charged with responsibility for regulating short sales, to keep the practice in bounds.

Fraudulent distributions of new and existing securities were to be discouraged by provisions requiring disclosure of all material information affecting a security's value, provisions bolstered by inclusion of stiff civil and criminal penalties. To avoid temptation, bankers were no longer to be allowed to perform both commercial and investment banking functions.

Trading practices on the exchanges were to be placed under continuous scrutiny. Known techniques of manipulative trading — pools, wash sales, matched orders, etc. — were either banned or permitted only under the strictest of supervision. Specialists making markets for stocks on exchange floors were barred from dealing with customers, curbing their capacity to be pool leaders. Finally, all exchange rules were to be subject to review by the

18 Pecora, *Wall Street Under Oath*, pp. 106–107, 263; Galbraith, *The Great Crash*, pp. 156–157; Carosso, *Investment Banking in America*, pp. 340–342; John Brooks, *Once in Golconda* (New York: Harper & Row, 1969), pp. 65–66.

Securities and Exchange Commission to assure that they promoted a fair market (protecting investors) and market efficiency (serving an economic rather than purely speculative function).

Our problem is to determine whether these market failures explain why government officials initiated the process which caused laws embodying these provisions to pass through Congress. Is it sufficient to claim that because of the moral laxity of financiers, the federal government intervened to construct more demanding and effective mechanisms of social control? The market failures hypothesis is clear: Because market failures caused the crash and the depression, they created an economic crisis putting pressure on government officials to act, if possible, to stop practices of illicit exchange, to restore confidence in financial markets, and to return business to normal. There are two difficulties with accepting this hypothesis.

One difficulty is establishing that the market failures actually caused the stock market crash. The point is not to deny that specific abuses occurred. At issue is whether their occurrence caused stock prices to depart significantly from prices to be expected from a market operating according to the model of perfect competition. There are several reasons to suspect that they did not. Careful quantitative research indicates, first, that speculative trading during the 1920s did *not* lead to extensive overvaluing of securities:

> The median price earnings ratio [for stocks] at the market peak [in 1929] could have been justified by earnings expectations that were not patently unreasonable.[19]

As important, short sellers in the 1930s were *not* able systematically to lower stock prices for their own profit, casting doubt generally on the hypothesis that "insider" traders could manipulate the course of stock prices.[20] It is possible to point to individual instances in which short selling led to huge profits. That is not at issue. At issue is whether short-selling was a generally effective tool for manipulating stock prices in a particular direction. But the evidence is that short-selling was not so effective. Trading pools organized for the purpose only sometimes earned a huge profit. And when profits were earned, typically, it was because short sellers went along with, rather than altering, the general price trend.[21] Finally, if the extent of fraudulent securities

---

19 Gerald Sirkin, "The Stock Market of 1929 Revisited," *Business History Review* (Summer, 1975), 223–231; Chandler, *America's Greatest Depression*, pp. 17–18.

20 Fred R. MacCauley, *Short-Selling on the New York Stock Exchange* (New York: Twentieth Century Fund, 1951).

21 Those who bucked the trend, as the famous speculator Jesse Livermore did in 1931, were frequently wiped out. As Livermore had argued in October, 1929, "it is very foolish to think that any individual or combination of individuals could artificially bring about

distributions is measured accurately by differences between new issue price behavior before and after federal requirements for disclosure were imposed, then the practice of securities fraud to sell new stock issues was *not* extensive: The price behaviors, before and after regulation, are not substantially different.[22] In short, the moral failures of leading financiers, real as they were, cannot be said to have caused the collapse of stock prices we associate with the crash of 1929.[23] If not, then we are hard pressed to argue that market failures supplied the original impetus for federal securities regulation.

Nevertheless, it could be argued that the market was perceived to have failed by witnesses of the event and that it is perceptions which count. Without denying the importance of these perceptions, noticing them now does not save the argument. In a causal argument, timing is important. While it is sometimes true that an effect precedes its cause in time, as when a child works hard in school to gain a good job in the future, the market failures hypothesis depends upon failures — in this case, perceptions of the failures — preceding the government action which responds to them. Here is the second difficulty: That did not happen here. The crash did not cause people generally to lose confidence in the market. If it did, they expressed their loss in a peculiar way. The number of individual shareholders, a measure of participation in the market, actually rose from between nine and eleven million in 1930 to between ten and twelve million in 1932, more than double what it was in 1927.[24]

a decline in the stock market." Or to stop it. The so-called banker's pool which Thomas Lamont of J. P. Morgan & Co. organized to staunch the stock market's crash never came close to succeeding. In the mass market for securities, created in this century, there is simply too much stock and too many traders to be able to manipulate prices at will. See Brooks, *Once in Golconda*, pp. 69–74, 279; *Commercial and Financial Chronicle*, October 26, 1929, p. 2619; Richard D. Wyckoff, *Wall Street Adventures through Forty Years* (New York: Greenwood Press, 1968, orig. 1930), pp. 148–149.

22 George J. Stigler, "Public Regulation of the Securities Market," *Journal of Business*, 37 (1964), 117–142; George J. Benston, "Required Disclosure and the Stock Market," *American Economic Review*, 63 (1973), 132–155. An argument is sometimes made that while the price behavior is not different when measured by means, it is different when measured by variability. See Irwin Friend and Edward S. Herman, "The S. E. C. Through a Glass Darkly," *Journal of Business*, 37 (1964), 382–405 and Seligman, *The Transformation of Wall Street*, pp. 561–568.

23 What did cause the stock market crash is an interesting question, but beyond the scope of this essay to treat. A general theory and history of financial crises, including the crash of 1929, can be found in Charles P. Kindleberger's *Manias, Panics, and Crashes* (New York: Basic Books, 1978).

24 N. R. Danielian, "Ownership of Securities in the United States," *The Securities Markets*, ed. Alfred Bernheim and Margaret Schneider (New York: Twentieth Century Fund, 1935), pp. 35–62; Adolph Berle and Gardiner C. Means, *The Modern Corporation and*

What did affect public confidence in the market was disclosure of particular moral abuses by Wall Street's leading financiers.[25] But this disclosure did not take place until *after* the Senate initiated its inquiry into stock exchange practices in 1932. Whatever effect public perception of the market failures subsequently had on the passage of federal securities law, it was a response to, not the cause of, government intervention which was already under way. The critical question, then, is what caused the Senate to initiate its investigation when it did, before the disclosure of market failures?

No complete understanding of the origins of federal securities law can ignore the disclosures of wrong-doing by financiers which led to the perception that the market had failed and needed reform. It is significant to say that the contents of the laws which passed are comprehensible only in the context of these disclosures. Nevertheless, it is also true that, despite this achievement, the market failures hypothesis in its simple form fails to explain what political processes led to the disclosure of market failures in the first place. The problem remains: What led public officials to extend the federal government's role to encompass securities regulation? What motivated them to press for this expansion? And, why did the proposed expansion succeed in being enacted?

Depression, Electoral Pressure, and Government Intervention

To deny that market failures caused the crash and initiated government action to regulate the market is not to deny the importance of general economic crisis as a condition for political action.

According to the developing structural theories of the state, economic depressions challenge the survival of capitalist systems and the legitimacy of existing distributions of goods and power which such systems sustain. Acting

Private Property, rev. ed. (New York: Harcourt, Brace and Jovanovich, 1968, orig. 1932), pp. 60, 331–334.

25 See Frederick Lewis Allen's portrayal of the public mood in his *The Lords of Creation* (Chicago: Quadrangle Books, 1966, orig. 1935), pp. 418–419. The depth of disillusionment is best measured perhaps by its lingering effects: A Gallup Poll of 1937 asked whether government regulation of stock exchanges has helped investors. The vast majority (69 %) answered yes; the rest answered no. The responses were politically partisan with more Democrats favoring regulation (83 % yes) than Republicans (47 % yes). But perhaps the most telling figure is that, when investors only were considered, 62 % thought regulation was helpful. George H. Gallup, *The Gallup Poll: Public Opinion 1935–1971* (New York: Random House, 1972), p. 72.

either in response to the demands of the capitalist ruling class or as a quasi-independent structure functioning to defend the long-term interests of that class, federal regulation of the economy is a political measure designed to prop up the capitalist system, to prevent overturning existing structures of domination.[26] The theory is based on the three-pronged proposition that officials are relatively autonomous of control by capitalists, including financiers; that they can pursue their interests through regulatory policies, even when these policies are strongly opposed by particular capitalist interests; and that they do so attempting to shore up their own position of advantage.[27]

To take the state's autonomy seriously forces recognition that, in our case, the federal securities laws were only one possible course of policy to pursue, that there was a range of policy alternatives extending from doing nothing to recommending — as Rexford Tugwell (and others) did — that the flow of capital should not be determined through markets but should be coordinated through administrative agencies.[28] Once recognized, questions of motive and purpose arise: Why did public officials press to do anything at all? And, why were their proposals sufficiently moderate as to reproduce rather than replace market mechanisms of capital control?

These questions, as Fred Block has shown, encompass the major theoretical problems a structural theory of the state is meant to solve.[29] Following Block's account, public officials pursue policies favoring the general interest of capital without capitulating completely to any particular capitalist interest. They do not oppose the general interest of capital because the state's own survival depends on maintaining a reasonable level of economic activity to finance its activities. Public officials are constrained to adopt policies which sustain business confidence to invest as required for economic growth. Yet, to keep power, they must also have public support, which may require adopting policies opposed by particular capitalists to minimize "class conflict," especially conflict over wages.

---

26 This is not to say, of course, that there are no constraints on governments, limiting the effectiveness of "state interventions." See Dietrich Rueschemeyer and Peter B. Evans, "The State and Economic Transformation," pp. 44–77.

27 See, e.g., James O'Connor, *The Fiscal Crisis of the State* (New York: St. Martin's Press, 1973); Nicos Poulantzas, *Political Power and Social Classes*, trans. Timothy O'Hagen (London: New Left Books, 1973); Fred Block, "The Ruling Class Does Not Rule: Notes on the Marxist Theory of the State," *Socialist Revolution*, 7 (1977), 6–28; and Eric A. Nordlinger, *On the Autonomy of the Democratic State* (Cambridge, Mass.: Harvard University Press, 1981).

28 Seligman, *The Transformation of Wall Street*, pp. 40–41.

29 Block, "The Ruling Class Does Not Rule."

Now the balance between these two sometimes conflicting concerns, to retain business confidence and public support, varies depending principally (but not entirely) on whether levels of economic activity are likely to be affected by the erosion of business confidence.[30] When they are not, typically during periods of crisis, either war or major depression, then the "veto" of capital over actions by public officials is reduced to a minimum. It is not eliminated. While firm in his belief that government ought to regulate business, Roosevelt was concerned not to pass securities laws so strict that they led to a "bankers' strike," in which enterprisers were discouraged from borrowing capital needed to build their businesses. (Indeed, such concerns explain in part the willingness of Roosevelt's administration to entertain amendments to the Securities Act during debate over the Securities Exchange Act in 1934). At the same time, however, it is precisely during national crises that the requirement for public support is both great and problematic. Consequently, crises like the Great Depression are periods when public officials are most likely to try to expand the government's role, especially to regulate economic activity, to minimize the intensity of "class struggles."

Theda Skocpol has shown that this general argument of Block's can be applied to construct a powerful explanation of New Deal labor policy.[31] It can also be applied to our case to explain why public officials were encouraged to press for federal securities controls. According to Block, such an expansion of the state's role should be tied to the "class struggle," and we shall argue that it can be.[32] To do so we have only to assume, with Skocpol, that the electoral contests of 1930 and 1932 were "an expression, albeit highly politically mediated, of class-based pressures from below ... to use state power for reformist and regulatory efforts."[33] Let us see how so.

The critical event creating the possibility for federal involvement in securities regulation was the opening in the Senate of an inquiry into stock exchange practices. More than any other event, this investigation was responsible for creating the public perception that the market had failed in ways which required a political response. Disclosures of deceptive and fraudulent trading practices by leading financiers stood in sharp contrast to the idea of "welfare capitalism" promoted by business leaders during the 1920s and based on the

---

30 *Ibid.*, pp. 14 – 15.
31 Theda Skocpol, "Political Response to Capitalist Crisis: Neo-Marxist Theories of the State and the Case of the New Deal," *Politics and Society*, 10 (1980), 155 – 202.
32 Block, "The Ruling Class Does Not Rule," pp. 21 – 22.
33 Skocpol, "Political Response to Capitalist Crisis," p. 185.

notion that they were reliable "trustees of the well-being of the American people."[34]

Although sometimes it is argued as though the idea to regulate securities transactions was confined to Democrats, credit for initiating this investigation belongs to Herbert Hoover.[35] After jawboning leaders on Wall Street for three years, trying unsuccessfully to persuade them to strengthen their self-regulation, it was Hoover who in 1932 endorsed a Senate resolution making possible an investigation of the stock market. Hoover's patience with the financiers was finally broken when his close friend and financial adviser, Senator Frederick Walcott, told him that stock speculators affiliated with the Democratic party planned to drive down stock prices simply to embarrass Hoover and to hurt his chances for reelection. The fact is significant for illustrating the influence of political struggle on the course of policy-making. Needing to retain public support to win reelection, Hoover asked for the investigation, which financiers opposed, and hoped through it to expose the "conspiracy" against him.[36] Hoover's action illustrates a central point: Disclosure of market failures here is simply a strategy of political action. Its purpose is to generate symbolic resources needed to define a program of action that responds to an electoral crisis.

Of course, it does not always work. The conspiracy was never proved, and the misdeeds revealed by the Senate's investigation in 1932 were mild in their degree of scandal when compared to those revelations made after Pecora took charge of the investigation in 1933. By themselves, they could not have led to enactment of federal securities laws and did not lead to Hoover's re-election. Still, Congressional investigation was begun and its revelations were sufficiently scandalous to encourage the Democratic party to promise, in their 1932 platform, to protect investors from the misrepresentations of securities promoters.[37] In Roosevelt, moreover, the Democrats chose a candidate for president who was perhaps more likely than Hoover to redeem such a campaign promise. Before the election, Roosevelt made plain his belief that financiers exerted a power too large and uncontrolled for a society already passed through the economic reorganization required by industrial revolution. "The day of the great promoter or the financial Titan . . . is over," he declared,

---

34 On the idea of "welfare capitalism," see Theda Skocpol and John Ikenberry, "The Political Formation of the American Welfare State," *Comparative Social Research*, 6 (1983), 114 – 116.

35 Taking credit for the Democrats is Moley, *The First New Deal*, pp. 229 – 232.

36 Brooks, *Once in Golconda*, pp. 135 – 140; Carosso, *Investment Banking in America*, pp. 229 – 232.

37 Cowing, *Populists, Plungers, and Progressives*, p. 72.

and it is a proper role for the federal government to modify and control their activities.[38]

Whether the import of that declaration was fully understood at the time is unknown. It was an assertion of old, but still lively progressive concerns about the concentration of banking and the possibility that that concentration put excessive power into the hands of financiers.[39] It appealed to those most likely to support expanding the government's role as regulators of financial interests, namely, to those living in the south and west. Since 1893, senators from these states had supported various legislative proposals to curb speculation to a much greater extent than eastern senators had.[40] And it was from these two regions that Roosevelt drew strong electoral support.[41] Without denying that Roosevelt pursued a policy consistent with his own political beliefs, constituency pressure and the arithmetic of electoral contests played no small role in establishing the policy of federal securities regulation. Over 80 percent of the senators from western and southern states voted for the Securities Exchange Act in 1934 despite the strong and effective opposition of Wall Street, while over 55 percent of the senators from eastern states opposed the bill.[42] Plainly, support from the south and west was a critical factor enabling Roosevelt to pursue and win adoption of his regulatory policies.

The major contribution of this structural theory lies in explaining the motivation of government officials to pursue expansion of the government's role regulating the securities market. It explains the original impetus to investigate financiers and the persistence of Roosevelt in pushing to pass federal securities laws, both in terms of (presumably class-linked) struggles to win electoral support in the midst of a depression.

It is clear in this context why disclosure of market failures did not precede (to cause), but followed (and was an effect of) initiation of government action to regulate the market. In order for government initiative to succeed, it had to define a particular program of political action that responded to the economic crisis and could attract a viable coalition of support. Both Hoover

38 Franklin D. Roosevelt, "The Commonwealth Address," *The People Shall Judge*, ed. Staff, Social Science Division, University of Chicago, vol. 2 (Chicago: University of Chicago Press, 1967), pp. 449 – 455. The address was originally delivered in 1932.

39 Louis D. Brandeis's book, *Other People's Money and How Banker's Use It* (New York: Frederick A. Stokes, 1932, orig. 1914), is perhaps the most famous statement of this concern.

40 Cowing, *Populists, Plungers, and Progressives*, p. 23.

41 John A. Allswang, *The New Deal and American Politics* (New York: John Wiley & Sons, 1978), pp. 48 – 49.

42 Cowing, *Populists, Plungers, and Progressives*, p. 273.

and Roosevelt perceived that disclosure of moral failings by Wall Street leaders would generate the symbolic resources needed for success in that endeavor. And both supported the Congressional investigation which was ultimately responsible for supplying the disclosures. But notice: Both did not succeed. Hoover's investigation led nowhere. The structural impetus to reform supplied by class struggle does not guarantee that state intervention will actually result in an expansion of the state's regulatory role. How then can we explain when regulatory expansion will occur? Why did Roosevelt's program succeed?

The Role of Political Contingency

Political contingencies play an important part shaping the expansion of government roles. Based on his analysis of the federal government's growth and transformation during the populist and progressive eras, Stephen Skowronek argues persuasively that "state building remains at all times a political contingency, a historical structural question."[43]

The assertion is not meant to support structural explanations about what motivates government officials to pursue expansionary policies. It aims to tell when their pursuits will succeed. Officials try to alter the institutions of government in response to perceived crisis or class conflict, and they do so in order to maintain their power and legitimacy. But whether they will successfully refashion institutions and relations between state and society is always a matter of uncertainty. The correlation between intentions and outcomes is unpredictable, because attempts to reform are mediated by preexisting institutional and political arrangements. How officials will respond to these arrangements cannot easily be foretold.[44]

Skocpol and Finegold add weight to Skowronek's emphasis on the influence of mediating institutional arrangements. Comparing the success of the Agricultural Adjustment Administration with the failure of the National Recovery Administration, they attribute the differences in outcome in large part to differences in the availability of institutions ready to support the intended work of each agency.[45] Contingencies, however, do not arise only from the

43 Stephen Skowronek, *Building a New American State* (Cambridge: Cambridge University Press, 1982), p. 285.

44 *Ibid.*, pp. 10–12.

45 Theda Skocpol and Kenneth Finegold, "Economic Intervention and the New Deal," *Political Science Quarterly*, 97 (1982), 255–278.

mediation of institutional arrangements. They may arise also from the differ-ential political capacities of actors recruited to fill roles which are structurally critical to implement a plan or program. Reference to contingency of this latter kind is needed to explain why New Deal proposals for federal securities regulation were finally adopted. The reason why is illustrated best perhaps by referring to the role played by Ferdinand Pecora. As counsel to the Senate Banking and Currency Committee investigating stock exchange practices, Pecora was singularly responsible for disclosures of wrong-doing by highly placed and well-known stock promoters and investment bankers. It is difficult to exaggerate the importance of these disclosures. They created the perception that there was a market failure significant enough in proportion to warrant legislative action. They persuaded some financiers to support passage of the Securities Act to keep the "good name of the investment banker" from being "dragged down" and led others to support the separation of commercial from investment banking. They supplied concrete examples of abuses which those drafting the securities bills would propose to abolish. They were, in sum, instrumental for securing passage of the original federal securities acts.[46]

It is essential to recognize how fortuitous it was that these disclosures were ever made. They were Pecora's distinctive achievement. Yet Pecora was not the first choice for the job of committee counsel, or even the second or third choice. Before him came William A. Gray, who actually held the post from April 1932, when the investigation began, through December 1932. To replace Gray, the committee made offers, in turn, to Samuel Untermyer, who had led the "money trust" investigation twenty years before, and to Irving Ben Cooper.[47] Both wanted the position, but, for quite different reasons, neither was able to serve. Only then was Pecora hired, as a fourth choice, and hired only to write a "final" report summarizing the committee's findings through 1932.

Matters changed when the committee chairman, the progressive Republican Senator Norbeck, asked Pecora to investigate the stock promotion of the defunct utility empire built by Samuel Insull. Norbeck's purpose was to demonstrate concern for his constituents in South Dakota who had suffered losses through these promotions. Pecora did much more. In only three days

46 Frankfurter, "The Federal Securities Act," pp. 53 – 54; James M. Landis, "The Legislative History of the Securities Act of 1933," George Washington Law Review, 28 (October, 1959), 29 – 49; Arthur W. Johnson, Winthrop W. Aldrich: Lawyer, Banker, Diplomat (Cambridge, Mass.: Graduate School of Business Administration, Harvard University, 1968), p. 150; Carosso, Investment Banking in America, pp. 351, 357, 371.
47 Raymond Moley, After Seven Years (New York: Harper & Brothers, 1939), pp. 176 – 177; Carosso, Investment Banking in America, p. 237.

of hearings, Pecora displayed his substantial investigative talents, getting the head of Halsey, Stuart, a major investment banking firm, to admit that their promotions of Insull's stocks were tainted by many conflicting interests and to reveal that they had hired an economics professor from the University of Chicago to "boom" Insull's shares on what was supposedly an unbiased, educational radio show. In light of these disclosures, the committee's work was continued, and Pecora was able to focus national attention on the moral failings of the country's leading financiers, with consequences we have already described.[48]

Now is it reasonable to give this credit to Pecora alone? The abuses had been committed. Would anyone in the same position have made the same or similar disclosures? Argument here is difficult because it implies the counter-factual, had Pecora not made his discoveries, then securities regulation would not have been forthcoming. That is not necessarily true. Roosevelt planned to seek federal securities law before Pecora made a single disclosure and, given his other legislative achievements, there are few (if any) grounds for believing that he would not have gotten some law passed.[49] The point, however, is that we cannot explain passage of the particular laws which did pass without referring to Pecora's disclosures. Moreover, it is possible to argue that others in the same position might not have made these disclosures. After all, William Gray held the job of committee counsel for nine months. During that time he made no similarly dramatic disclosures, there was no perception of widespread market failure based on his work and no impetus for reform.[50]

This is not to argue that Pecora's achievements were single-handedly responsible for successful passage of federal securities laws. They were important, but not all-important. Consider, for example, the similar achievements of Samuel Untermyer. More acerbic, and perhaps less persuasive than Pecora in his handling of the "money trust" investigation, Untermyer nonetheless documented the deceptive and manipulative practices of stock trading well enough to cause editors of many daily and periodical journals, not all of which were muckraking, to conclude that there might have been abuses which justified federal regulation.[51] To correct the abuses, Untermyer drafted a bill to regulate stock transactions through the Post Office, an arrangement which drew no support from Congress or Wilson. Nevertheless, Untermyer stuck

48 Ibid., pp. 328 – 330; Pecora, Wall Street Under Oath.
49 Freidel, Franklin D. Roosevelt, pp. 70 – 74; Moley, The First New Deal, pp. 307 – 308.
50 Carosso, Investment Banking in America, pp. 325 – 326.
51 Literary Digest, (14 January 1913), pp. 1 – 3, (8 February 1913), pp. 261 – 263.

doggedly beside his proposal, refusing to compromise, and so dashed hopes for establishing federal securities control at that time.[52]

What distinguished the success of New Deal from the failure of "money trust" proposals was the quality of legislative draftsmanship and the capacity to compromise which characterized the New Deal program. The importance of legal drafting became evident early in Roosevelt's administration. Roosevelt wanted to introduce a bill to regulate stock exchanges during his first days in office. Untermyer was retained, before Roosevelt was inaugurated, to draft the measure. But Untermyer was still rigidly attached to the idea of regulation through Post Office control and, in essence, reproduced the bill which failed a generation before, forcing Roosevelt to postpone consideration of exchange regulation until 1934. Turning instead to regulation of securities issuance, Roosevelt submitted to Congress a loosely written bill that was ill-conceived in many details and easily argued against by financiers opposed to any federal securities controls. Roosevelt was wisely advised by his Congressional leaders to abandon hope for passing this measure.[53]

With no prospects for establishing the sought-after securities regulation, Roosevelt's assistant, Raymond Moley, contacted Felix Frankfurter − a student of Brandeis, professor of law at Harvard, and confidant of Roosevelt − asking for help. Frankfurter immediately recommended three of his protégés, James Landis, Thomas Corcoran, and Benjamin Cohen, as men able to devise the appropriate statutes. Here is testimony to the worth of good writing. Within a few days, these three did write a bill to regulate securities issuance which survived the best efforts of Wall Street's attorneys to criticize it. As a result, the bill passed easily through Congress to establish the first instrument of federal securities control.[54]

Yet beside skillful writing, compromise is required to ensure successful passage of a measure. Financiers were disturbed by the strict moral requirements of the Securities Act which, as we noted, made all underwriters liable for the total amount of a securities offering, no matter what percentage of the offering they were responsible for selling. Despite the promises of "welfare capitalism," financiers were reluctant to shoulder the fiduciary responsibility these liability provisions imposed. They wished to qualify the degree to which

52 Arthur S. Link, *Woodrow Wilson and the Progressive Era* (New York: Harper Torchbooks, 1963), p. 70; Cowing, *Populists, Plungers, and Progressives,* p. 62.

53 Freidel, *Franklin D. Roosevelt,* pp. 341 − 344; Parrish, *Securities Regulation and the New Deal,* pp. 44 − 56; Moley, *The First New Deal,* pp. 308 − 312.

54 Seligman, *The Transformation of Wall Street,* pp. 63 − 72; Freidel, *Franklin D. Roosevelt,* pp. 345 − 350; Parrish, *Securities Regulation and the New Deal,* pp. 56 − 68; Moley, *The First New Deal,* pp. 312 − 315.

they were "trustees acting for others." They exerted great pressure on members of Roosevelt's administration to seek amendments softening the liability provisions of the act, and they let it be believed that they would fail to bring out any major securities issues until the amendments were passed.[55] Roosevelt bristled under the pressure, particularly under the threat of a "bankers' strike," so much so that he nearly sacrificed the political goal to establish federal securities control.

After publicly admonishing bankers in the fall of 1933, reminding them that their government must be leader and judge even over them, Roosevelt backed his admonishments in February 1934 by supporting a strict securities exchange bill drafted by Cohen and Corcoran with help from Pecora's staff. Though a model of draftsmanship, the measure overestimated the degree of market regulation which Roosevelt's Congressional constituency was prepared to support.[56] The bill effectively banned any speculative trading on the floor of the exchange. Worse, by proposing to segregate broker from dealer functions, it virtually denied brokers of any opportunity to participate in the underwriting business, which would have meant bankruptcy for many small broker-dealers in the south and west and the demise of regional stock exchanges. Met then by the well-organized resistance of financiers, so strong that even fresh disclosures by Pecora could not overcome it, and opposed by many across the country, the bill had no chance for passage. It stood to be Roosevelt's first major legislative defeat, dealing a serious blow to the president's prestige.[57]

Under this threat, Roosevelt sought compromise. He agreed to amend the securities exchange bill. He shifted regulation from the Federal Trade Commission to a newly created Securities and Exchange Commission which Wall Street (erroneously) believed it might control. He evaded the issue of broker-dealer segregation by assigning the matter to the Securities and Exchange Commission for future study and legislative recommendation. By this device, for which Landis takes credit, opposition to the measure by financiers was split as regional brokers, no longer worried about the threat of segregation, came now to back the measure.[58] And, hardly less significant, he agreed to

55 Seligman, *The Transformation of Wall Street*, pp. 76 – 80; *Roosevelt and Frankfurter, Their Correspondence: 1928 – 1945*, ed. Max Freedman (Boston: Little, Brown, 1967), pp. 157 – 159.

56 Arthur M. Schlesinger, Jr., *The Coming of the New Deal* (Boston: Houghton Mifflin, 1958), p. 500; *Roosevelt and Frankfurter*, pp. 195 – 196.

57 Seligman, *The Transformation of Wall Street*, pp. 85 – 93.

58 James M. Landis, *Reminiscences of James M. Landis* (New York, Oral History Collection, Columbia University), pp. 200 – 201.

amend the Securities Act, in particular, to limit the civil liability financiers assumed when underwriting new securities issues and to lower the standard to be used when judging their behavior from that of a fiduciary to that of an ordinary prudent man.[59] With these changes, more than enough members of Congress could freely support the measure to assure its passage and, not incidentally, to salvage Roosevelt's prestige.

These compromises may seem to indicate a failure by Roosevelt to achieve his purpose, that he buckled to the opposition of financiers. That judgment is too strong. Without these compromises, no securities exchange bill would have passed, and the Securities Act might well have been amended into impotence. With the compromises, New Dealers successfully expanded the government's role to encompass securities regulation, fulfilling an ambition left unfulfilled in the wake of "money trust" hearings twenty years before. That it was possible to succeed this time depended, in the last analysis, on the availability of legal draftsman able both to write tight legislation and to compromise strategically when required to gain the larger objective, something Untermyer had been unable to do.

Their availability, it is my main point, was a fortuitous event – one that could not be counted on, one which an earlier and similar situation of perceived market failure official ambition to regulate never called forth. And if the argument is correct, it confirms Skowronek's general point (which we noticed earlier): The success of officials at expanding the government's role depends on political contingencies which are not determined entirely by the perception of crisis or by the structural interests to which officials would respond.[60] The origins of federal securities regulation, in sum, are far more complex than the simple hypothesis of market failure makes it seem. We are misled by a mechanistic model that begins with the moral laxity of financiers and proceeds through the crash and depression to government investigation and intervention. The historical order of events does not necessarily reproduce that causal order.

The depression created electoral pressures causing political leaders to investigate the stock market before any knowledge of previous market failures was disclosed. Disclosure of market failures – specifically of moral deception and fraud by leading financiers – was important when it occurred. It generated the critical symbolic resources needed politically to define a regulatory program that expanded the state's control over the market. Successful use of investigations for this purpose, however, cannot be taken for granted.

59 Seligman, *The Transformation of Wall Street*, pp. 93–94.
60 Stephen Skowronek, *Building a New American State.*

The art of investigation to create a program for reform around which an effective political coalition might be built has not yet been routinized and defies bureaucratization. Even when the art is highly refined, as it was by Pecora, it may not always succeed. Compromises were required to assure passage of the law, and these compromises established limits on the range within which the state could exercise its control.

As finally passed, the legislation established the principle of federal control over the stock market. It required corporate officials and investment bankers to disclose information about the conditions of firms whose securities were sold to the public. It forbade commercial banks and securities dealers from associating with one another to underwrite and distribute new securities issues. It forbade traders on the exchanges from employing trading techniques supposedly useful for those trying to manipulate stock prices. And it created the Securities and Exchange Commission to ensure that these changes in market conduct actually occurred.

But the purposes for which this control was to be exercised were no longer entirely clear. The initially strong moral emphasis embodied in the original Securities Act, especially in its civil liability provisions, reflected the intensity of public concern over the gross moral laxity in the conduct of some financiers. These provisions were essentially removed from the Securities Act within a year in a compromise to win passage for the Securities Exchange Act. Moreover, for the same reason, the fragmented, loosely coupled system of large and small regional markets was preserved under private control, an arrangement which was bound to make exertion of regulatory authority more difficult. How such laws would affect the moral order of the market could hardly be foreseen.

Chapter 3

Market Ideology and the Organization of Trading

To show how the new federal securities acts affected the market, we must look first at their effects upon the norms which govern stock trading. Trading, after all, is the central activity of the market. Beliefs about how one ought to trade are, therefore, critical for the constitution of the market's normative order. There are three questions, then, which we have to ask in this chapter: What beliefs guided how market participants thought they ought to trade before the federal securities acts were passed? How were those beliefs altered after the new laws were imposed? And what consequences did these changes in belief have for the organization of stock trading? The questions assume my thesis that beliefs did in fact change. They changed, I shall argue, in response to legal requirements on corporations to disclose information about their financial condition and to proscriptions against certain manipulative techniques. Before explaining how so, we must briefly examine the general character of these beliefs — or "market ideologies" — and their importance to our understanding of the organization of trading.

Market ideologies, as I define the term, are essentially beliefs about how we should measure the value of capital. They help traders to determine the relative worthiness of different stocks. They define certain factors as more important than others to consider when figuring out which stocks to buy and which to sell, in what amounts, and at what price. And they provide a theory to explain why and when stock prices vary as they do.

The theory, of course, may not be objectively accurate. Stock market participants are not empowered with any special ability to predict the future course of stock prices. Like any other act of fortune-telling, such prediction is (presently) beyond the capacities of the human mind. Except under special circumstances, as we have in the case, say, of insider trading, the act of stock trading is filled with uncertainty. That is why these beliefs are indispensable to the market. Absent any interpretive framework, the fluctuation of stock prices appears to be entirely capricious, an unordered event. Human beings generally are loath to act in the face of uncertainty, and they avoid doing so unless they possess some collectively defined response that lends a deterministic character to their proceeding, even if the response is mythic. For those in the stock market, the "unreliable" and "mercurial" nature of stock prices "stimulates hard-headed search for firmer ground" which beliefs about why stock prices change evidently provide.[1]

The importance of these beliefs for our purposes lies less with the psychological security they bestow than with their effect on market structure. Participants in the market focus their attention on the factors these beliefs identify as important, and they guide their choice of relationships and their activities according to what these beliefs prescribe. These beliefs, in other words, are like an operating code for the market, a code that critically determines the organization of trading, or structure, which we observe in the market. The organization of stock trading, in short, is constituted by market ideologies, by beliefs about stock prices and why they change.[2]

The converse of this argument is also true. Market structure must accommodate the prescriptions of a particular operating code before that code can be institutionalized. Here we indicate alternative possibilities by which market structures change. So far as beliefs can be acted out and are adhered to by market participants, they affect market organization. Should the content of these beliefs change, so too will the market's structure. But when beliefs adhered to once cannot be acted out in the present, when market structure no longer accommodates them, then the effect of these beliefs on market organization whithers. In time, they will be replaced by alternative beliefs.

1 The quotation is from a market analyst, Nicholas Molodovsky, "Valuation of Common Stocks," *Financial Analysts Journal*, 15 (February 1959), 98. But the idea is not entirely new to sociology. As Arnold M. Rose once observed, "before economic forces can exert their influence on prices, they must be interpreted ... in the minds of men so as to form a belief as to the course of future trends in stock market prices. It is this belief which determines prices directly ..." *Kyklos*, 19 (1966), 287. Empirical confirmation of Rose's argument is found in Wayne E. Baker, "The Social Structure of a National Securities Market," *American Journal of Sociology*, 89 (January 1984), 775 – 811.

2 Though infrequently noted in the literature on organizations, all institutions are constituted by a particular correlation of beliefs and patterns of action. No car is built, no war is fought, and no government bureaucracy is run in the absence of shared beliefs about how to transform raw materials into finished products, about the strategies and tactics essential to debilitate an enemy, or about the appropriate managerial techniques for motivating clerical staff. A review of the available literature is contained in Lee S. Sproull, "Beliefs in Organizations," *Handbook of Organizational Design*, ed. Paul C. Nystrom and William H. Starbuck, vol. 2 (New York: Oxford University Press, 1981), pp. 203 – 224.

In the case before us, it is the latter event which takes place. Federal securities laws altered patterns of trading in the market in ways that made it impossible any longer to follow long-held, what I shall call "materialist," beliefs about what makes stock prices change. At the same time they facilitated adoption of "pragmatic" beliefs, beliefs which before the 1930s could not compete successfully for recognition within the market, because their prescriptions could not be acted on. It was as a result of this change from "materialist" to "pragmatic" beliefs, a change induced by law, that the organization of stock trading was transformed.

Before the New Deal: Materialist Ideology Organizes Trading

Beliefs about stock prices, about what they stand for and why they change, are in fact beliefs about how we should measure the value of capital. Stock prices, after all, are the product of collective attempts to assess the present worth of the equity accumulated within a particular business enterprise. Two views dominate about how this assessment should be made.[3] On one side are the "materialists" for whom capital consists of physical goods. The value of capital for materialists equals the sum of the current market prices for these goods. On the other side are the "pragmatists" for whom capital is a fund to be deployed for earning income. The value of capital for pragmatists is measured by the consequences of fund deployment, that is, by the capitalized present value of all the income the fund is likely to earn. Both views find defenders among those close to the market. But until the 1930s, materialist beliefs prevailed, as they did generally among economists, and it is materialist beliefs which organized the market.

The ideas of John Moody, who began his career as a publisher of financial statistics in 1900, illustrate the way materialist beliefs were applied. In his book on *The Art of Wall Street Investing* (1906), Moody attributes differences in the price behavior of bonds, railroad stocks, and stocks of industrial

---

3 John Hicks, "Capitalist Controversies: Ancient and Modern," in *Economic Perspectives* (Oxford: Clarendon Press, 1977), pp. 149–165, esp. 151–152. Notice that Hicks employs the terms "materialist" and "fundist." I substitute the term "pragmatic" for "fundist" to emphasize the importance of future earnings for this position, that is, the pragmatic dwelling upon the importance of the consequences of capital deployment. Although our terms are different, our meanings are the same.

companies to the relation each kind of security had to the corporation's real property.[4] Bond prices were more or less stable, because they were secured contractually by the assets of the company. Railroad stock prices were also stable, though less stable than bonds. As with all stocks, these did not represent claims backed by assets, but actual ownership of property left over after all debts were paid. The only entitlement they carried was to benefits produced by use of the property, such benefits if received being paid out at the directors' discretion as dividends. The reason for the price stability of railroad stocks, Moody claimed, was that the value of railroad property had risen so much that the customarily limited claims of stockowners were relatively secure; they were not much affected by additional borrowings or changes in earnings.[5] In contrast, the price behavior of industrial stocks was erratic, and for the good reason that it was uncertain whether real property stood behind them. Moody wrote:

> As is well known, nearly all the newer industrial corporations are greatly over-capitalized and, as a result, the common stocks are of a very speculative nature ... [and] do not represent anything except voting power and future hopes.[6]

For Moody, all depended on the accumulation of real property. The level and stability of stock prices were tied to the net value of real property which corporation's owned.

Materialist beliefs supply an explanation for why stock prices change and suggest a practical guide for trading stocks successfully, that is, with a profit. The secret is to know where the property is. The significance of such knowledge was made very clear in the primary market where stocks are sold for the first time. To limit their risk, promoters of corporate reorganizations working during the gilded age tried to persuade corporate owners to accept new stock rather than cash in exchange for the promoter's right to sell the new stock publicly. In addition, they wanted to sell as many shares as possible to increase the capitalization of the new enterprise. But should the owners think the promoters were trying to capitalize the corporation for too great an amount, more than the value of the property on hand, then the owners would insist on cash payment. They were confident, given cash, that they could buy all the new overcapitalized stock they wanted later on, and at low prices. Demand for cash payment set limits on how far promoters could go in selling shares in new industrial combinations. The key point is that

---

4 John Moody, *The Art of Wall Street Investing* (New York: Moody Corporation, 1906), chap. 2.
5 *Ibid.*, chap. 4.
6 *Ibid.*, p. 70.

determination of the limits was based on assessment of the value of corporate property by those in a position to know.[7]

Not everyone was equally well placed to determine whether stocks were adequately backed by assets, and so many were reluctant to buy them. Under these circumstances, promoters searched for some means to overcome investor resistance to stock promotions. (Profits from successful promotions before the 1930s could net over twenty percent of the offerings' total value.) On the advice of investment bankers, they divided stock capitalization into two categories. One category, of preferred stock, would be backed by the earning capacity of the company and secured by fixed assets, while the other, of common stock, stood for uncertainty, risk, and anticipated growth. A benefit of this division was that the combined value of the preferred and common shares usually exceeded the value of the stock they replaced.[8] As Navin and Sears put it:

> So long as the "trust" certificates had represented risk as well as investment value, they had little appeal for the conservative moneyed man. But once the two aspects had been separated, the worth to each — to the conservative investor and to the rash speculator — was increased.[9]

Thus the amount of capital that could be floated in the market was increased by a kind of differentiation.

Notice that sometimes knowledge was certain that no property stood behind the stock. It was not uncommon early in the century for subscribers to preferred stock issues to receive a "bonus" share of common stock to sweeten the pot. Here stock is a vehicle for pure speculation. This direct appeal to the speculative element offended some who saw in it a subversion of the "great industries of the nation into mere tools of the gambler and the speculator, eventually resulting in the great injury of a nation of industries."[10] But reaction against speculation was far from universal. Students of the market believed that risk was an inevitable aspect of exchange, necessary to commerce, and necessary for someone to assume for trade to expand.[11] Popular writers

7 Thomas R. Navin and Marion V. Sears, "The Rise of a Market for Industrial Securities, 1887 – 1902," *Business History Review*, 29 (Summer, 1955), 105 – 138.

8 *Ibid.*, pp. 131 – 133; Vincent P. Carosso, *Investment Banking in America* (Cambridge, Mass.: Harvard University Press, 1970), p. 24.

9 Navin and Sears, "The Rise of a Market for Industrial Securities," p. 120.

10 James B. Dill, "Industrials as Investments for Small Capital," *Annals of the American Academy of Political and Social Science*, XV (May, 1900), 111.

11 Henry Crosby Emery, *Speculation on the Stock and Produce Exchanges of the United States* (Westport, Conn.: Greenwood Press, 1969, orig. 1896); Carl Parker, "Government Regulation of Speculation," *Annals of the American Academy of Political and Social Science*, XXXVIII (1911), 444 – 472; Governor's Committee on Speculation in Securities

applauded the speculative aspects of stock trading precisely because it was representative of the American "gambling spirit" which they believed was responsible for the nation's growth.[12]

Underlying this praise, however, was an important moral lesson. In a time when disclosures of financial information by corporations were by no means common and when disclosures made were not always reliable, uncertainty about the course of stock prices could not be overcome by most adherents of materialist beliefs. Therefore, only those able heroically to embrace the uncertainty of stock trading should enter the market. All others should avoid it altogether.[13]

Who then embraced uncertainty? On what grounds? And with what consequences for the social organization of stock trading? The crucial qualification, following Moody, was knowledge about whether a particular corporate stock actually represented fixed assets and, if so, what the value of those assets were. The more assets and the greater their value, a materialist would argue, the less volatile the changes in a stock's price were supposed to be. Anyone who knew what property values were was in a position of advantage, and this was true whether the values were great or small. If they were great, the materialist trader knew that the stocks represented a sound and stable investment good to own outright. If they were small, the materialist trader knew that the stock's price movements would be volatile and supposedly

and Commodities, *Report* (dated 1909) as reprinted in W. C. Van Antwerp, *The Stock Exchange from Within* (Garden City, N.Y.: Doubleday, Page, 1913), pp. 415–417 (hereafter referred to as Hughes's Committee, *Report*, after Charles Evans Hughes, convener of the committee and then governor of New York).

12 See, e.g., Edwin Lefevre, "The American Gambling Spirit," *Harper's Weekly*, 47 (May, 1903), 704–705. There he writes:
Every business man speculates, not occasionally, but all the time. His business is founded upon it. The stockrail mill-owner, the woolen manufacturer, the restaurant keeper, all speculate. Americans are great business men because they are great gamblers. It is not that they are foolishly reckless, but that they are braver, less appalled by the possibility of disaster (p. 704).

13 Read in the Hughes's Committee, *Report*:
A real distinction exists between speculation which is carried on by persons of means and experience, and based on an intelligent forecast, and that which is carried on by persons without these qualifications. The former is closely connected with regular business. While not unaccompanied by waste and loss, this speculation accomplishes an amount of good which offsets much of its cost. The latter does but a small amount of good and an almost incalculable amount of evil ... The problem, wherever speculation is strongly rooted, is to eliminate that which is wasteful and morally destructive, while retaining and allowing free play to that which is beneficial ... The most fruitful policy will be found in measures which will lessen speculation by persons not qualified to engage in it (p. 417).

subject to manipulation. In such cases, he might borrow money to buy the stock in hopes of driving its price up, or borrow stock to sell short in hopes of driving its price down; then he would close the transaction — selling at a high price or buying (to replace the borrowed stock) at a low price — hoping to catch a profit off the induced price fluctuation. For such a game to work, however, all stock traders could not be equally knowledgeable.

Knowledge about property values was not equally distributed among market participants, and this fact was crucial for determining the social organization of stock trading while the materialist ideology was dominant.

Market participants were arranged in a hierarchy with their relative position based upon one's access to accurate knowledge about corporate property values. At the top of this hierarchy were investment bankers and corporate insiders, people whom Moody called "masters of capital."[14] Moody was referring to such familiar figures in American financial history as J. J. Hill and E. H. Harriman, H. H. Rogers and William Rockefeller, and, of course, J. P. Morgan, for they apparently controlled how much if any property would stand behind stocks sold to the public. Their common knowledge about "true values" could lead sometimes to dramatic contests among them. In 1901, for example, Hill and Harriman in combination cornered the stock of the Northern Pacific Railroad, driving its price sky-high. By itself, the property was not so valuable and could not justify the price bid for its stock. But Hill and Harriman battled one another for control, because either one could merge the railroad with their other railroad holdings to establish a virtual monopoly over the western portion of the nation's transportation system.[15]

Sometimes investment bankers used their control over property deliberately to mislead less knowledgeable investors about the value of corporate assets. Rogers and Rockefeller withdrew Anaconda Copper from the Amalgamated Copper combination, substituting for it a property of meager value, but they kept silent about the switch to maintain Amalgamated's high stock price and enriched themselves as a result by $36,000,000.[16] By knowing what values existed where and by being in a position to create (or deplete) values if need be, many thought that investment bankers and corporate insiders could virtually assure the success of their undertakings.

14 John Moody, *The Masters of Capital* (New Haven: Yale University Press, 1919).
15 *Ibid.*, pp. 89 – 109. Neither one was powerful enough to wrest control from the other. In a compromise, imposed by J. P. Morgan, Hill and Harriman shared control over the Northern Pacific through joint ownership of the Northern Securities Company. The Supreme Court later judged this arrangement to be an unlawful monopoly. The company was liquidated in 1904.
16 Thomas Lawson, *Frenzied Finance* (Westport, Conn.: Greenwood Press, 1968, orig. 1905), pp. 23 – 32; Louis Filler, *The Muckrakers* (University Park, Pa.: Pennsylvania State University Press, 1976), pp. 176 – 184.

Below them in the hierarchy were stock manipulators and traders operating on the floor of the exchange. They were professional speculators. Prominent names here are James R. Keene, Thomas Lawson, and Jesse Livermore. They did not possess direct knowledge about property values. They did possess highly developed skills at stock trading. They knew well how to employ matched orders and wash sales to create the appearance of trading volume when in fact there was none (or not so much).[17] And they knew (or seemed to know) how to organize trading pools to coordinate trading either to raise or to lower a stock's price.[18]

These were skills investment bankers and corporate insiders valued and could use. As a result, these speculators were frequently well connected with those who knew where real values lay. They worked on their behalf. J. J. Hill hired Keene to buy shares of the Northern Pacific Railroad in the operation which quickly led to Hill's shared cornering of the market in that stock.[19] Rogers and Rockefeller hired Lawson to promote distribution of the Amal-gamated Copper stock at a high price even without the Anaconda Copper. This was to be done through market manipulation which was the common way to promote new stock issues at the time.[20] A committee appointed in 1908 by New York's Governor Hughes to investigate securities speculation concluded that speculators' "connections with corporations issuing or con-trolling particular securities" and "their familiarity with the techniques of dealings on the Exchange" enabled them to "manipulate values," "to move prices up or down," and so "in some degree" protected them "from the dangers" encountered by other stock traders.[21]

Below the professional speculators came the "tipsters, the windbags, and the unqualified optimists."[22] They were people with capital, some experi-ence and knowledge of general conditions of business, but without specific knowledge of property values or special skills in trading. Some of these were earnest people with scruples who believed that they could be helpful

---

17 Matched orders and wash sales are two techniques for generating trading volume in a particular security without actually affecting share ownership. The purpose is to promote the interest of others in trading the stock, creating a trend in the stock's price, and then to trade against the trend to catch a profit. For formal definitions turn to Chapter 2, note 8.

18 Richard Wyckoff, *Wall Street Adventures through Forty Years* (Westport, Conn.: Green-wood Press, 1968, orig. 1930), pp. 130, 148 – 149; Edwin Lefevre, *Reminiscences of a Stock Operator* (Larchmont, N. Y.: American Research Council, 1964, orig. 1923).

19 Moody, *The Masters of Capital*, p. 103.

20 Lawson's, *Frenzied Finance*, pp. 23 – 32; Hughes Committee, *Report*, pp. 421 – 422.

21 *Ibid.*, pp. 418 – 419.

22 Merryle Stanley Ruykeyser, "Wall Street's Speculative Optimism," *The Nation*, (Novem-ber 14, 1928), 514; Hughes Committee, *Report*, p. 419.

to others by passing on what they learned about property values from reading newspapers and broker circulars or by listening to the radio. Some were without scruples – Raliegh J. Curtis and A. Newton Plummer, for example, who were employed by equally unscrupulous people during the 1920 s boom to spread false tips about stocks through the mass media.[23] Most, however, were trading quietly for their own account, though with what success is most uncertain. They were hampered in their dealings by requirements to pay interest and commission charges which investment bankers and professional speculators could avoid and by their lack of definite knowledge which left them prey to turns of luck. The hoped for, and occasionally realized, gain kept them at it, but only until "a serious or ruinous loss force[d] them out of the 'Street'."[24]

Last of all, on the bottom, were the "lambs," the people shorn in the market, whom the Hughes Committee refers to delicately as "inexperienced persons."[25] They were the tip takers. They bought stocks naively, acting on whatever information they may have heard or relying blindly on impulse. And they were habitués of bucket shops where they simply bet on stock price movements without actually buying or selling shares.[26]

The overarching importance of knowledge about property values lies in its central place within materialist beliefs about how to understand the level of stock prices and to explain why stock prices change. It is the central tenet of the materialist market ideology that stock prices are determined by the market value of physical property which corporations own, net of all indebtedness. Before the federal securities laws were passed in the 1930 s, for reasons we shall notice momentarily, there was no strong contending belief about which any rival organization of stock trading might form. There is no evidence that any alternative organization was ever contemplated, beyond the reformers' often expressed wish to exclude the unqualified from trading stocks. The stock market was a stable organizational form; patterns of trading were consistent with and reinforced by the dominant market ideology and vice versa. Stability, however, even long-lasting stability, is not the same thing as invulnerability to change.

23 U.S. Congress, Senate, Committee on Banking and Currency, *Stock Exchange Practices* (Washington, D.C.: Government Printing Office, 1932), pp. 447 – 161, 601 – 620.
24 Hughes Committee, *Report*, p. 419.
25 *Ibid.*
26 *Ibid.*; Patton Thomas, "The Bucket Shop in Speculation," *Munsey's*, (October, 1900), 68 – 70; Wyckoff, *Wall Street Adventures*, pp. 160 – 161, 258 – 266; Lefevre, *Reminiscences of a Stock Operator*, pp. 1 – 54.

Ideological Shift from Materialist to Pragmatic Beliefs

A notable achievement of the federal securities laws was to undermine the social organization of trading based on materialist beliefs. The principal instruments of this destruction were, first, the prohibition of manipulative stock trading and, second, the requirement that corporations issuing stocks make periodic public disclosures of their financial condition. There is nothing about either of these actions which casts doubt on the validity of materialist beliefs. To the extent that matters disclosed by corporations included information about the market value of their physical property, disclosure requirements might even be said to have supported materialist beliefs. How then did they contribute to an ideological shift within the market from materialist to pragmatic beliefs?

Undermining Materialist Beliefs

To begin, federal securities law substantially undermined the power of investment bankers within the market by requiring that bankers choose to be either commercial bankers or investment bankers, but not both. The effect of divorcing these two functions, at least in the short run, was to cut off the investment bankers' access to and control over the large amounts of capital deposited in commercial banks. Without so much capital to control, the extent of their influence was measurably curtailed.[27] Moreover, the new laws made it impossible legally to continue to act on materialist beliefs. Much of the profit to be gained from trading as a materialist came from engaging in manipulative trading of stocks whose value was uncertain. But manipulative trading practices, to create the appearance of heavy trading volume and wide swings in stock prices, were banned. Section 9 of the Securities Exchange Act explicitly forbade use of wash sales or matched orders, the spread of false or misleading information, or any other means artificially to raise or to depress stock prices. And early on, the Securities and Exchange Commission made clear its determination to enforce this prohibition by successfully prosecuting a violator, M. J. Meehan, a well-known and otherwise respected stock operator of the "old school."[28] Notice that the law never casts doubt on the

27 Mark S. Mizruchi, *The American Corporate Network, 1904–1974* (Beverly Hills: Sage, 1982).
28 Rudolph L. Weissman, *The New Wall Street* (New York: Arno Press, 1975, orig. 1939), pp. 127–137.

materialist premise that manipulation can occur and might succeed. On the contrary, it accepts the premise, but rejects the practice. Under the law, securities trades are meant to facilitate transfer of ownership of property, not speculation.

Given the trading hierarchy created by materialist beliefs, enforcement of this act alone would seem to preclude virtually everyone from trading except investment bankers and corporate insiders. As long as they alone possessed knowledge of corporate property values, only they could trade stocks without speculating. The intent of course was not to exclude people from the market. It was rather to include all those who wished to participate, but to include them on the same terms that investment bankers and corporate insiders were included. To make this possible, the Securities Act required corporations to disclose information about their financial condition before issuing new stocks to the public, and to update their disclosures periodically if any of their securities were listed on a registered securities exchange. The usefulness of these disclosures to investors is currently a matter of debate. Disclosure requirements were modeled after the practice of British accountants. They were not devised to meet well-defined needs of investors trying to evaluate the quality of a stock.[29] Nevertheless, the hierarchical social organization of the trading depended on differential access to just such information about corporate financial conditions. When this information was publicly distributed, the hierarchy based on materialist beliefs could not long endure.

Again, it is worth repeating that a requirement to disclose information about corporate financial conditions casts no doubt on materialist beliefs. If federal securities laws only altered the way these beliefs were institutionalized, the materialist ideology might have retained its position of dominance.

In fact, the laws did much more. Besides undermining the organization of trading built upon materialist beliefs, federal securities regulation facilitated a reorganization of the trading based on pragmatic beliefs, beliefs that stock prices are determined by the rate of earnings on a capital fund rather than on a value of a corporation's physical property. How it did so is a question we will need to consider. Before we do, though, it is necessary to discuss the substance of pragmatic beliefs as they were foreshadowed before the 1930s and then fully elaborated thereafter.

29 Homer Kripke, "Can The SEC Make Disclosure Policy Meaningful?" in *Economics of Corporation Law and Securities Regulation*, ed. Richard A. Posner and Kenneth Scott (Boston: Little, Brown, 1980), pp. 331–332; James M. Landis, "The Legislative History of the Securities Act of 1933," *George Washington Law Review*, 28 (October, 1959), 34.

The Rise of Pragmatic Ideology

Earlier I said that until the 1930s there was no strong contender to rival materialist beliefs as a basis for market organization. That is not to say that there were no contending beliefs. Charles H. Dow, a founder of the *Wall Street Journal*, rejected the materialist doctrine that only knowledge about physical property values could allay uncertainties regarding stock prices. Dow argued forcefully that stock price change was an orderly process, the order of which could be detected by careful observation of historical price trends. He tried to instruct the readers of his newspaper in the proper methods of observation and in the art of interpreting what they observed, so hopefully they could translate their observations into practical decisions to buy stocks or to sell. In 1902, S. A. Nelson published a popular version of Dow's method in a slim volume on *The ABC of Stock Speculation*. Yet the ideas were not meant simply for popular consumption. Dow's theory was systematically extended by William Peter Hamilton, Dow's successor as editor of the *Wall Street Journal*. Hamilton's work, published as *The Stock Market Barometer*, was highly regarded. On its merits, Hamilton was elected a fellow in the Royal Statistical Society.[30] None of this makes Dow's theory true. I know of no research to substantiate its claims. Yet here we have an attempt, apparently a relatively persuasive attempt, to break free from the constraints of the dominant materialist beliefs. The problem with Dow's theory — and others like it — was its failure ever to specify the mechanism or mechanisms which determined the course of stock price movements. As a result, it was difficult, if not impossible, to put into practice, and its persuasive powers were limited.

A more serious challenge to materialist doctrine was posed during the 1920s by the work of Edgar L. Smith.[31] Like Dow, Smith believed that the uncertainties of stock trading could be reduced by understanding the history of stock price movements. Unlike Dow, Smith offered a compelling reason why. Tracing stock prices back to the mid-nineteenth century and comparing their trends with trends in corporate earnings, Smith noticed that over the long run, after allowing for the effects of dividend payments, stock prices regularly grew at a compound rate determined by the corporation's rate of earnings. By making this point, Smith clearly abandons the materialist for the pragmatic

---

30 Robert Rhea, *The Dow Theory* (New York: Barron's, 1932); William Peter Hamilton, *The Stock Market Barometer* (New York, n. p., 1922); S. A. Nelson, *The ABC of Stock Speculation* (New York, n. p., 1902).

31 Edgar L. Smith, *Common Stocks as Long-Term Investments* (New York: Macmillan, 1923).

view of capital worth. Stock prices are decided by how much the corporate fund will earn, not by how much the corporation's physical property is worth.

This was an attractive theory. Adopting it made it possible to believe that common stocks of corporations with rising trends in earnings are sound investments no matter what price is paid for them.[32] For small investors in the 1920s looking for alternatives to their Liberty Bond investments acquired during the First World War, and for speculators as well, such an assertion, if true, took much of the worry out of stock investing. Many argue, in fact, that dissemination of Smith's theory in the mid-1920s was influential in drawing small investors into the market.[33] That is not to say that Smith's theory of pragmatic beliefs generally had much effect on market organization during that period. In fact, they could not.

It was central to Smith's analysis that trends in stock prices be compared to trends in corporate earnings. But this was not possible to do. The data were not generally available. Economists urged corporations to disclose earnings data; the New York Stock Exchange required corporations to make such disclosures as a condition for listing their securities. But corporations for the most part ignored these urgings and refused to comply with stock exchange rules. Secrecy was common. What disclosure there was was not always helpful. Accounting standards of the day were not so well-developed as to permit uniform and comparable disclosure of income and expense, assets and liabilities, and some were prepared to take loose standards as a license to write fiction.[34] In these circumstances, however persuasive, pragmatic beliefs could not be acted on. Like all beliefs without effect on action, they were not to be taken seriously as organizing principles. They could only be refined and tested in the academician's mind, as in fact they were.

During the 1930s, pragmatic beliefs about why stock prices change were carefully articulated and defended. In 1934, Benjamin Graham and David Dodd first published their famous work on *Security Analysis*. In that book they rely on purely pragmatic criteria for determining the intrinsic value of a corporate stock. It is not property value per se, but the ability to deploy capital to earn income which is decisive in rendering one's judgment about

---

32 Benjamin Graham and David L. Dodd, *Security Analysis*, 2nd ed. (New York: MacGraw-Hill, 1940), pp. 354–355.

33 *Ibid.*, pp. 351–361; Chelcie C. Bosland, *The Common Stock Theory of Investment* (New York: Ronald Press, 1937), p. 4.

34 David F. Hawkins, "The Development of Modern Financial Reporting Practices among American Manufacturing Corporations," *Business History Review*, 37 (Autumn, 1963), 135–168; William Z. Ripley, *Main Street and Wall Street* (Boston: Little, Brown, 1927), pp. 210–213.

stock prices. For them two factors enter in. First to enter are the results of a careful, skeptical examination of the elements affecting the corporation's future earnings potential — e.g., general economic prospects, probable industry growth, market shares, and dividend payout rate. It was upon this examination that an assessment of the corporation's value was based. The second factor was the comparison of the corporation's value, determined by analysis, with its market value, established by the current stock price. The critical question was whether the stock price to be paid was more or less than a "prudent business man" would pay for the opportunity "to invest in a private undertaking over which he could exercise control."[35] Writing during the time when federal securities laws were being framed, they were far from sanguine about how easy it would be to make these judgments. Nevertheless, they believed that it was possible in principle to do. Once done, and this is their main point, if inspection shows the stock's market price to be far less than the corporation's intrinsic value, then "a true investment opportunity" has been discovered.[36]

Four years after publication of *Security Analysis*, John Burr Williams published his doctoral dissertation on *The Theory of Investment Value*. He agreed with Graham and Dodd that appropriate determination of a corporation's intrinsic value based on assessments of earnings capacity was essential to wise stock investing. Yet he wanted to put determination of that value on a firmer footing than they had done. He believed he could do so by defining the value of a stock "as the present worth of all dividends to be paid upon it."[37] A stock is worth, to put it crudely, "only *what you can get out of it*."[38]

By defining what can be gotten from a stock as the simple sum of the value of expected dividends discounted by the interest rate sought by the investor, Williams made easier what was most difficult in Graham and Dodd's treatment, namely the calculation of a corporation's intrinsic value. But he did not depart from their pragmatic premise. The critical determinant of future dividends is the level of earnings upon the capital fund. It is no easy matter to estimate future corporate earnings; indeed it is arguably impossible for any one to do it consistently year in and year out.[39] To attempt to do so at all

---

35 Graham and Dodd, *Security Analysis*, pp. 367–368.

36 *Ibid.*, p. 371.

37 John Burr Williams, *The Theory of Investment Value* (Amsterdam: North-Holland Publishing, 1958, orig. 1938), p. 55.

38 *Ibid.*, p. 58, original emphasis.

39 The impossibility of predicting corporate earnings has been thoroughly documented and made the basis of a sustained criticism of the pragmatic ideology by economists in the 1960s and 1970s. See Lawrence Fischer and James H. Lorie, "Rates of Return on

requires thorough research and special training. Williams warns that experts, specializing by industry, will have the advantage in such work, and it is experts at securities analysis whom he expects to be first to gain from the conclusions of their work. Those who are quick to follow the expert's advice, however, will also stand to gain.[40]

There was substantial evidence in support of these pragmatic beliefs which Williams and Graham and Dodd helped to establish. In large part, and in consonance with their approach, the evidence consisted of original analyses of particular stock histories incorporated in their volumes. (A full thirty percent of the pages of William's book are given over to case materials.) In addition, in 1939 Alfred Cowles and his associates published their *Common Stock Indexes* which was a study of stock price behavior from 1871 to 1938.[41] The study showed beyond doubt that "earnings, dividends, and prices are bound together by a real and definite relationship."[42] It is important to emphasize that these were not merely theories backed by evidence without any practical application. The idea that knowledge about corporate earnings systematically pursued could help investors construct a relatively high-yielding, but safe portfolio of corporate stocks had enormous practical consequences. Individuals could confidently regard stocks as investments, because they could know what was necessary to overcome the uncertainty of stock price behavior. They could, that is, so long as the data were available and a class of experts was formed able to interpret the data. Here is where the new federal securities laws entered in to facilitate a new organization of the market based on pragmatic beliefs.

Investments in Common Stocks," *Journal of Business*, 37 (January, 1964), 1–24; Lawrence Fischer, "Outcome for 'Random' Investments in Common Stocks Listed on the New York Stock Exchange," *Journal of Business*, 38 (April, 1965), 149–161; Ian M. D. Little and A. C. Rayner, *Higgledy, Piggledy Growth Again* (Oxford: Basil Blackwell, 1966); Michael Jensen, "The Performance of Mutual Funds in the Period 1945–1964," *Journal of Finance*, 23 (May, 1968), 389–416. The criticism shook confidence in the claims that experts could consistently pick stocks that would outperform the market. (The relevance of such a criticism has declined in the 1980s for large investors who can afford to hedge their stock investments through options and futures contracts; see Benjamin M. Rowland, "Roll the Dice and Cross Your Fingers," *New York Times Book Review* (December 14, 1986), 35.) Yet, even the critics of pragmatic beliefs agree with the central claim, namely, that the price of a stock today is determined by tomorrow's earnings on the corporation's capital fund.

40 Williams, *The Theory of Investment Value*, p. 36.
41 Alfred Cowles, *Common Stock Indexes* (Bloomington, Ind.: Principia Press, 1939).
42 Molodovsky, "Valuation of Common Stocks," p. 25.

Both the Securities Act of 1933 and the Securities Exchange Act of 1934 guaranteed public availability of reliable financial information needed to invest according to pragmatic theories. In addition, they helped to assure that experts would analyze this information, to assure that its significance would become widely known. In other words, framers of the federal securities acts did not presume that the public was qualified either to interpret or to act independently based on the financial materials they required to be disclosed.[43] On the contrary, they presumed, as William O. Douglas explained in 1933, that investors were generally incompetent to judge the adequacy of securities for themselves.[44] Either a lack of training or intelligence or else concern for speculative profits was supposed to blind them to the truth. This made disclosure not less but more important precisely because it would facilitate the cause of investment research by experts. "The judgement of these experts," Douglas asserted, "will be reflected in the market price;" no less important, "investors who seek [expert] advice will be able to obtain it."[45]

Securities Analysts and the Pragmatic Organization of Trading

The presumption that expert investment analysts, not ordinary investors, would analyze the information which corporations disclosed encouraged lawmakers to demand complex reports. Complex reports would accurately reflect the truth about a corporation's financial situation. Only a few and the most qualified would be able easily to understand them. But that was the point. Lawmakers anticipated that participants in the market would rely on a profession of experts to guide their stock trading.

Theirs was a peculiar hope, however, for no well-defined professional group was ready to step into the breach to fulfill the role which Douglas and others clearly expected to be fulfilled. There was no dearth of people willing to offer their advice on stock investments, of course. The number of brokers rose dramatically all through the boom of the 1920s and did not decrease dramatically during the depression.[46] But the reputation of brokers as financial

43 Kripke, "Can the SEC Make Disclosure Policy Meaningful?", p. 340.
44 William O. Douglas, "Protecting the Investor," *Yale Review*, 23 (1933), 523 – 524.
45 *Ibid.*, p. 524.
46 The number of branch offices maintained by members of the New York Stock Exchange rose from 662 in 1920 to 1,658 in 1930. This high figure was not maintained, but in

experts was hurt, understandably, by the decline in stock prices. And they were perceived in the public mind, not incorrectly, to be salesmen working on commission.

Another claimant of the financial expert's role was the "statistician." Statisticians were researchers who gathered various financial statistics about companies and the economy. Theirs was an occupation that had been commonly found within brokerage firms since the turn of the century. And they had some rudimentary sense of themselves as performing a special job. Statisticians in Chicago formed an Investment Analysts Club in 1925, followed by statisticians in San Francisco, who formed their own group in 1929, and in Los Angeles, who did so in 1931.[47] Yet they too were unlikely candidates for the role of financial expert. Their research had not been instrumental to decisions about what stocks to buy and sell. Fewer than ten percent of 330 investment trusts — forerunners of our mutual funds — doing business in 1930 had any research departments employing statisticians to advise their portfolio managers. Typically, their work was thought to be part of the advertising function. They supplied information to draw people's attention to the market.[48] Congressional investigations into the speculative boom of the 1920s revealed that the information they released, in the form of "tips" and "news releases," was not always truthful, but sometimes served as a prop to support stock manipulation.

Nevertheless, despite their handicaps, statisticians moved quickly to meet the need for investment experts. They tied successful performance of their role to mastery of the new research developments coming out of the nation's business schools. With their role performance organized about the cognitive core of pragmatic investment theory, they restyled their job title, now calling themselves "professional security analysts."[49] They would be the experts able

1934 1,215 branch offices were still in operation, and the number of branch offices never fell below 1,057 (in 1940) during the whole depression. Even this low number is far above the figure for 1920. Nonmembers of the exchange who maintained wire connections with a member firm actually increased in number over the decade of the thirties from 3,024 in 1931 to a high of 4,238 in 1938, dropping off thereafter to 3,825 in 1940. See New York Stock Exchange, *Year Book — 1940* (New York, 1940), pp. 26 – 27.

47 Richard W. Lambourne, "The Evolution of Financial Analysts' Professional Standards," *Professional Standards of Practice*, ed. M. H. Earp and John G. Gillis (Charlottesville, Va.: Financial Analysts Research Foundation, 1978), p. 65.

48 See H. Parker Willis and Jules I. Bogen, *Investment Banking* (New York: Harper & Brothers, 1929), p. 55 and Wilson Fels Payne, The Analysis and Research Department in Certain Types of Fiduciary Companies, M. A. Thesis, University of Chicago, 1930.

49 Richard Whitely has recently traced the close relationship between "business finance"

accurately to interpret the vast quantities of new information being produced by corporations in response to the recently passed federal securities laws. Even brokers interested in forwarding their own claims as financial experts began to enroll in large numbers in the New York Stock Exchange Institute to take, among other things, courses in investment and security analysis.[50] By studying the very matter which security analysts (formerly statisticians) claimed to know, they lent legitimacy to the analysts' claim that they were indeed the experts on whom investors would wisely rely.

By 1937, analysts in New York City were sufficiently numerous, re-spected, and well organized to form a professional association. In 1945, they began to publish a journal devoted to articles on pragmatic methods of analysis and on applying the methods in particular cases. That same year they agreed to a code of ethics that pledged them to the independent search for truth about securities values. Professionalization of security anal-ysis was a movement growing rapidly outside New York as well and, in 1947, was large enough that a national federation of local chapters of securities analysts was formed.[51]

Though employed primarily by brokers, their professional ideal of auton-omy and the evident need for independent status (if the public would have confidence in them) was recognized by the brokerage community. Speaking before the Society of Security Analysts in New York City in 1945, Emil Schram, then president of the New York Stock Exchange, acknowledged that investors depended heavily on the information supplied by the analysts' research reports:

and "financial economics" in his article, "The Transformation of Business Finance into Financial Economics: The Role of Academic Expansion and Changes in U. S. Capital Markets," *Accounting, Organizations, and Society*, 11, 2 (1986), 171 – 192. But he confines his attention, wrongly I think, to the period following the Second World War. The movement to establish business schools to promote the use of scientific research and scientific management was widespread by the 1920s. (See James H. Bossard, "University Education for Business: A Survey," *Journal of Business*, 4 (July, 1931), 64 – 77 and Walter J. Matherly, "Present and Probable Future Needs for Collegiate Business Education," *Journal of Business*, 4 (July, 1931), 45 – 63.) It is no small part of my argument that early research developing the pragmatic ideology was done in business schools. Without this early mutual influence between "business finance" and "financial economics" I would, perhaps, have a different tale to tell.

50 Enrollments grew from 1,685 in 1929 – 1930 to a high of 5,397 in 1933 – 1934. New York Stock Exchange, *Year Book – 1940* (New York, 1940), p. 30.

51 See Lambourne, "The Evolution of Financial Analysts' Professional Standards," pp. 65 – 66; "Code of Ethics," *The Analysts Journal*, 1 (January, 1945), 49.

> I hope this society will seek to remain independent. It should not permit itself to be influenced by anyone in the important work which it performs. In other words, it should preserve its intellectual freedom.[52]

He encouraged the analyst to behave like an "ethical doctor," doing his best "regardless of the financial and professional consequences," and he was adamant that they should succeed in this.

> The very essence of the Stock Exchange principle is that judgment as to security values should be arrived at on the basis of facts … that those who scorn factual information and competent advice and who buy and sell securities on the basis of tips, rumors, hunches and impulses are misusing the facilities of our market.[53]

This was a very strong declaration affirming the market's conversion from materialist to pragmatic beliefs, and the important place security analysts held in making that conversion a practical reality. It was, of course, only partly based on the rational persuasiveness of pragmatic investment theories.

Of all the structural elements of professional status — association, code of ethics, cognitive base, colleague control, institutionalized training, licensing, and work autonomy — the financial community willingly granted security analysts all but work autonomy.[54] Unlike doctors or lawyers, who were largely self-employed at that time, securities analysts continued to be hired employees working primarily for brokerage firms or investment companies. Their employers had no interest in interfering with their research, but they did hope to profit from the pragmatic promise that good research should insure superior portfolio performance. And it was in the various ways that this hope was realized that we find the organization of stock trading transformed from its simple hierarchical form, under materialist beliefs, into a structure much more complex and polycentric.

The uses of investment research to support pragmatic trading were varied. Charles Merrill, founder of Merrill Lynch, believed that investors wanted to learn how to invest in stocks and were willing to work to do so. To meet their need, and as a way of promoting his business, he gave away the research reports prepared by his staff of security analysts without charge to any who

52 Emil Schram, "A Message to the Society," *The Analysts Journal*, 1 (April, 1945), 11.
53 *Ibid.*, p. 13.
54 As Magali Sarfatti Larson observes, the structural elements of the general form of a professional project are not always to be manifest in particular historical situations; they are resources to be mobilized when the political situation permits. Securities analysts did gain power, in the 1930s, relative to their broker-dealer employers and they expanded their power through the 1960s. But they were not all-powerful. Their power was channeled for the benefit of profit-seeking financiers. See generally Larson's *The Rise of Professionalism* (Berkeley and Los Angeles: University of California Press, 1977).

asked. At the same time he put his sales representatives on salary rather than on commission so they would not be suspected of giving advice to buy or sell merely to raise their income. These changes set standards that other brokerage firms were quick to follow and eventually to elaborate upon. The New York Stock Exchange, for example, began to promote the idea that small investors were crucial to the strength of the economy, an idea it announced under the banner of "people's capitalism" and supported with a "monthly investment plan" for buying stocks on an installment basis.[55]

There was an alternative to Merrill's approach of distributing so much information as broadly as possible. It was to form professionally managed investment funds and to encourage individual investors to own stock indirectly by purchasing shares of these funds. These mutual funds were not a new idea in the 1930s, but they were an investment vehicle that heretofore had not been exploited on a large scale. It was only when linked with pragmatic trading – under the name of "growth stock investing" – that the mutual fund "industry" began to grow explosively. The main idea of growth stock investing was put forward in 1938 in a report of the National Investors Corporation which stated:

> The common stocks of growth companies – that is, companies whose earnings move forward from cycle to cycle, and are only temporarily interrupted by periodic business depressions – offer the most effective medium of investment in the field of common stocks, either in terms of dividends or longer term capital appreciation.[56]

To this pragmatic idea, emphasizing corporate earnings, a second was added. Because the rate of increased earnings for growth stocks would, by definition, exceed the rate of aggregate economic growth, the market price for growth stocks would appreciate at a rate no less than the rate of inflation. The significance of this was not lost on the investing class. As investment adviser T. Rowe Price put it:

> Back in the 'thirties when Franklin D. Roosevelt took us off the gold standard, I was convinced we were in for a period of unending inflation with a few interruptions. I figured that if we bought stocks whose earnings were growing faster than the economy I could protect myself and my clients against inflation.[57]

As we shall see in the next chapter, similar concerns were instrumental not only for explaining the growth of mutual funds, but for explaining the growth of stock investing by financial institutions generally.

55 Robert Sobel, *Inside Wall Street* (New York: Norton, 1977), pp. 104 – 107; Martin Mayer, *Wall Street: Men & Money* (New York: Harper & Brothers, 1955), p. 117.
56 Quoted in Graham and Dodd, *Security Analysis*, p. 364.
57 Quoted in *Forbes* (July 1, 1969), 62.

Yet we must be clear, growth stock investing was not something everyone could do. Graham and Dodd recognized this early on when they said it requires more than examination of statistics and records to identify a growth company; it also requires a "considerable supplement of special investigation and of business judgment."[58] In their view, the difficulty of picking growth stocks was great enough that their purchase by individuals was better called imprudent speculation than prudent investment.[59] Mutual funds, however, like trust companies and other institutional investors, unlike individual investors, could afford to hire the analytical expertise required to do it well. The growth stock approach to pragmatic investing through institutional investors was an attractive and prudent alternative that also relieved individuals of doing all the study that Charles Merrill expected of them.

Organizationally, the rise of security analysts was critical in determining the impact of pragmatic beliefs on the market. When individuals went to Merrill Lynch to learn about investments, they learned from studying reports prepared by analysts. When mutual funds required that supplement of special investigation and business judgment, they too depended on security analysts. By the 1950s, individuals and financial institutions both believed that security analysts were competent experts, able to discriminate sound from unsound investment. In 1958, *Business Week* credited analysts with providing the "new faith" that bolstered stock prices. The magazine noted particularly that recovery of stock prices from the "dip" in 1957 was selective, those stocks gaining most in value which had shown the best gains in earnings. "This 'rational' recovery is largely due," it continued, "to the growing importance of institutional investors who have large research staffs to help guide them."[60] The evident success of the pragmatic approach to stock investing convinced even the conservative executives of the American Telephone and Telegraph Company to agree to place up to 10 percent of their $2.6 billions in pension fund assets into common stocks.

Their success through the 1950s and 1960s made some analysts wary. In the issue immediately following the one that praised their good work, *Business Week* reported that "the great fear is that the present passion for common stocks will go too far."[61] Analysts were worried that the "elevated status of equities" might cause prices to rise uncontrollably. "Then, if earnings did not live up to their pomise, there could be a major market decline." The decline in stock prices in 1961, against most analysts' predictions, confirmed their vulnerability to empirical contradictions. But it did not erode their faith in

58 Graham and Dodd, *Security Analysis*, p. 366.
59 *Ibid.*, p. 725.
60 *Business Week* (September 20, 1958), 32.
61 *Business Week* (September 27, 1958), 142.

the benefits of analysis. When one analyst commented that his colleagues were in "about the same situation as the political pollsters were in 1948 after Truman beat Dewey," he implicitly affirmed his belief that progress in developing the methods of security analysis would improve the reliability of their predictions just as methodological advances had aided pollsters.[62]

Demand for more elaborate research by institutional investors, by mutual funds, insurance companies, and increasingly by managers of trust (especially pension trust) funds continued to grow through the 1960s. As it did, analysts pressed their search for a basis to claim status as a learned profession.[63] Even without that high status, the emoluments and powers attached to their offices within the financial community grew to sizeable proportions.[64] By the mid-1960s, the size of these rewards was based rather less on whether analysts' predictions about future events were correct and rather more on how soon they could be shown to be correct. Some saw that this emphasis on short-term "performance" could produce a "whithering" of prudence.[65] Most accepted demonstrated performance as fulfillment of the pragmatic promise to overcome the uncertainties of stock trading.[66]

Although there may be some resurgence of the materialist outlook in the recent growth take-overs, especially of hostile take-overs, in the 1980s, the bulk of trading in the market continues to be organized around pragmatic beliefs. Instead of being a hierarchical structure dominated by a few investment bankers and their stock operator associates, we have a market institutionally organized in multiple sectors, each one having its own hierarchy of market-power and prestige based on the reputation of in-house securities analysts, who busy themselves studying the financial data which the federal securities laws, passed in the 1930s, first made it mandatory for corporations to disclose.

It is tempting, but wrong, to suppose what we have argued here offers a complete explanation of the decline of influence of investment bankers and the rising influence of institutional investors guided by quasi-professional securities analysts. A complete explanation must take into account the broad secular transformation of market-based, capitalist societies from their early

62 *Business Week* (January 21, 1961), 116.
63 C. Stewart Sheppard, "The Professionalization of the Financial Analysts," *Financial Analysts Journal* (November 1967), 39 – 41; Douglas A. Hayes, "Potential for Professional Status," *Financial Analyst Journal* (November, 1967), 29 – 31; Marshall D. Ketchum, "Is Financial Analysis a Profession?" *Financial Analyst Journal* (November, 1967), 33 – 37; Earp and Gillis, eds., *Professional Standards of Practice.*
64 Sobel, *Inside Wall Street*, pp. 136 – 139.
65 Waid R. Vanderpool, "Whither the Prudent Man?" *Barron's* (April 18, 1966), 5.
66 Martin Mayer, *New Breed on Wall Street* (New York: Macmillan, 1969).

to their more advanced forms.[67] Even broad transformations, however, are made up of smaller parts. What we have shown is how much this particular transformation of the stock market occurs as a result of a shift in market ideology brought about by the passage of federal security laws.

Federal securities laws, in sum, had a double effect on the social organization of stock trading so far as market ideology is concerned. By prohibiting manipulative trading practices, they made it impossible to continue acting on materialist beliefs, which presumed speculative practice was the way to profit from stock trading. And by forcing corporations to disclose information about their financial condition, they broke the monopoly of access to information on which the materialist organization of the market was based and made it possible to institutionalize pragmatic methods of stock trading. These effects were only partially anticipated. Reformers, who meant to curb speculation and to promote public disclosure of financial data, did not comprehend how their action would reorganize beliefs about how one ought to trade. Nor did they imagine how such a change in normative beliefs would reorganize stock trading. They certainly did not foresee, what we must now turn to consider, that altering this critical element in the market's moral order would justify further normative reconstruction and help to promote the rise of institutional stock investing.

67 See, e.g., Mark S. Mizruchi, *The American Corporate Network, 1904–1974* (Beverly Hills: Sage, 1982); Vincent Carosso, *Investment Banking in America* (Cambridge, Mass.: Harvard University Press, 1970); and, more generally, John Zysman, *Governments, Markets, and Growth* (Ithaca: Cornell University Press, 1983).

Chapter 4

The Rise of Institutional Stock Investing

Besides governing how one ought to trade, market norms govern with whom one ought to trade. These norms create boundaries around the market. They regulate access to the market. They distinguish social actors who are supposed to be able to withstand the risks which stock trading entails from those who are not. But they are not established on the basis of objective criteria. They are socially formed in response to competitive and political factors and struggled over by those in and out of the market. This chapter focuses on a successful struggle to redraw the stock market's boundaries, to redefine its norms of access, to permit institutional investors to put their funds into stocks. And it links the success of the struggle to the effects of federal securities regulation.[1]

For most of its history, the stock market has been perceived by many to be a wastrel and dangerous form of speculation. Rather than a store of value, stock speculation was thought to be a drain on wealth. As a result, state governments erected boundaries around the market when it began to grow large late in the nineteenth century. They passed statutes (or, sometimes, constitutional amendments) forbidding corporate and personal trustees from using funds in their care to purchase corporate stocks.[2] And the boundaries

---

1 The important role of boundaries is often recognized in the literature on organizations. See, e. g., James D. Thompson, *Organizations in Action* (New York: McGraw-Hill, 1967), pp. 39 – 50 and W. Richard Scott, *Organizations: Rational, Natural, and Open Systems* (Englewood Cliffs, N. J.: Prentice Hall, 1981), pp. 179 – 206. The two main ideas guiding this chapter, that boundaries function to contain uncertainty and that they are changed by external environmental as well as by internal organizational pressures, are at the center of this literature. Nevertheless, organization theorists have tended to focus on formally simpler cases of single organizations or organizational forms. At this point, no strong theory exists to guide us in the more complex case involving boundaries within a field of organizations not all of one type.
2 Austin Wakeman Scott, *The Law of Trusts*, 2 nd ed., 5 vols. (Boston: Little, Brown, 1956), vol. 3, p. 1698.

were effective. Before the late 1930s, less than ten percent of all stock outstanding was held in the portfolios of financial institutions.[3]

During the late 1930s, through the 1950s, however, norms proscribing stock investment by financial institutions were overturned. They were replaced by norms which encouraged them to invest in stocks. And in the 1950s and 1960s, we witness the first wave of an enormous growth of institutional stock investing. By the late 1960s, financial institutions became the dominant players in the stock market. Having progressed so far, they pressed on, trying, with mixed results, to gain access to the market's technical core – the trading floor – by becoming full-fledged members of stock exchanges, having the same privileges and benefits of membership which brokers do. (The consequences of their doing so will be the subject of chapter 5.) What was the impetus for such a change? Who led the movement to reform state laws which had restricted institutional stock investment? What arguments were used to persuade state legislators that legal boundaries to stock investment ought to be removed? And, why were they persuasive?

The principal thesis of this chapter is that norms limiting institutional stock investing were overturned largely because of the new adherence to pragmatic beliefs about the safety of stock trading, a change which we have just traced to passage of the federal securities acts of 1933 and 1934. In saying this, I do not mean to ignore the influence of material factors. The Great Depression narrowed the field of securities in which financial institutions could safely invest, and fears about inflation (stoked by government deficits run first to fight the depression and then to fight the Second World War) caused leaders of financial institutions to search earnestly for high yield investment. Given the uncertain investment climate, they lobbied against laws restricting their investment discretion. They lobbied specifically for powers to invest in stocks, as opposed to other investment vehicles, because they were persuaded by pragmatic arguments that they could trade stocks safely. The compellingness of this argument, coupled with confidence in the federal securities laws to contain irresponsible speculative activity, caused state legislators to agree with institutional financial leaders and to change the law. This success gave a crucial boost to the most obvious and dramatic development of the stock market since the 1930s, the rise of institutional stock investing.

3 Raymond W. Goldsmith, "The Historical Background: Financial Institutions as Investors in Corporate Stock Before 1952," *Institutional Investors and Corporate Stock*, ed. Raymond W. Goldsmith (New York: National Bureau of Economic Research, 1973), p. 78.

Before weighing the evidence for this argument, we have first to consider why boundaries were erected to limit the access of financial institutions to the stock market and to assess whether they were effective.

The Origins and Effects of Boundaries Limiting Access to the Market

We can safely assume that financiers welcomed buyers and sellers of stock from all quarters of society, even fiduciaries who managed portfolio for the benefit of others, so long as they had the material resources to back up their orders to trade. It was not financiers who built walls around the stock market to limit who could invest in stocks. Constraints on stock investing were the creation of state governments for reasons we have now to explore.

Historical Origins of the Boundaries

The role state governments played in limiting market access was a bequest of English legal history. Though common law inherited from England predates the development of large-scale financial institutions, it dealt with the analogous case of the investment of estates by trustees for the benefit of widows, orphans, and charitable foundations. Through our colonial period until 1859, English common law presumed that trust assets should be held in land. Exceptions were granted when estates held substantial amounts of cash to permit investment in securities, but only in government bank annuities at three percent, the famous British consols. This singular investment was not chosen for the lack of any alternative. While there were not many joint-stock companies before the nineteenth century, there were some. Stocks of corporations had been traded in England since late in the seventeenth century. These, however, were believed to be especially risky speculations — a belief borne out by the spectacular burst of the South Sea Bubble in 1720 — and inappropriate to hold in trusts.[4]

4 Mayo A. Shattuck, "The Development of the Prudent Man Rule for Fiduciary Investment in the United States in the Twentieth Century," *Ohio State Law Journal*, 12 (1951), 491–492; C. Allison Scully, *The Purchase of Common Stocks as Trust Investments* (New York: Macmillan, 1937), pp. 1–6; George W. Keeton, *The Investment and Taxation of Trust Funds* (London: Sir Isaac Pitman & Sons, 1964), pp. 4–6.

When state governments in America took over the role of regulating trustee investments from England, they did not at first apply the same strict and conservative investment policy. Perhaps it would have been impossible. The supply of investments safe as British consols was not large in the new republic, and the thirst for capital was virtually unquenchable. In New England, trust funds were used to establish mills and industries and other speculative commercial ventures.[5] That they could be used in this way was affirmed by the Supreme Judicial Court of Massachusetts in 1830. Deciding the case of *Harvard College v. Amory*, the court wrote:

> All that can be required of a trustee to invest is that he shall conduct himself faithfully and exercise sound discretion. He is to observe how men of prudence, discretion and intelligence manage their own affairs, not in regard to speculation, but in regard to the permanent disposition of their funds, considering the probable income, as well as the probable safety of the capital to be invested.[6]

This "prudent man" rule of trust investment did not definitely constrain fiduciaries in the exercise of their powers. Trustees were free to place funds in whatever securities they believed best suited the beneficiaries' needs. They were free to decide for themselves whether a particular enterprise was a safe investment.

The policy of freedom was comparatively short-lived. By the mid-nineteenth century, such liberality was far less well appreciated, and the prudent man rule, adopted by other states besides Massachusetts, was replaced by the rule of "legal lists" in which the state specifically defined by statute what were safe investments appropriate to be placed in trusts. This turn of events was designed explicitly to prohibit trustees from investing in corporate stocks. The pivotal case justifying the reasons for such a prohibition was decided in 1869 when the New York court, in *King v. Talbot*, decided that the prudence required of a trustee could never justify speculation, particularly stock speculation. At the least, stock speculation violated the trustee's duty to maintain control over investments:

> The moment the fund is invested in bank, or insurance, or railroad stock, it has left the control of trustees; its safety and the hazard, or risk of loss, is no longer dependent upon their skill, care, or discretion ... and the terms of the investment [unlike bonds] do not comtemplate that it will ever be returned to the trustee.[7]

---

5 Shattuck, "The Development of the Prudent Man Rule," p. 493.

6 *Harvard College v. Amory*, 9 Pickering (Mass.) 446 (1830).

7 *King v. Talbot*, 40 N.Y. 88 – 89 (1869), quoted by Bascom H. Torrance, "Legal Background, Trends, and Recent Developments in the Investment of Trust Funds," *Law and Contemporary Problems*, 17 (1952), 130.

Under this decision no prudent man would ever purchase or retain any share of corporate stock. This return to the original English precedent regarding trust investment would prove too strict for most states to follow completely, but its conservative tone and direction did become the model others followed. Even Massachusetts began to place restrictions on stock investments by trustees.[8]

Through the second half of the nineteenth century initiative for regulating fiduciary investment passed from the courts to state legislatures. Most states passed laws, like the British law of 1859, which specified a list of securities safe enough for trustee investment. By this time, however, state laws broadened their horizons to specify lists of "legal investments" not only for trustees over estates, but also for rapidly growing mutual savings banks, and, after 1906, for life insurance companies, too. Typically, trustees were required to invest funds in their care with the sole aim of conserving the principal amount so it could always earn income for the trust's beneficiaries. What securities qualified as conservative varied from state to state, but there was this common thread: Securities thought safe enough to qualify for prudent, that is, for conservative, investment regularly included local municipal bonds and bonds of the home state, federal government bonds, and the stocks and bonds of specific local public utilities and transportation companies.[9] As a practical matter, this meant that institutional investors were denied general access to the stock market. Or, better put, financiers in the stock market were denied general access to the wealth controlled by fiduciaries, whether personal trustees or institutional investors.

Perhaps the reason for these restrictive laws will seem plain, especially to those with a slightly cynical turn of mind. Trustees, after all, were constrained to purchase securities issued to finance public projects and construction of the economic infrastructure. Investment laws were a tool for state legislatures to ensure the supply of capital they required to foster economic development.[10] Yet, without denying operation of political self-interest, it was not the only motive at work. There were paternalistic considerations as well. Some states forbade their legislatures from passing laws to permit trustees to invest in stocks, no matter what the purpose; this was done by constitutional provision. Pennsylvania's constitution had such a provision from 1873 to 1933, as did Colorado's

8 Shattuck, "The Development of the Prudent Man Rule," p. 495.
9 Montgomery Rollins, *A Compilation of Laws Regulating the Investment of Bank Funds* (Boston: n. p., 1905); James G. Smith, *The Development of Trust Companies in the United States* (New York: Henry Holt, 1928), p. 429; Alan L. Olmstead, *New York City Mutual Savings Banks, 1819–1861* (Chapel Hill: University of North Carolina Press, 1976), pp. 78–79.
10 For a detailed study of this practice see Olmstead, *New York City Mutual Savings Banks*, pp. 74–96.

until 1951, Wyoming's until 1966, and as the constitutions of Alabama and Montana continue to have today.[11] Even when states moved to liberalize their policies, the steps they took were carefully measured. In 1935, the Advisory Legislative Council to Governor George C. Perry of Virginia recommended that fiduciaries be permitted to invest in preferred stocks only if the issuing corporations met definite quantitative criteria of fiscal stability, stringent enough to assure that the principal invested was not at jeopardy and that dividends would be paid.[12] New York did not allow trustees any discretion to invest in stocks from 1869 until 1950 and then their discretion was limited; stocks could make up no more than thirty-five percent of the trust fund's value.[13]

Reticence about the wisdom of allowing trustees free rein to invest in stocks was not without an explanation. At the same time states began to pass more restrictive laws to control trustee investment, they also passed the first general incorporation statutes. Rather than charter each corporation by specific legislative enactment, corporate charters were granted to any applicants who met the qualifications stated in the general law. Here was a significant delegation of the state's authority to its citizens. Though surely a spur to economic growth, this delegation presented opportunities to incompetent and disreputable people, as well as to more substantial entrepreneurs, to grasp for the public's capital. Many states tried to limit these opportunities through laws attempting to maintain some minimum standards of prudence in matters of capital structure and of honesty in promises made by corporate officers to shareholders and prospective shareholders. But these laws were notably unsuccessful. It is likely that their impotence to ensure the quality of stocks aroused paternalistic concerns within state legislators to protect trustees from the vagaries of the stock market.[14]

Effects of Limiting Access to the Market

Historical details about the portfolios of trust funds and financial institutions are not plentiful. What data are available suggest that the barriers erected to

11 Scott, *The Law of Trusts*, p. 1698; William Franklin Fletcher, *Supplement to Scott on Trusts*, 3 rd ed. (Boston: Little, Brown, 1982), p. 50.
12 "Widening the Field of Trust Investments," *Trust Bulletin*, (December, 1935), 22 – 24.
13 Earl S. MacNeill, "New York's Trust Investment Statute," *Banking*, 42 (1950), 54.
14 Louis Loss, *Securities Regulation*, 3 vols. (Boston: Little, Brown, 1961), vol. 1, pp. 120 – 121; Louis Loss and Edward Cowett, *Blue Sky Law* (Boston: Little, Brown, 1958), pp. 3 – 10; Gerald D. Nash, "Government and Business: A Case Study of State Regulation of Corporate Securities, 1850 – 1933," *Business History Review*, 38 (Summer 1964), 146 – 154.

keep fiduciaries from investing in the stock market were generally effective.[15] That is not to say that fiduciaries failed to invest in stocks at all. In 1900, four states — Kentucky, Maryland, Massachusetts, and Rhode Island — still adhered to the prudent man rule, giving trustees significant discretion to invest in stocks. These four were joined by Vermont, in 1908, and North Carolina, in 1928.[16] Moreover, most states which subscribed to the legal list rule did not simply prohibit stockholding, but varied in the degree of their restrictiveness. Many states, as noted already, permitted stock investment in local utility and transportation companies, and many also permitted retention of inherited stocks either temporarily, to give trustees a chance to dispose of the shares in a favorable market, or permanently, if the trust's grantor requested that the exception be made. In any case, grantors of personal trusts could always obviate the state laws when drawing up their trust deeds by specifically granting trustees power to invest in stocks. As a result, fiduciary stockholdings equaled just under seven percent of all stock outstanding in 1900, rose slightly to just under ten percent after the First World War, and remained at that level until the late 1930s.[17]

Were they free to do so, there is some reason to believe fiduciaries would have held more stock than they did. A 1925 survey of personal trusts administered in 255 bank trust departments supplies evidence that when the grantor of the trust empowered trustees to invest in stocks, trustees showed no hesitancy in doing so, and did so to a greater degree than they did with trust funds governed by the state's legal list rule.[18] Perhaps stronger evidence for the constraint of laws comes from examining the portfolio of life insurance companies early in this century. Traditionally adverse to speculative holdings, investments by life insurance companies were not legally restricted until 1906. Then, in the wake of disclosures that some life insurance company funds were used to finance stock speculation by company officials, New York passed a strict law, subsequently copied by many other states, which prohibited life insurance companies from investing in stocks.[19] The effects of this prohibition

15 Raymond W. Goldsmith, "Basic Considerations," *Institutional Investors and Corporate Stock*, ed. Raymond W. Goldsmith (New York: National Bureau of Economic Research, 1973), pp. 11, 21.
16 Shattuck, "The Development of the Prudent Man Rule," p. 502.
17 Goldsmith, "The Historical Background," p. 78.
18 Smith, *The Development of Trust Companies*, pp. 415–453.
19 Morton Keller, *The Life Insurance Enterprise, 1885–1910* (Cambridge, Mass.: Harvard University Press, 1963), pp. 246–259; Andrew Brimmer, *Life Insurance Companies in the Capital Market* (East Lansing, Mich.: Bureau of Business and Economic Research, Michigan State University, 1962), pp. 62–70.

show up in aggregate financial statistics: In 1900, before the law was passed, corporate stock represented 3.6 percent of their portfolio assets, but in 1912 and thereafter until 1952, stocks represent just 2.0 percent of their assets.[20] The 1952 date is significant because it was not until 1951 that New York liberalized its law of 1906 to permit life insurance companies once again to invest in stocks. After that, stockholding by life insurance companies clearly increased to take up a larger proportion of their assets than at any other time, even before 1906. What was true for life insurance companies was generally true for other financial institutions as well.

From the late nineteenth century to the late 1930s, state laws effectively regulated the investment powers of trustees to prevent them from investing in stocks. Attempting to limit the uncertainty of trust investments, they actually defined the outer boundary of the stock market, limiting access to the market. All those who were not trustees were free to participate in the stock market if they had the means and will to do so. Trustees, however, could not be stock market participants. Financiers would have to be content to attract the wealth of individuals trading for their own account. The wealth controlled by trustees, especially by corporate fiduciaries, was for all practical purposes ruled out of bounds. Yet it would not always be so, and it is time now to discover why not.

Removing Boundaries to Stock Investing

The years between 1930 and 1952 saw significant changes in the law regulating the investment powers of trustees. In 1930, only six states permitted trustees full discretion to invest in stocks. But before 1952 was out, twenty-three states would overthrow their restrictive legal list statutes and adopt instead the more liberal prudent man rule. Six more states would modify their legal list statutes to allow trustees to invest some portion of their funds in corporate stocks. By the period's end, in other words, there had been a significant shift in consensus about the appropriate domain of the stock market, and the high boundary protecting trustees from the vagaries of stock investing was torn down. Thirty-five states, the largest and wealthiest among them, allowed trustees to buy and sell stocks for their accounts.[21]

20 Goldsmith, "The Historical Background," p. 78.
21 Shattuck, "The Development of the Prudent Man Rule."

Such a radical shift in "domain consensus" can be explained only in part by the response to changing material circumstances in the market, even circumstances as traumatic as those brought about by the Great Depression.[22] Beliefs about the value of stock investing and about the value of alternatives to stock investing had also to change during this period, and the changes in beliefs had to be institutionalized before trustees and, in particular, before institutional investors, could become participants in the stock market. These changes may have come unexpected by observers in the 1920s, but they could not have occurred without some deliberation and organized social movement. Circumstances were ripe for undermining normative restrictions on fiduciary stock investing in the 1930s.

Material Factors Weakening Support for Limits on Stock Investment

What strength the restrictions enjoyed depended on the validity of two assumptions: First, that bonds were relatively safer investments, more permanent and so less speculative than stocks, and, second, that there was and always would be an adequate supply of legal list securities offering a reasonable return on investment. So long as both assumptions appeared to be true, then it would seem that the legal list statutes successfully limited the uncertainties of trust fund investment without hurting the interests of income beneficiaries. In the 1930s, both assumptions proved demonstrably false.

The supply of legal investments shrank relative to demand in the 1930s, sending prices up and yields down. The problem was caused in part by the rapid growth of trust funds. Despite the depression, between 1926 and 1938 the number of trusts managed by national banks increased from 26,053 to 135,615, while the value of trust assets increased from $922.3 million to $9,419.0 million. The average trust nearly doubled in value from $35.4 thousand to $69.4 thousand, even though nominal prices in 1938 were more than fifteen percent below their 1926 levels.[23] These funds had to be invested somewhere. With the number of eligible places restricted by law, prices paid for approved securities naturally rose which had the effect of decreasing the rate of income earned. Aggravating matters, some bonds thought to be secure, and included on the legal lists of some states, went into default. Even when

22 James D. Thompson, *Organizations in Action* (New York: McGraw-Hill, 1967), pp. 28–29.
23 *Ibid.*, p. 449.

they did not default, they no longer represented the security they once did. Under changing economic conditions and the standards imposed by the Pennsylvanian law, one observer noted that three-fourths of the railroad bonds eligible for trust investments in the 1920s were not legally qualified in 1942.[24] Under these circumstances, complaints mounted that the volume of legal securities was too small and their yields too low, forcing many trusts to keep trust funds idle or virtually idle in bank savings accounts. This of course was to the detriment of trust beneficiaries dependent on trust income.[25]

Not only was the supply of legal investments inadequate, but their safety relative to stocks was no longer legally assured. Public policy changed under the New Deal to erode creditor's rights. A principal objection to stock investing was that after the money was let go, trustees no longer commanded any control over it; the corporation whose stock was bought did not intend ever to return it. There was no way to regain the funds except by selling the shares in the stock market; and what shares would gain (or lose) from such a sale, no one could tell. Bonds, in contrast, which were included on legal lists, not only promised to repay the money lent on some definite future date; they also frequently contained provisions allowing the creditor to recall the loan, in effect, to demand repayment early. Trustees were protected by provisions which promised to repay loans not in the paper currency of the day but in gold. So long as these provisions were included in bond agreements and enforced by the courts, bonds were safer and more permanent investments than stocks. But neither recall provisions or gold clauses survived the depression. New laws of bankruptcy, passed during 1933 and 1934, permitted courts to readjust the terms of debt without particular reference to recall provisions. Some state laws simply forbade foreclosure on mortgages. Also in 1933, as part of Franklin Roosevelt's policy to devalue the dollar, a bill was passed suspending the gold clause, requiring all creditors to accept legal tender money in satisfaction of the debt. The effect of this law, given the change in the dollar price of gold from $20.67 per ounce in 1933 to $35.00 per ounce in 1934, was all at once to reduce the face amount of bonds with gold clauses by over forty percent. However necessary the policy may have been to meet the emergency of depression, it made it difficult to argue that bonds were an especially secure investment compared to stocks.[26]

24 Ann K. Bender, "Prudent Investor Rule in the Investment of Trust Funds," *Temple University Law Quarterly*, 16 (1942), 219.
25 "Widening the Field of Trust Investments," p. 22; Bender, "Prudent Investor Rule," p. 218; Scully, *The Purchase of Common Stocks*, pp. 30–31.
26 Scully, *The Purchase of Common Stocks*, pp. 27–28, 33–41.

Debating the Idea of Stock Investing

The combined effect of undermining the assumptions on which legal lists were based was rather to create than to limit uncertainties in the management of trust funds. These uncertainties spurred trustees to oppose legal list statutes and to lobby instead for adoption of prudent man rule statutes allowing them discretion to decide for themselves which securities, stocks or bonds, were best suited for their portfolios. Their opposition to legal list laws represented a radical change in the habit of mind that had traditionally guided trustees, a change that would have been unthinkable even a few years before.[27] Of course, it was a change that only occured after intense debate among trustees. After all, the traditional understanding was that the primary purpose of trusts was to conserve trust funds, not to hazard them by trading stocks.

Louis S. Headley, a midwestern banker and once president of the Trust Division of the American Bankers Association, led the defense of the traditional conception of fiduciary duty. Addressing the American Banking Association's Mid-Winter Trust Conference in New York, where a prudent man trustee investment bill was pending before the state legislature, Headley told his colleagues that the issue was whether they would continue to be trustees or would instead become "gentlemen adventurers."[28] The issue was raised very sharply he thought by the claims Mayo A. Shattuck had made about the trustee's duty.

Shattuck, a prominent Boston trust attorney, argued that trustees should worry more about increasing the value of trusts than about maintaining the value of trusts as measured by dollars. Headley quite correctly believed that Shattuck's claim ran counter to any traditional understanding of the trustee's role. In the 1939 edition of his classic work on trusts, Austin Wakeman Scott wrote plainly that

> the primary purpose of a trustee should be to preserve the trust estate, while receiving a reasonable amount of income, rather than to take risks for the purpose of increasing the principal or income.[29]

Nevertheless, Shattuck defended his departure from tradition on the grounds that inflation undermined the purchasing power of trusts. Failure to manage trust funds with an eye toward increasing money values meant reducing the

27 Smith, *The Development of Trust Companies*, p. 442 – 444.
28 Louis S. Headley, "Trustees or 'Gentlemen Adventures'?" *Trusts and Estates*, 88 (1949).
29 Scott, *The Law of Trusts*, vol. 3, p. 1666; Torrance, "Legal Background, Trends, and Recent Developments," pp. 134, 137 – 138.

purchasing power of beneficiaries, the very people whom the trust grantor meant to support.[30]

This argument, so far as Headley was concerned, fell on deaf ears. To follow Shattuck's advice, trustees would have to do more than buy common stocks as permanent investments for the dividends. They would have to buy and sell stocks in anticipation of capital gains. "It is better," he argued, "that the trustee should use principal if necessary than that he should risk it for profits ... the purpose of conservation is not to enrich the future but to protect the present."[31] In any case, Headley went on, now dodging the matter of principle, it was far from certain statistically that stocks provided a hedge against inflation. A similar argument was advanced in 1952 by Bascom H. Torrance, who chaired the Trust Investment Study Committee of the New York State Bankers Association.[32]

Still there were other arguments in favor of stock investing which persuaded trustees to change their mind. In addition to the inadequate supply of legal investments, there was an incentive provided by the usually high return available on stocks as compared with bonds. In 1945, stocks yielded income of 4.2 percent as compared with a yield on corporate bonds of only 2.6 percent and on state and local bonds of only 1.7 percent.[33] A survey of trust officials conducted in the same year by the American Bankers Association found that the first and foremost advantage which trustees saw in adopting the prudent man rule was the opportunity "to procure more satisfactory income for the life beneficiary."[34] I am bound to add that a large part of the revenue trustees are paid for their services is based upon the income which trust funds earn.

There was, secondly, a concern that legal list statutes were too inflexible to apply in a rapidly changing investment environment. In New York, for example, the volume of legal investments dropped from $7.6 billion in 1931 to $2.6 billion in 1939 because securities qualifying as "safe" before the depression could not meet the requirements for safety (continuing interest

30 Mayo A. Shattuck and Louis S. Headley, "Whither Trusteeship?" *Trusts and Estates*, 89 (1950), 92–95, 120–125.
31 Headley, "Trustees or 'Gentlemen Adventures'?" p. 91.
32 Torrance, "Legal Background, Trends, and Recent Developments," pp. 144–150.
33 James J. O'Leary, "Trends of Yields on the Investments of Financial Institutions," *Law and Contemporary Problems*, 17 (1952); see also, more generally, Roger G. Ibbotson and Rex A. Sinquefield, *Stocks, Bonds, Bills, and Inflation: Historical Returns, 1926–1978* (Charlottesville, Va.: Financial Analysts Research Foundation, 1979).
34 Report of the Committee on Prudent-Man Rule of Trust Investments, Section of Real Property, Probate and Trust Law, American Bar Association, *Proceedings of Meetings, December 17–18, 1945* (South Hackensack, N. J.: Red B. Rothman & Co., 1972, orig. 1946), p. 94.

payments, maintenance of collateral, etc.) once the depression's full force was felt.[35] Presumably state legislators could revise their legal lists year by year. But such a solution would raise as many difficulties as it resolved. Trustees who purchased bonds included on one year's list must inevitably face a dilemma if the bonds were subsequently dropped from the list. Liable to sell at a premium while on the list, the bonds would sell at a discount when off. Consequently, trustees could not easily maintain both the value of the trust and its compliance with the law. Even forgetting these practical difficulties, there is the further problem that frequent revisions of legal lists impose on state legislators the burden of prophesying what securities will be prudent investments. It is not a burden which legislators, by calling, are peculiarly well-suited to bear.[36] Under the circumstances, the best solution appeared to be to delegate responsibility for securities selection to the trustees who did the investing. If they chose to invest in stocks, so be it.

But most important, in my view, was that trustees came to believe that they could safely invest in stocks. While some were uncertain whether they might invest in stocks for gains, many looked forward to the chance to offset losses with gains, and few if any worried out loud about the risk of loss.[37] Their sanguine attitude can be attributed in part to the belief that stock investing was no longer speculative. Writing in 1937 in favor of stock investing by trustees, C. Alison Scully asserted that "the possibility that the business of the Standard Oil Company of New Jersey or other of the great industrial companies might be so conducted that the investment in stock would vanish is so remote as to be silly."[38] From our perspective, of course, given the experience of collapses and near collapses by Penn Central, Lockheed, Chrysler, W. T. Grant, and others, that possibility seems insufficiently remote.

They commonly argued that the requirements for investing safely in stocks were known and could be met. The central requirement was to know as much as possible about the corporation before investing in its stock. Prescriptions for doing this were hardly lacking and can be quickly summarized: Determine whether its stock price is stable, or fluctuates widely; compare the stock price with the value of corporate assets and with the corporation's future business prospects; examine the capital structure and financial condition of the company to determine whether it is sound; and evaluate the management to determine whether they are capable. Compare one corporation with another; study specific industries to place each stock into perspective; examine

35 Shattuck, "The Development of the Prudent Man Rule," p. 500.
36 Bender, "Prudent Investor Rule," p. 219.
37 Report of the Committee on Prudent-Man Rule of Trust Investments, *Proceedings*, p. 96.
38 Scully, *The Purchase of Common Stocks*, pp. 26–27.

trends of growth, decay, and of technological change which might affect stock values. Study trends in prices. Companies which capitalize earnings at higher or lower ratios than common should receive close scrutiny, for an opportunity to buy or sell may be in the making. Consider also what experts, who are informed and qualified to judge, have to say about which stocks are satisfactory to buy and prudent to hold. Such was their advice.[39] The purpose was to base stock trades on specific empirical knowledge, systematically gathered and analyzed. When this was done, trustees argued, it would prove difficult to regard them imprudent for investing in stocks. The argument sounds pedestrian today. Fifty years ago, in the midst of a depression, it was not. What was the basis of their confidence about how to invest in stocks.

The Role of Federal Securities Law

Although it was no new idea to do research before investing in stocks, it was an idea virtually impossible to implement before the 1930s. Information about the financial conditions of corporations was difficult to come by. The habit of regular disclosure to shareholders was not yet well established. When financial reports were released, they varied greatly in their level of detail, in the assumptions on which they were based, and in their reliability. Of course, they were impossible to use for comparative purposes. As a result, trustees could not have conducted the research necessary to decide which stocks to buy or sell. Nor could anyone else.

What changed during the 1930s to make the trustees' argument plausible (and now pedestrian) was the passage of the federal securities acts of 1933 and 1934. A central feature of these acts was to require periodic, reliable, and comparable disclosure of a vast array of information about the financial condition of corporations issuing new stocks to the public and of corporations whose stocks were listed on the stock exchanges. The objective utility of the information which the Securities and Exchange Commission required to be disclosed is debatable. But, at least it made information available where there was none before. With this information in hand, trustees could perform the actions they proposed. If they lacked the expertise to do it themselves, they could hire the recently professionalized security analysts to do the research for them.

---

39 *Ibid.*, p. 37; Richard P. Chapman, "Investing Trust Funds under the Prudent Man Rule," *Trust Bulletin*, 23 (1944); R. S. Walker, "Investment of Trust under the So-Called 'Massachusetts Rule'," *Connecticut Bar Journal*, 13 (1939).

The importance of the new federal securities laws was not confined to assuring the supply of financial information. When Bascom Torrance answered the question, why do trustees invest in stocks, he noted the more extensive information which facilitates studying stocks. But he noted also that

> the markets in which they [stocks] are traded are more firmly regulated and less subject to manipulation which at times in the past gave them risks wholly unrelated to investment values.[40]

The importance of stricter market regulation is also acknowledged by the substance of New York's law authorizing trustees to invest in stock. According to it, common stock may be purchased only if the issuing corporation has at least some securities registered with the Securities and Exchange Commission (and so must periodically disclose financial information) and the stock is listed on an exchange registered with the Securities and Exchange Commission (and so is subject to stricter regulation of trading).[41] This combination of the flow of information and the stricter oversight of stock trading, which the federal securities laws created, persuaded trustees that they could escape from the morass created by legal list statutes and gain a higher income for their trusts by investing in stocks.

Encouraged by this new belief in the safety of stock investing, the Trust Division of the American Bankers Association decided in 1942 to coordinate a nation-wide campaign to replace legal list with prudent man statutes. They began by devoting a large part of that year's Mid-Winter Trust Conference to discuss the prudent man rule, a practice continued for the next ten years. A committee was formed to develop a proposed model statute. Mayo Shattuck was brought in to assist with the legal drafting. The job was done by November 1942, published in booklet form, and, by arrangement with state banking associations, the model statute was introduced as a bill into state legislatures across the country.[42]

Success from these efforts was not immediate, but it was far from slow. Within two years, six states adopted the prudent man statute, and among them were such large states as California, Illinois, and Texas. These were important accomplishments. Each of these states were dominant in their respective regions and could be expected to exert influence on the legislative efforts of neighboring states. Perhaps more importantly, the legislature in

---

40 Torrance, "Legal Background, Trends, and Recent Developments," p. 151.
41 MacNeill, "New York's Trust Investment Statute," p. 54; Frank G. Sayre, "Prudent Man Rule for Trust Investments," *Trust and Estates*, 89 (1950), 706.
42 Emerson Lewis, "The Prudent Man Investment Rule," *Illinois Bar Journal*, 35 (1946), 65–66; MacNeill, "New York's Trust Investment Statute;" Bender, "Prudent Investor Rule," p. 218 n. 17.

Pennsylvania, which rejected the measure once, had agreed to consider it again – it finally adopted a modified prudent man rule in 1951 – and the New York legislature agreed to study the matter.[43]

Gaining passage of the prudent man rule in New York was the major goal, for most trust funds were (and are) administered in New York City, and New York law governing trust investment policy has been influential nationally. As was done in other states, the strategy adopted was to document that most personal trust funds were already managed according to the prudent man rule as allowed by the deed of trust. In fact, in New York, it was estimated that only twenty percent of the personal trusts (but still over $4 billion) were administered by the legal list.[44] This meant that trustees had experience investing in stocks, that their belief about the safety of stock trading was not simply theoretical. A next step in their campaign, hardly insignificant, was to supply evidence that trust funds administered under the prudent man rule were invested as safely as the legal list trusts and yet were able to earn roughly one percent more income per year.[45] Such arguments, supplying ideological justifications drawn from the federal securities acts, minimizing the extent of the change, and documenting the improvement in trust earnings, proved effective tools in legislative lobbying. New York adopted a modified prudent man rule for personal trusts in 1950 and followed up in 1952 by freeing life insurance companies, pension funds, and savings banks to invest in stocks as well.

It was not long before the consequences of this new freedom were felt, for the investment portfolios of financial institutions were growing in size. From 1939 to 1949, financial assets under the control of institutional investors grew by a factor of 5.3 from $13.9 billion to $73.9. But stockholdings grew by a factor of only 2.5, rising from $3.8 to $9.5 billion. In contrast, however, from 1949 to 1958, financial assets under the control of financial institutions doubled, increasing to $142.8 billion, while stockholdings increased by a factor of 4.5 to $42.8 billion with most of the increase occurring after 1953. While the rate of increase in stockholding would slow as the base expanded, financial institutions steadily increased the proportion of their portfolios placed in corporate stocks throughout the 1950s and 1960s, until by 1970 more than half of their total investments were invested in the stock market, up from only 12.9 percent in 1949.[46] The conclusion seems plain. The change

43 Lewis, "The Prudent Man Investment Rule."
44 MacNeill, "New York's Trust Investment Statute."
45 Chapman, "Investing Trust Funds under the Prudent Man Rule," p. 10; Torrance, "Legal Background, Trends, and Recent Developments," pp. 151–155.
46 These data have been calculated from Raymond W. Goldsmith, Robert E. Lipsey, and Morris Mendelson, *Studies in the National Balance Sheet*, vol. 2 (Princeton: Princeton

in law permitting institutional stock investing reflected a real shift in the preferences of institutional investors for stockholding and supplied the opportunity for that new preference to be acted out.[47]

We have here, in sum, a general accounting for the beginnings of the growth of institutional stock investing. It is not an exhaustive account to be sure. Investments by property insurance companies were never subject to supervision under the legal list rules. Stock investing by mutual funds, which grew rapidly during the 1940s and after, can only indirectly be tied to the events discussed here. Stock investing by personal trusts was, in a sense, self-liberating because trust grantors were free to empower trustees to follow the prudent man rule; and there is every evidence that they did so in increasing numbers through the 1930s, 1940s, and 1950s.[48] But stock investing by life insurance companies, savings banks, and pension funds could only have been freed from legal list restrictions by political action. Their fate was significant, for their growth was largely responsible for the dominance of institutional investors in the stock market today.[49]

If the account given here is correct, the political action required to reconstruct market norms governing who ought to trade – to tear down barriers to fiduciary stock investing – occured in large part as a second-order consequence of the federal securities laws. Without these laws, it would have been impossible for trustees to believe that they could trade stocks safely, and it would have been unlikely that state politicians could have risked dismantling restrictions on institutional investment which bore the approval of three centuries.

University Press, 1963), pp. 300–315 and the *Federal Reserve Bulletin* (1971), pp. A71.15–A71.21.

47 One critic of an earlier version of this argument complained that "almost all the growth in the ownership of common stocks by institutions in this country is attributable to the growth of private pension funds" and, by inference, had nothing to do with the change of law. What the complaint ignores is the changing preference for stockholding by the institutional managers of pension funds. Just over twenty percent of pension fund assets were held in stocks before 1953. That percentage rose to over sixty percent by the 1970s where it has remained. Changes in preference for particular kinds of assets cannot be explained by the rate of total portfolio growth.

48 Compare Smith, *The Development of Trust Companies*, p. 429 with Bender, "Prudent Investor Rule," p. 220, Donald L. Kemmerer, "The Marketing of Securities, 1930–1952," *Journal of Economic History*, 12 (1952), 461, and MacNeill, "New York's Trust Investment Statute."

49 Robert M. Solodofsky, *Institutional Holdings of Common Stock, 1900–2000* (Ann Arbor: Bureau of Business Research, Graduate School of Business Administration, University of Michigan, 1971).

We might pause at this point to consider what we have learned about the process of normative reconstruction. Whether we examine shifting beliefs about how one ought to trade or who ought to trade, the substantive change which took place (as described in this chapter and the preceding one) took place at the initiative of market participants in the pursuit of their own interests. They responded to the constraints of regulatory law to be sure — especially to the disclosure of information and the prohibition of manipulative trading techniques. Statisticians used their control over the information financial disclosure supplied to transform their role as public relations researchers into the quasi-professional role of securities analysts able to advise people as experts about how to trade stocks safely. Institutional investors, especially bank trustees, built on the new market ideology which securities analysts touted and on the relative absence of manipulative trading to free themselves from constraining investment restrictions which had kept them out of the market and made adequate performance of their fiduciary role more difficult. In sum, while federal regulation provided no certain technology to link the pursuit of private interests to some public good, private actors within the market seized what it offered to pursue their own good. It was as a consequence of their pursuit rather than any particular plan or intention that the market's normative order was reformed. Now it is time to explore the longer-run consequences of this normative reconstruction to see how it affected the processes of market control.

Part III

Unintended Consequences for Market
Control

Chapter 5

Unraveling Regulatory Control

Business in the stock market is allocated among a series of (variously important) stock exchanges and a loosely knit over-the-counter market. How
business is allocated is obviously a matter of no small importance for market
participants. The decision is not based on general consensus. Rather, it is a
historical accommodation, the outcome of struggle among conflicting interests
carried on by competitive means. If they persist through time, the mechanisms
which enforce a particular accommodation are "sanctified." They take on a
degree of legitimacy; they seem to represent an unalterable order of things.
That, of course, is an illusion. They are creatures of conflict, and they persist
only so long as competitive conditions do not shift in ways substantially to
alter the balance of power among market participants.

By the early 1960s, it was evident that the rise of institutional stock investing
threatened such a shift. That is to say, acting out the new moral order of the
market was not a stabilizing event. Competition for business in a market
characterized by institutional investors was by no means the same as competition for the business of individual investors. The volume of business was
much greater with financial institutions in the market, and so was the
concentration of order flow. Unlike individuals who traded in round lots of
100 or 200 shares, financial institutions traded in large blocks of 10,000 or
even 100,000 shares. There was enormous profit to be earned from handling
the high volume generated by institutional orders. Yet, because of the concentrated order flow, there was also a large risk for broker-dealers and for
the stock exchanges that failure to obtain institutional orders would cause a
precipitous drop in their revenue, prestige, and power within the financial
community. In these new circumstances, adherence to traditional market rules,
which had limited conflicts of interest, unraveled, and the "natural" harmony
which seemed to mark relations among participants in the market dissolved
into rancor that would endure for more than a decade.

In this chapter, we shall examine the unraveling of these traditional regulatory controls. Our purpose is to explain how institutional stock investing

upset the competitive status quo to trigger a crisis of social control sufficiently severe to drive the market to the brink of collapse. The argument has two parts. Institutional stock investing was a catalyst for breaking down traditional accommodations among market participants. But it was the ineffective response to this breakdown by market leaders and regulators which prevented any new accommodation from being reached and caused the breakdown to devolve toward institutional failure.

Traditional Accommodations Subject to Challenge

The business between broker-dealers, investors, and stock exchanges had been divided traditionally on the basis of three "regulatory" principles.[1] The form these principles took varied with historical circumstances, to meet the particular competitive threat market leaders faced, but each one was of long standing in the history of the stock market with roots reaching into the nineteenth century. Many market participants believed that stock exchanges could not function without them. And they were not alone in their belief. In the 1930s, the Securities and Exchange Commission, exercising its authority to review exchange rules, preserved these principles virtually without change. Only in the wake of institutional stock investing were they called into question.

Three Regulatory Principles

The three principles which limited conflicts between market participants can be listed as follows: (1) to maintain a market based on mediated exchange, i. e., in which buyers and sellers only met through brokers; (2) to restrict off-board trading, i. e., not to allow exchange-listed stocks to be traded over-the-counter; and (3) to eliminate direct price competition among brokers by charging fixed commission rates.

The first principle excluded anyone but brokers from having direct access to the trading floor. Trading on the stock exchange (as opposed to "over the counter") was never meant to be a direct confrontation between buyer and seller. Exchange was to be mediated by brokers acting as agents for buyers

---

1 Norman S. Poser, "Restructuring the Stock Market: A Critical Look at the SEC's National Market System," *New York University Law Review*, 56 (November-December, 1981), 888.

and sellers and, incidentally, earning their income as a result. This principle of mediated exchange was preserved by restricting memberships on stock exchanges to partnerships formed for the express purpose of conducting a securities business. By this rule, buyers and sellers of stocks − particularly institutional stock investors − could not join stock exchanges, trade for their own account, or bypass brokers and broker commissions.

The second principle prohibited trading of exchange-listed securities in the over-the-counter market. Restriction took the form of a rule which required members of the New York Stock Exchange to obtain permission from exchange officials before being allowed to trade listed securities "off board." The purpose of this rule was two-fold. It was to maintain the New York Stock Exchange's near monopoly on the flow of orders to buy and sell the securities it listed. It was also to limit competition between exchange specialists, who are charged to make markets in exchange-listed stocks, and over-the-counter market dealers, who were not exchange members, but who nevertheless tried to earn their living by making a market − the so-called third market − in exchange-listed stocks traded off board.

Without doubt, the New York Stock Exchange would have preferred an even more restrictive rule.[2] In 1940, to bolster sagging trading volumes, it announced its intention to enforce an old provision carried over from its constitution of 1863 which forbade exchange members, on threat of expulsion, to trade listed securities anywhere but on the New York Stock Exchange. If enforced, this rule would have driven many regional stock exchanges out of business, leaving the New York Stock Exchange with an undisputed monopoly of the stock trading business. Quite apart from the antitrust implications of such an action, if allowed to stand, it would have violated the 1936 amendments to the Securities Exchange Act which explicitly authorized the Securities and Exchange Commission to approve trading of exchange-listed securities on regional exchanges. This protection of the interests of regional exchanges was not based on economic need. (A case could be made that trading all shares in one market would provide greater liquidity and so a fairer price than would be set if trading was fragmented among many markets.) It was based rather on political considerations. Regional exchange financial interests only agreed to support passage of the Securities Exchange Act of 1934 on the condition that the legislation in no way threaten their continuing existence. To preserve this agreement, Jerome

2 The details in this paragraph and the next are drawn from Joel Seligman, *The Transformation of Wall Street* (Boston: Houghton Mifflin, 1982), pp. 233 − 235; cf. Roberta Karmel, *Regulation by Persecution* (New York: Simon and Schuster, 1982), pp. 136 − 137.

Frank, chairman of the Securities and Exchange Commission in 1940, blocked the New York Stock Exchange's attempt to monopolize the order flow in exchange-listed securities by forcing it to adopt rules letting its members trade without penalty in Exchange-listed securities on other exchanges. His action, however, did not eliminate all trading restrictions. Restrictions against trading exchange-listed securities "off board" in the over-the-counter market were allowed to stand and, in fact, were tightened further in the 1960s.

The third principle eliminated direct price competition among brokers who belonged to the same stock exchange, a practice as old as the exchange itself. In 1792, when brokers first combined to establish what became the New York Stock Exchange, they agreed to charge the same fixed minimum commission on trades as a fee for their services. This fixed price agreement helped to establish the New York Stock Exchange as a rule-making body with legitimate authority to regulate the conduct of its members, to oversee their compliance with market rules. In return for the public good of market regulation, members of the exchange received the private benefits conferred by price monopolies. By requiring that every member charge the same minimum commission, brokers assured one another that no competition among them would be based on the price client's paid for their securities. Violators of this agreement faced possible expulsion from the exchange or lesser sanctions levied, after 1935, by the Securities and Exchange Commission. In practice, no elaborate machinery was required to assure compliance. Competition kept fees charged at the minimum level, and the minimum fee – a small fraction of the principal value of the securities bought or sold – did not seem to leave room for price cutting, if profits were to be earned. It did not, that is, until institutional investors entered the market.[3]

Each of these principles, it should be clear, instituted an anticompetitive practice. Mediated exchange prevented free competition between brokers and their customers; off-board trading restrictions prevented, or at least minimized, competition between exchange members and dealers in the third market; and fixed commission rates limited competition among brokers belonging to the same exchange. It is ironic, of course, that the stock market, symbolically

---

3 Appearances, in fact, were deceiving. Fixed rates were established at higher rates than they would have been had competition been unrestrained. Evidence that there was room for price cutting, at least in recent years, comes from observing what happened to commissions after fixed rates were dropped in 1975. They declined, on average, by fifteen percent. See Hans R. Stoll, *Regulation of the Securities Markets* (New York: New York University Press, 1979), p. 2.

representative of a free-market economy, should itself be constituted by anticompetitive practices. But it is not surprising. A purely competitive market is a rare social event. Like all economic actors, financiers seek to define and sustain a role for themselves within the markets, and market organizations seek to define and sustain a role for themselves as well. This process may occur solely through exchange. More often it involves political negotiations and agreements to narrow the scope of competition.[4]

To limit competition, however, is not to rid the market of conflicting interests among market participants. Investors excluded from the trading floor by the principle of mediated exchange nevertheless have a strong incentive to minimize the costs of trading through brokers and to seek out the particular market in which transaction costs are low. Members of the exchanges will be willing to abide by market rules which prevent them from trading shares elsewhere than on exchange floors only so long as their compliance does not put their own business at risk or too severely limit their opportunities for profit. Fixed commission rates, for example, actually created a cleavage of interests between large and small brokerage firms. Because fixed rates effectively eliminated price competition among firms, they encouraged non-price competition. As a practical matter, this meant large firms could offer their clients a variety of "free" services, ranging from investment research and information services to the safekeeping of customers' securities, which small firms could not afford to do. As a result, small firms were put at a competitive disadvantage which they could accept only if minimum commission rates were kept at a level high enough that they, too, could make money.[5]

We are not remiss, in other words, if we regard these principles not as axioms, accepted by everyone as an ideal basis for market order, but as accommodations of conflicting interests, accommodations that are liable to break down when the compromises on which they are based no longer seem to supply satisfactory roles for market participants to follow. Just such a breakdown began to occur early in the 1960s when the legitimacy of each of these principles was seriously challenged.

---

4 The idea that people engaged in the same business will frequently conspire to limit competition for their own advantage was made famous by Adam Smith, *The Wealth of Nations*. A more recent treatment of how the search for a particular role within a market affects the constitution of markets is to be found in Harrison White, "Where Do Markets Come From?" *American Journal of Sociology*, 87 (November, 1981), 517–547.

5 Walter Werner, "Adventure in the Social Control of Finance: The National Market System for Securities," *Columbia Law Review*, 75 (November, 1975), 1263.

Challenging Anticompetitive Practices

Challenges were based on the argument, which was certainly true, that anticompetitive practices were proscribed by antitrust laws dating back to the Sherman Anti-Trust Act of 1890. The first hint that antitrust arguments might be an effective weapon to undermine the exchanges' anticompetitive practices came in 1963. In that year, the U. S. Supreme Court decided the case *Silver v. the New York Stock Exchange*.[6] At issue was whether the New York Stock Exchange could arbitrarily deny access to communication links between its trading floor and other brokerage firms when the other firms were not members of the exchange. The court ruled that the exchange could do so (though not arbitrarily, without due process), even though its action was an anticompetitive practice in obvious violation of the antitrust laws. It could do so because the Securities Exchange Act implicitly gave it that authority. But, and this was the encouraging word for would-be challengers of stock exchange rules, the Securities Exchange Act "did not automatically repeal the antitrust laws with respect to any actions which the Exchange had authority to take."[7] Repeal was limited to the minimum extent necessary to achieve the goals of federal securities regulation.

The decision opened a pandora's box. One could argue that these three principles were necessary to maintain the existing organization of the stock market. But that was not the issue. How necessary were they to make the federal securities laws work? That was certainly debatable. Originally promulgated in eighteenth and nineteenth centuries, they were not derived from federal securities law. They are examples of private regulations which until the 1970s were, in Norman Poser's phrase, "acquiesced in" by the Securities and Exchange Commission.[8] As was perhaps to be expected then, in the wake of the *Silver* decision, those who thought they might profit from doing so filed suits attacking various aspects of the exchange's fixed commission regime and threatened to sue the exchange to force it to abandon its off-board trading restrictions.[9] Whatever their merits, these suits and threats of suits created great uncertainty for exchange leaders during the 1960s and early 1970s about whether these principles – and so, we might suppose, whether the exchange system itself – would survive into the future. Adding to their uncertainty

6 See 373 *U. S.* 341 (1963).

7 David L. Ratner, *Securities Regulation* (St. Paul, Minn.: West Publishing, 1978), p. 189.

8 Poser, "Restructuring the Stock Market," p. 896.

9 Three suits were filed and one against the fixed commission rate regime and suit was threatened against off-board trading restrictions.

was the support these suits received from government officials. The Antitrust Division of the Justice Department lobbied actively in Congress and with the Securities and Exchange Commision to bring an end to the market's anticompetitive practices.[10] Congress was not especially sympathetic to the exchanges' cause either. In 1965, Manuel Cohen, then chairman of the Securities and Exchange Commission, asked Congress to consider amending the securities laws to grant antitrust immunity to the exchanges in all areas subject to commission oversight. His request was flatly refused.[11]

These challenges did not arise from a sudden ardor to see antitrust laws enforced. Antitrust laws had been on the books long before the federal securities acts were first passed and yet had not been used to strike against exchange monopolies. The challenges were made in the 1960s and not before because the influx of institutional stock investing greatly altered the stakes of market participation.

The root problem was the fixed commission rate. Exorbitantly high commissions paid by institutional investors caused them to be alert for any opportunity to lower (or to avoid paying) their transaction costs. Institutional investors had much to gain, for example, if off-board trading restrictions were removed. Their removal would allow the over-the-counter market in exchange-listed securities – the "third" market – to grow much larger and stronger because third-market dealers which belonged to no exchange were not bound to charge the fixed commission rate. Given the excess profits it generated on large trades, third-market dealers could easily quote a better aggregate price for a trade than could be had on the exchange. Even with off-board trading restrictions in place, which is to say, even excluding participation in the third market by the largest broker-dealer firms, third-market trading volumes grew at a very rapid rate, more than twice that of trading volumes over the New York Stock Exchange between 1965 and 1970.[12] Institutional investors had much more to gain, of course, if the fixed commission rate could be abolished or, alternatively, if they could share in the benefits of the fixed commission regime by becoming members of the major stock exchanges.

We should not attend myopically to the details of these competing interests, however, and miss the broader view. What we witness in the market of the

10 Seligman, *The Transformation of Wall Street*, pp. 386 – 387, 480 – 481n.

11 *Ibid.*, pp. 385 – 386. See also Werner, "Adventure in the Social Control," and Ratner, *Securities Regulation*, pp. 188 – 190.

12 Susan M. Phillipps and J. Richard Zecher, *The Securities and Exchange Commission and the Public Interest: An Economic Perspective* (Cambridge, Mass.: MIT Press, 1981), p. 96.

1960s is a clash between two long-term effects of the federal securities law. By facilitating the shift from materialist to pragmatic beliefs, federal securities regulation indirectly promoted the growth of institutional stock investing. But, as that growth was realized, it served ironically to upset the traditional accommodation among conflicting market interests, a balance that federal securities regulation had, since the 1930s, worked to preserve. What was to be done?

Failure to adjust anticompetitive practices would actively dissuade institutional investors from continuing to participate in the market, something which worked against the general interests of nearly every broker-dealer and exchange. Yet how could the anticompetitive regulatory principles be altered, how could a new accommodation among market participants be reached, without a radical restructuring of the exchange? Very few broker-dealers and very few exchanges looked forward to any such restructuring. The principles upon which the status quo was maintained, after all, had been designed to protect their various particular interests. (If their interest were now under attack, they needed protection all the more.) And the Securities and Exchange Commission was too weak to redefine the situation, to force a realignment of these interests. In the event, by indecision, the choice was made to attempt both to maintain the regulatory status quo and to encourage the growth of institutional stock trading. The choice was not a happy one. It is perfectly clear, in hindsight, that it was a choice bound to promote conflict among market participants and eventually to lead the market to the brink of organizational collapse.

The Catalyst of Market Strain

The market's problems arose in the first place as a direct result of the enormous growth of stock trading volumes during the 1940s, 1950s, and 1960s. Though these volumes were small when compared to current volumes of over thirty billion shares each year, they were large compared to the dry times of the 1930s and grew exponentially. During the 1960s, the average daily volume of shares traded over the New York Stock Exchange nearly quadrupled. The dollar value of all stock trading rose to a similar degree from $45.3 billion dollars in 1960 to over $176.3 billion 1969. This growth rate (not matched in the 1970s, but exceeded since then) represented a doubling of the rate of growth experienced in the 1940s and 1950s.[13] What lay behind this rapid growth? And, why was it a problem?

It is only partially correct to attribut the increase in trading volume to the rise of institutional investors. We have witnessed a general expansion of the market since the Second World War, to include expanded participation by individual shareholders. Their numbers rose from five million in 1950 to twenty million in 1965 and thirty million in 1970, from less than five percent to over fifteen percent of the population.[14] Nevertheless, the growth of their business should not become the main focus of our attention. The relative importance of individual stock investors declined during the twenty-five year period following the war. While their trades accounted for the majority of shares traded during the 1950s, their preponderance quickly declined thereafter until, by the 1970s, individual traders accounted for only one-third of total share volume. Moreover, they were net sellers of stock through the 1950s and 1960s.[15] And they traded in relatively small lots, which, as a technical matter, posed no serious problems for broker operations or market control.[16]

Nevertheless, the more important source of growth in trading volumes was the expansion of stock trading by institutional investors. Financial assets under their control rose enormously during this period from $92.4 billion in 1953 to $488.3 billion in 1973. If they had continued to invest 18.7 percent of their securities portfolios in stocks as they did in aggregate in 1953, this rise in assets alone would have meant an inflow of $74.0 billion into the stock market, more than enough to pay individual investors for all the stocks they sold. In fact, the preference for stockholding among institutional investors over this twenty year period was much higher than 18.7 percent. Free to invest in stocks, as they were not before the war, they invested 46 percent of all the new money they received in the stock market, most of this in stocks listed on

---

13 New York Stock Exchange, *Fact Book* (New York, 1980), p. 64; U. S. Securities and Exchange Commission, *Fiftieth Annual Report* (Washington, D. C.: Government Printing Office, 1984), p. 109.

14 Lewis H. Kimmel, *Share Ownership in the United States* (Washington, D. C.: Brookings Institution, 1952), p. 139; New York Stock Exchange, *Shareownership 1981* (New York, 1982), p. 1.

15 New York Stock Exchange, *Public Transaction Study, Fourth Quarter 1980* (New York, 1981), p. 5; Helen Stone Tice and Virginia A. Duff, "Basic Statistical Data," in *Institutional Investors and Corporate Stock*, ed. Raymond W. Goldsmith (New York: National Bureau of Economic Research, 1973), pp. 329–331.

16 Remember, trades generated paperwork that had to be processed by hand in those days; there were physical limits on trading which, with computers, do not exist to the same degree today.

the New York Stock Exchange.[17] By the mid-1960s, institutional stock investors had displaced individual investors as the largest source of trading volume
over this exchange, and by the 1970s they consistently accounted for over
half of the trading over the New York Stock Exchange.

Growth of institutional trading did not only mean increasing volume, it
also meant increasing the average size of a trade.[18] This fact is full of
significance for the organization of the stock market. Because commissions
were tied to the total dollar value of the trade, trades by institutional investors
generated many more times as much income as trades by individuals. And
because the cost of processing (say) a 100,000 share trade was by no means
1,000 times greater than the cost of processing a 100 share trade, institutional
trades under the fixed commission regime generated very high levels of profit.
The rapid growth of institutional trading volume, in short, created special
incentives for brokers to specialize in serving institutional investors and
supplied them with good reason to support continuing enforcement of the
fixed commission rule.

Institutional investors were well aware, of course, that their business was
exceptionally profitable for brokers. They sought ways to divert some portion
of the profits derived from their trades to their own benefit. Two radical
proposals were offered, both of which seriously threatened the dominant
position of the New York Stock Exchange within the stock market. One was
to allow institutional investors to join stock exchanges directly as seatholders
or indirectly as major partners of member firms. To permit this would reduce
the commissions paid by institutional investors who were also "brokers."
(Brokers paid lower fees to one another than they charged to "public" clients.)
But it would also end the monopoly over the trading floor on which the
livelihood of brokers depended. It was to abandon the principle of mediated
exchange. The New York Stock Exchange was unalterably opposed to any
such arrangement. It strictly enforced its rules to prevent nonbrokers from
gaining memberships, especially the rule which required broker members to
be organized as partnerships rather than corporations. Because most institutional investors were incorporated, they were formally unqualified even to
apply for membership. As we shall see, however, successfully holding the line

17 Figures compiled from Raymond W. Goldsmith, Robert E. Lipsey, and Morris Mendel-
   son, *Studies in the National Balance Sheet of the United States* (Princeton: Princeton
   University Press, 1963), vol. 2, pp. 300–315; *Federal Reserve Bulletin*, (March, 1971),
   A71.15–A71.21.
18 Susan M. Phillipps and J. Richard Zecher, *The SEC and the Public Interest* (Cambridge,
   Mass.: MIT Press, 1981), pp. 124–125; New York Stock Exchange, *Fact Book* (New
   York, 1980), p. 66.

during this battle proved to be a pyrrhic victory for an exchange leadership also anxious to preserve the fixed commission rate regime.

The second proposal was equally threatening to brokers. It was to eliminate fixed commission rates, to permit direct price competition among brokers. The New York Stock Exchange once again was in the forefront of opposition to this proposal. Leaders of the exchange were adamant that its member firms had to comply with the fixed commission schedule. (They even argued on several occasions in the late 1960s that the minimum rates should be raised.) Their insistence stymied, but did not entirely prevent, direct price competition, for the exchange could not and did not stop nonmember firms from making markets in the stocks it listed. Securities dealers in the over-the-counter market, led by Donald Weeden of Weeden & Co., created what they called the "third market" for New York Stock Exchange stocks. Prices of stocks trading in the "third market" were comparable to prices on the floor of the exchange, but the total cost of a transaction was less because third-market dealers were not bound to charge the exchange's minimum commission. Giving bargain rates, third-market dealers cut deeply into the volume of business done over the New York Stock Exchange: In 1965, third-market dealers did 3.4 percent of the exchange's dollar volume value. Their market share more than doubled to reach 8.5 percent by 1972.[19]

The leaders of the New York Stock Exchange were confronted with a curious organizational dilemma. If they responded to the demand for concessions in the fee structure by abandoning the fixed commission rule, the private benefits encouraging exchange membership would be curtailed and their power over the membership would decline. If the fixed commission rule was retained and no concessions were granted, the benefits of exchange membership would be sustained, but the exchange's share of the business, its control over the order flow, would erode, as in fact it did in the face of third-market competition. In either case, the outcome was to undermine the basis for the exchange's existence.

In practice, the alternatives were not so stark. Some brokers were willing to offer concessions to institutional investors, but only if doing so did not involve abandoning the fixed commission rule which was the source of their excess profits. The result was *sub rosa* deviation from the fixed commission schedule. Reciprocity was a common practice. Investment management companies were more likely to trade through brokers selling shares of mutual funds they managed, while bank trust departments were more likely to trade

19 Phillipps and Zecher, *The SEC and the Public Interest*, p. 96.

through brokers who kept deposits in their bank.[20] Brokers not able to perform a desired service in return for business agreed instead to "give up" a portion of their commission, paying it to another broker designated by the institutional trader, presumably one to whom the trader owed some debt.[21] When exchanges or "give ups" could not be arranged, all types of goods and services – ranging from investment research, office equipment and supplies to vacations in exotic places and sexual favors – could be "purchased" by institutional investors using the commission dollars their clients paid, supposedly, for executing orders.[22] At best, the consequence of these practices was to make the true price of securities vary by quite a lot and unpredictably from broker to broker. It was hardly a satisfactory resolution of the problem.

While leaders of the New York Stock Exchange worked hard to defend anticompetitive practices against these attacks, other market participants tried to gain some benefit for themselves by joining in. Third-market dealers, led by Weeden & Co., heavily advertised their ability to handle large institutional "block" trades, i. e., trades of 10,000 shares or more, and to do so at prices superior to those offered over the exchange. They encouraged the erosion of off-board trading restrictions.[23] Even member firms of the exchange began to bridle under exchange restrictions. Mediated exchange was bolstered in part by a rule which barred member firms from raising capital by selling shares in their firm to the public. The aim was to keep institutional investors from gaining indirect membership in the exchange through the purchase of shares in member firms. Yet, by 1969, the need for new capital both to finance large institutional trades (and to pay for the back-office operations necessary to process them) was so great that member firms could no longer afford to be bound by this restriction. One firm, Donaldson, Lufkin, and Jenrette, announced in April 1969 that it was "going public" to raise capital even if that meant resigning its exchange membership. It was predominantly an institutional firm and could always sell shares in the third market. Other members also desperate for capital could easily follow suit. Exchange leaders were faced, then, with a determined opposition which could lead to the loss of members who would no doubt reestablish themselves as competitive third-market dealers, and forced to compromise. They altered exchange rules to allow firms to be publicly owned. But to maintain the principle of mediated

20 Ibid., pp. 23 – 25.
21 John Brooks, The Go-Go Years (Dublin: Gill and Macmillan, 1973), pp. 150 – 151; Chris Welles, The Last Days of the Club (New York: Dutton, 1975), pp. 74 – 79.
22 Robert Sobel, Inside Wall Street (New York: W. W. Norton, 1977), p. 136.
23 Welles, The Last Days of the Club, pp. 55 – 60.

exchange, there was this proviso: No member corporation could be owned by a corporation not itself in the brokerage business.[24]

Leaders of regional stock exchanges displayed no similar loyalty to the principle of mediated exchange. Beginning in 1965, they allowed institutional investors to join their exchanges. As regional exchange members, institutional investors could trade securities listed on the New York Stock Exchange at a fraction of the cost of trading directly in New York. Not incidentally, trading volumes on regional stock exchanges began to grow. By the early 1970s, the livelihood of some regional exchanges, notably the Philadelphia-Baltimore-Washington Stock Exchange, depended heavily on business brought by its institutional members.[25]

In sum, the regime of fixed commission rates when applied within an institutional stock market created such a large opportunity for broker-dealer firms to earn excess profits that few were content simply to abide by market rules as they were applied for decades before. Institutional clients and brokers sought every means either to avoid paying the hig commission charge or to capture institutional business by charging fees just below the fixed commission charge. The result usually was to undermine the legitimacy of and adherence to anticompetitive practices. Put in other words, there was more competition within the market in the 1960s — price competition, competition between broker-dealers and their institutional clients, and competition among markets — than there had been at any earlier time in this century. The force of this competition pushed uniformly in one direction. It drew trading volume away from the New York Stock Exchange toward the over-the-counter market and the regional stock exchanges.[26] If allowed to continue in this direction, the traditional primacy of the New York Stock Exchange was threatened, and persistence of the principle of mediated exchange was cast into doubt.

According to simple economic theory, we might expect such competitive pressures to cause exchange leaders to modify their rules — at least to modify the fixed commission rate schedule — to recapture their business.[27] If markets

---

24 *Ibid.*, pp. 96–98; Seligman, *The Transformation of Wall Street*, pp. 470–473; U. S. Congress, Senate, Subcommittee on Securities of the Committee on Banking, Housing, and Urban Affairs, *Securities Industry Study* (Washington, D. C.: Government Printing Office, 1973), pp. 70–71.

25 Seligman, *The Transformation of Wall Street*, pp. 470–473; U. S. Congress, *Securities Industry Study*, pp. 68–73.

26 It even encouraged the development of an automated market, called Instinet, which allowed institutional investors to trade directly with one another, bypassing broker-dealers altogether.

27 Even according to some sociological theory. See Huseyin Leblebici and Gerald R.

are truly self-regulating, here was the opportunity for self-regulation to show. But it did not. Regulatory officials and stock exchange leaders failed to act decisively either to enforce or to adjust market rules to accommodate an institutional market. Instead, broker-dealers used market rules deceptively, pretending to obey them in order to keep profit margins high while avoiding them in fact to undercut one another in the hot pursuit of institutional business. Competition among them worked inharmoniously to undermine the operating principles which helped to define the market's "self-regulatory" structure, and it did so without erecting any alternative controls in their place.[28] The result was an unraveling of the anticompetitive regulatory policies, a kind of de facto deregulation. Why was this the outcome? And, what were its effects?

Ineffective Regulatory Response

We must be very careful in specifying what the matter with the market was after institutional stock investors entered the arena. It would be easy to conclude that the change in the scale of market trading was the sole cause upsetting well-established institutional controls, redefining the market situation in such a novel way that broker-dealers could hardly be faulted for engaging in whatever behavior seemed likely to gain them a part of the profitable institutional business. The lure of institutional business was very strong and, in conjunction with a general rise in stock prices, it may have suggested to some broker-dealers the possibility of earning unlimited wealth. Under such circumstances, we should not be surprised to witness a kind of anomic adventurism, reminiscent of behavior in a gold rush. Nevertheless, such adventurism is to be expected only under certain specific structural circumstances.[29] In markets, it is to be expected only when there is a prior loosening of traditional restraints that might otherwise have been expected to curb competition by raising the costs of deviance; when there is, in short, a failure of regulatory leadership. It was such a failure that occurred and for two primary reasons.

Salancik, "Stability in Interorganizational Exchanges: Rulemaking Processes of the Chicago Board of Trade," *Administrative Science Quarterley*, 27 (1982), 227–242.

28 See Amitai Etzioni, "Encapsulated Competition," *Journal of Post-Keynesian Economics*, 7 (Spring, 1985), 300.

29 See Gary G. Hamilton, "The Structural Sources of Adventurism: The Case of the California Gold Rush," *American Journal of Sociology*, 83 (May, 1978), 1466–1490.

An Imbalance of Power

First, fiscal evisceration of the Securities and Exchange Commission in the 1950s altered the balance of regulatory power to favor the exchanges over the commission itself. To accommodate President Eisenhower's policy to balance the federal budget, resources and staff available to the Securities and Exchange Commission were cut drastically even though the market was undergoing rapid expansion. With a skeletal staff and limited resources, the commission fell behind in its work and attempted to adapt by relying on the investigatory apparatus of state authorities and on the regulatory abilities of leaders of the stock exchanges and of the National Association of Securities Dealers which oversaw conduct within the over-the-counter market. Delegated power is difficult to exercise well. In retrospect, it is clear that recession of strict federal oversight promoted an efflorescence of fraudulent stock issues and speculative trading abuses, concentrated on the American Stock Exchange, the likes of which had not been seen since the 1920s. There was a definite deterioration of standards applied to govern market conduct during the early post-war period.[30]

If delegated power is difficult to exercise, it is more difficult still to recall. In 1961, the Securities and Exchange Commission was revived under President Kennedy's administration.[31] Infused with resources, it acted promptly and decisively to correct the worst abuses in the market. It suspended those connected with shady trading practices, removed exchange officers who had

30 Sobel, *Inside Wall Street*, pp. 170–173; Seligman, *Transformation of Wall Street*, chap. 9.

31 President Kennedy's attitude toward regulatory agency's was informed by the Landis Report, named for its author, James Landis, former member of the Federal Trade Commission, Civil Aeronautics Board, and Securities and Exchange Commission as well as one of the authors of the federal securities acts. In the 1930s, Landis was sanguine about the prospects for increasing the efficiency of governmental regulation by creating more and more agencies to do the job. In subsequent years, he changed his mind, believing that regulatory agencies were too susceptible to political pressures, bureaucratic inertia, and the malaise of poor political leadership. By 1960, when he was asked by Kennedy to write a report on the matter (as a guide for appointments), Landis was convinced that the quality of leadership possessed by the chairman of each agency was the most important factor for revitalizing agencies: "Good men can make poor laws workable, poor men will wreak havoc with good laws," or so he said. See Donald A. Ritchie, "Reforming the Regulatory Process: Why James Landis Changed His Mind," *Business History Review*, 54 (Autumn, 1980), 283–302 and James M. Landis, *Reminiscences of James M. Landis* (New York: Oral History Collection, Columbia University, 1975).

breached the trust of their office, and oversaw a reorganization of the government of the American Stock Exchange.[32] But this was not enough for the Securities and Exchange Commission to regain its former stature as an agency of control on Wall Street. After nearly a decade of federal regulatory neglect, leaders of the market's self-regulatory agencies no longer believed it was necessary for them to consult with the Securities and Exchange Commission about important matters concerning the rule of their markets. (Consultations had been standard practice from 1935 through 1953.) And commissioners appointed to the Securities and Exchange Commission in the 1960s accepted their belief. Their acceptance of this arrangement, of course, seriously limited their strength to enforce market regulations forcefully, even when there was clear evidence that such enforcement was necessary and not otherwise forthcoming.

Congress was not quite so accepting of this division of regulatory labor. In 1961, in the aftermath of the trading scandals over the American Stock Exchange and amid reports that trades were not settling promptly, Congress authorized the Securities and Exchange Commission to undertake a *Special Study of the Securities Markets* to be completed by 1963. The *Special Study* was limited in its approach and criticized by some for assuming the need for government regulation of markets.[33] Yet it was thoroughly done and it was not uncritical of market regulation. On the contrary, it found fault with industry self-regulation in almost every field of market activity, including selling practices and back office problems, fixed commission rates, and disciplinary procedures. Fault was found also with the passivity of the Securities and Exchange Commission. It urged the commission to become more actively involved in adjusting the market to its new circumstances, at least by studying the problems of market structure associated with fixed commission rates. It anticipated that market structure was to be fundamentally transformed by the growth of institutional stock investing coupled with developing computer technologies. And it recommended several regulatory reforms.[34] As a result of this study, the securities acts were amended in 1964 to extend disclosure requirements to include securities issues trading only on the over-the-counter markets and stiffened barriers of entry into the securities business to help assure that only knowledgeable and financially solvent people took up the trade. These were not controversial reforms. But neither Congress or the

32 Brooks, *The Go-Go Years*, pp. 26 – 54.
33 See, e.g., George J. Stigler, "Public Regulation of the Securities Market," *Journal of Business*, 37 (April, 1964).
34 Securities and Exchange Commission, *Special Study of the Securities Markets* (Washington, D. C.: Government Printing Office, 1963).

President stood so firmly behind the idea of regulatory reform that a controversial bill could withstand lobbying by private interests to pass into law.[35] Nevertheless, the study did succeed in specifying accurately the regulatory problems the market faced in an era of institutional stock trading.

The Securities and Exchange Commission only partially heeded the warnings sounded by the *Special Study*. It did study important matters of market structure; in particular, the anticompetitive practices of fixing commission rates and restricting off-board trading. Completed in 1965, both studies doubted that either practice was justified.[36] But the Commission remained a passive regulatory force. Its reports were not made public. Nor were they used to cause exchange leaders to alter their rules. Rather the commission, conservative in outlook, quietly negotiated with exchange leaders hoping to gain their voluntarily agreement to modify, if not abolish, their anticompetitive practices.

The commission's soft-pedal approach toward gaining rule reform is the second reason for the failure of regulatory leadership. The deference shown by commissioners to the exchange leadership was not repaid in kind. Exchange leaders would not act. They believed anticompetitive practices were necessary to constitute markets and that the commission had no authority to compel them to change their rules. And on the last point, at least, they were right. The Securities Exchange Act authorized the commission to *review* exchange rules, not to *initiate* changes in rules. As a result, exchange leaders rigidly refused to make any change in their rules except those they thought would strengthen the financial position of their particular market organization. Because the interests of various market participants were conflicting, this produced a chaotic pattern of industry self-regulation. The New York and American Stock Exchanges pressed the commission to end institutional memberships on regional exchanges; third-market dealers pressed for an end of off-board trading restrictions; and institutional investors pressed for the abolition of fixed commission rates or, at least, for volume discounts.

Moving Toward the Brink of Collapse

With no unity of interest or effort, there could be no agreement about how to revise market rules, but only a rapid deterioration of market organization

35 Seligman, *The Transformation of Wall Street*, pp. 311–323.
36 *Ibid.*, pp. 388, 391–402; Ernest Bloch and Arnold V. Sametz, *A Modest Proposal for a National Securities Market System and Its Governance* (New York: New York University, Graduate School of Business Administration, 1973), p. 19.

as the old rules became increasingly irrelevant, except as tools to pursue private interests. The signs of this deterioration became obvious to all during the late 1960s when brokers failed to settle on the trades they executed over the floor of the exchange. By December 1968, in fact, the trade settlement system had virtually broken down. Unsettled trades accumulated at an alarming rate through the last three quarters of the year rising from $2.6 billion in April to $3.1 billion in September to $4.1 billion by the end of the year.[37]

Difficulties in settling trades could be traced to record trading volumes which where wholly unanticipated by the members or the leadership of the New York Stock Exchange. Few if any brokers, for example, had automated their back office operations. Most clerical work associated with settling trades, therefore, had to be done by hand. Their lack of preparedness was considerably aggravated by the fact that so many of the trades consisted of institutional orders. Bank trust departments, for example, legally were required to segregate assets for each of their accounts. The requirements greatly increased the number of stock certificates in circulation, as separate certificates were needed for each account. It also increased the number of stock transfers required to remove stock from the seller's into the buyer's name. Stock transfer procedures, moreover, were much more complex and took longer to complete when stock was registered in the corporate or legal name of the institution, as was customary for public pension funds and insurance companies. The effects of rising volumes, multiple certificates, and legal transfers combined so that on average the number of days required to transfer stock was over four rather than the mandated two business days. Where transfer was required to settle a trade, as it often was with institutional trades, waiting so long made it necessary to fail several days before making settlement.[38] The significance of these (perhaps tedious) details about settling and not settling trades lies with its impact on the financial strength of brokerage firms.

Despite having large incomes, brokers did not accumulate a sufficient stock of permanent capital to permit them to process the large volume of transactions which characterized trading in the institutional market. They did not, in large part, because they could not. Search for capital was limited by exchange restrictions which would not allow firms to become publicly owned corporations able to raise money for themselves in the capital market. These

37 Ernest Bloch, "Securities Markets under Stress: 1967–1976," in *Impending Changes for Securities Markets*, ed. Ernest Bloch and Robert A. Schwartz (Greenwich, Conn.: JAI Press, 1979), p. 5.
38 U. S. Congress, Senate, Subcommittee on Securities of the Committee on Banking, Housing, and Urban Affairs, *Clearance and Settlement of Securities Transactions* (Washington, D. C.: Government Printing Office, 1972), pp. 94–98, 321, 353.

restrictions, remember, existed so that the exchange could retain tight control over the exchange's membership. If shares of member firms traded publicly, institutional investors could gain the advantages of membership simply by purchasing enough shares to control a member firm.[39] But this tactic for restricting membership hurt brokers in need of equity capital to expand fixed investments in operational facilities.

In 1970, the level of fails subsided to $ 2.7 billion, yet even that lower figure represented eighty-four percent of total broker-dealer equity capital. If fails were distributed among firms in proportion to their capital, then the net equity capital position of all firms was severely strained. Of course, fails were not distributed in proportion to capital. Firms with little capital or poor accounting systems – and the latter category including some very large firms – were rather more likely to fail on trades than others.[40] These firms were in serious financial difficulty.

In theory, their difficulty should have been detected and limited by the Securities and Exchange Commission which had responsibility for monitoring the financial health of brokerage firms. The commission was alerted to the impending crisis by customer complaints about unsettled trades, the number of which rose sharply in 1966. Yet through 1967 and 1968, the commission continued to defer to exchange officials, allowing them to regulate member-firm operations and finances.[41] It allowed its offers of help to be quietly set aside until May 1968. At that point, the New York Stock Exchange agreed to inspect every major brokerage firm in the country with the commission by its side. These inspections revealed, to the commission for the first time, the depth of the operational difficulties underlying failures to settle trades on time, and they indicated the direct connection between a firm's operational health and its financial well-being.

Finally, the commission began to act, warning firms that advertising for business it could not process was fraudulent, threatening to suspend the registration of firms which did not curtail operations until clearing up their accounts, and persuading the New York Stock Exchange to cut back to a four day trading week. But these actions came too late to alter the course of events, and even late in 1968 the commission would agree that primary

39 Welles, *The Last Days of the Club*, p. 97.
40 Egon Guttman, "Broker-Dealer Bankruptcies," in *Modern Securities Transfer*, rev. ed. (Boston: Warren Gorham & Lamont, 1976), p. 34; Securities and Exchange Commission, *Study of Unsafe and Unsound Practices of Brokers and Dealers* (Washington, D. C.: Government Printing Office, 1971), pp. 95 – 122.
41 See, e. g., Securities and Exchange Commission, Securities Exchange Act Release No. 34 – 8024 (January 18, 1967), p. 3.

regulatory responsibility for member-firm operations and finances rested with the exchanges. The result was inevitable. Between 1969 and 1970 over 100 broker-dealers went bankrupt or were forced involuntarily into mergers.[42]

Nothing comparable to this had ever occured before, not even during the depression of the 1930s. The New York Stock Exchange had established a special fund of $25 million to pay the debts of failing firms so customers would not sustain any losses, but this fund was soon exhausted. Even an infusion of $30 million more, money taken from a building fund, was not able to pay all claims which by August 1970 were known to equal $60 million. Before the end of 1970, the failure of another large firm, Goodbody & Co., added $23 million more to total claims. At this rate, the exchange could not reasonably continue to assess its membership for the money needed to protect investors from losses due to broker failures.[43] It had to go to Congress hat in hand asking that lawmakers provide public insurance to protect investors.

Fortunately for the exchange, a bill to insure customer deposits with brokers had already been filed in Congress in 1969 by Senator Edmund Muskie. Under these strained circumstances, the bill began to receive careful attention. There was substantial agreement among legislators, members of the Securities and Exchange Commission, and the financial community that the insurance provided for by the bill was necessary to retain public confidence in the market. Yet lawmakers were not pleased that self-regulation by the exchange and oversight by the Securities and Exchange Commission had so plainly broken down.[44] They agreed to pass the Securities Investor Protection Act in December 1970. The act pledged $1 billion of federal money to insure customer deposits with brokers and created the Securities Investor Protection Corporation which, like the Federal Deposit Insurance Corporation, would be a self-financing quasi-public insurance corporation. The act also explicitly defined the commission's powers to include inspection of the condition of exchange member firms. In this one area at least the powers of self-regulation, the powers of stock exchange leaders and of officials of the National Association of Securities Dealers, were clearly subordinated to those of the commission. But the lawmakers agreed to this "bail out" only after the bill's sponsors added provisions for an immediate and comprehensive Congressional investigation

42 Securities and Exchange Commission, *Study of Unsafe and Unsound Practices*, p. 27; Welles, *The Last Days of the Club*, pp. 243–283.
43 Hurd Baruch, *Wall Street: Security Risk* (Baltimore: Penguin Books, 1971), pp. 71–72: Welles, *The Last Days of the Club*, p. 245; Guttman, "Broker-Dealer Bankruptcies," pp. 48–50.
44 Donald T. Regan, *A View from the Street* (New York: New American Library, 1972), pp. 154–155.

of the stock market's organization and regulation.[45] Congressional reaction, in other words, signified no approval of the de facto deregulation which, under competitive pressures and lax regulatory leadership, had been allowed to occur.

If there is a single lesson to be learned from these events, it is that market order is not a spontaneous creation; market rules are not self-adjusting. Markets are institutions whose adaptation to a changing environment, successful or not, is determined by the exercise of authority. In this case, it was not successful. When authority was exercised, it was exercised rigidly, to preserve privileges − accommodations − which could be justified, perhaps, in a market dominated by individual investors, but not in a market dominated by institutional investors. The traditional regulatory principles were not successfully adapted to the market's new situation. They were not enforced either.

Institutional stock investors avoided the principle of mediated exchange by trading on the third market (or among themselves without brokers) and by seeking memberships on regional exchanges. Exchange members refused to charge institutional stock traders the full minimum commissions, but engaged in price cutting, disguised as the provision of various goods and services. Exchange leaders themselves were reluctant either to change or to enforce capital requirements designed to defend market boundaries and to assure the financial integrity of their member firms. Meanwhile, the Securities and Exchange Commission, though more attuned to what the situation required, lacked both the power and the influence to make market participants and exchange leaders behave any differently.

The long-term consequences of acting out the market's new moral order − its new beliefs about how and with whom one ought to trade − undermined adherence to traditional market rules on which institutional stability had come to depend. The result was to unleash an opportunistic pursuit of private interest that "worked" only to erode the institutional integrity of the market and the financial integrity of key market participants. It was to create an unstable institution which was bound to fail over the long run as, in fact, it did. And in response, Congress committed itself to reform the market's regulatory structure, to devise some means to restore the market's stability, to discipline the pursuit of private gains by (at least some minimal) concern to preserve the institutional viability of the market as a whole. Precisely how and with what success this could be managed is a topic for the next chapter.

45 Ibid., pp. 37 − 140; Baruch, *Wall Street*, pp. 70 − 84.

Chapter 6

The Limits of Regulatory Reform

The failure of so many broker-dealer firms and the inability of viable firms to settle trades in a timely fashion appeared to many in Congress in the early 1970s "as perhaps the single most dramatic technical failure of the free enterprise system."[1] Congressional willingness to make the federal government a lender of last resort, to rescue bankrupt brokerage firms, guaranteed the economic trustworthiness of key market participants and may thus have prevented a collapse of confidence in the stock market as an organizational mechanism through which to raise and value corporate capital. But it did not address the fundamental problem, the failure by leaders of the stock exchanges and by regulators within the Securities and Exchange Commission adequately to exercise their authority to adjust the market organization to changing economic and technological circumstances.

It was this fundamental problem which members of Congress sought to address. The problem, as they saw it, was to maintain the organizational viability of the private capital market system in the context of economic and technological change. The solution proposed was, not exactly a return to laissez-faire, but it was a conservative response, an affirmation of and attempt to apply principles of neoclassic economics to market reform. Congress hoped to employ "free competition" as a means to create the incentives and discipline for market leaders to adjust their markets to shifting competitive pressures. The role for government regulators was to assure that market participants did nothing to constrain the operation of competitive forces. Were these objectives possible to achieve?

The question resists any simple answer. Though the aims of Congress were stated relatively clearly in an act to reform market regulation along these lines – the Securities Reform Act of 1975, the hypotheses of this conservative movement for reform were never tested. Nor could they be. Federal securities

---

1 U. S. Congress, Senate, Subcommittee on Securities, Committee on Banking, Housing, and Urban Affairs, *Regulation of Clearing Agencies and Transfer Agents: Hearings on S. 2058, July 11 – 12, 1973* (Washington, D. C.: Government Printing Office, 1973), p. 1.

laws organized the market's governance structure in a way that fragmented market interests and weakened regulatory leadership by the Securities and Exchange Commission. The result was to prevent the aggregation of political and material interests needed to implement the act as Congress intended. Rather than remake the regulatory system as Congress directed, the commission concentrated on piecemeal reforms on which it could reach some agreement. Their cumulative effect has been to limit the extent of regulatory reform and to reinforce the existing market structure.[2]

Movement to Create a Competitive National Market System

The policy, implied by the Securities Investor Protection Act passed in 1970, that broker-dealers and their market organizations should not be allowed to slip into bankruptcy was explicitly affirmed by the Securities Reform Act of 1975. It declared that "the securities markets are an important national asset which must be preserved and strengthened."[3] At issue was precisely how this preservation and strengthening was to be done.

To address this issue, Congress conducted over ten investigations between 1970 and 1975. These investigations addressed a range of matters from the details of the clearance and settlement of securities transactions to consideration of the state of the "securities industry" as a whole. In addition, Congress received two important reports from the Securities and Exchange Commission, one detailing the unsafe and unsound practices of broker-dealers which led to their financial crisis in the late 1960s and the other, a broader study begun in 1968, assessing the growth and impact of institutional investing on capital markets generally.[4]

The influence of these studies, especially of the *Institutional Investor Study*, is difficult to exaggerate. This study, authorized by Congress in 1968, but not completed until 1971, was unique for being led by university-based economics instead of lawyers. The result was to give voice to a new conservative

---

2 Donald C. Langevoort, "Information Technology and the Structure of Securities Regulation," *Harvard Law Review*, 98 (February, 1985), 754–755.

3 *Securities Exchange Act*, sect. 11 A(a) (1).

4 For an overview of these investigations and their relation to passage of the Securities Reform Act in 1975 see Harvey A. Rowen, "The Securities Acts Amendments of 1975: A Legislative History," *Securities Regulation Law Journal*, 3 (Winter, 1976), 329–346.

movement that saw in "free market" processes a tool for achieving federal policy objectives. Neoclassical economists, notably George Stigler and his colleague Milton Friedman, had criticized federal regulatory policies, claiming that government regulation rarely if ever achieved its declared purpose to promote the public interest, and they backed their claims by substantial empirical research.[5] Their case was bolstered by new developments in economic theory.

It had become axiomatic for social scientists and policymakers to notice that no real markets met the stringent assumptions made by economists in their models of perfect competition. Consequently, the benefits supposed to be achieved by perfect competition could not be realized through imperfect markets. Government regulation was justified, therefore, to correct allocative distortions (and abuses) that resulted from market imperfections. The strength of this argument was seriously challenged in the 1960 s when empirical research showed that markets could depart very far from perfection and yet still be "efficient markets." Efficient markets were "fair" in the sense that current prices so quickly and fully reflected public knowledge about the product traded that even those with privileged information could not often make use of it to achieve superior returns at the expense of the less knowledgeable.[6] If the "efficient market" hypothesis was true, then the benefits of competition could be achieved even from imperfect markets, as long as they were efficient, and the justification for government regulation was correspondingly thrown into doubt. No regulator of persons or institutions in the pursuit of their own interests could be more effective than competition itself. So the neoclassical economists argued.

While the neoclassical position was never unopposed either in academic or government circles, it gained in political influence through the late 1960s and 1970s. It gained in part because of the persuasiveness of the research which supported its propositions. It gained also in response to an intractable series of negative changes within the domestic and global economy: the failure of Penn Central, the end of the boom in stock prices (which had been virtually uninterrupted since the Second World War), rates of inflation high enough to cause then-President Nixon to impose peace-time price controls and to abandon international convertibility of the dollar into gold at $35 per ounce, a slowing of the rate of economic growth, and the shock of the first oil embargo.

5 See, e. g., George J. Stigler, *The Citizen and the State* (Chicago: University of Chicago Press, 1975).

6 James H. Lorie and Mary Hamilton, *The Stock Market: Theories and Evidence* (Homewood, Ill.: Richard D. Irwin, 1973), p. 71.

These negative economic developments caused uneasiness among policymakers, especially when they could not be readily offset by following traditional Keynesian approches. There was a willingness on the part of many in government to return to the tradition of free enterprise as they understood it.

It was in this context that Congress and the staff of the Securities and Exchange Commission were persuaded that anticompetitive regulatory practices in the market were the immediate cause of the market's organizational problems and that the main purpose of efforts to reform stock market regulation was to assure that these anticompetitive practices were overturned.[7] Here, then, was the program of regulatory reform which Congress sought to establish when passing the Securities Reform Act of 1975. The program was divided into two parts.

What Congress Sought to Do

First, anticompetitive practices had to be eliminated, beginning with fixed commission rates. The importance of this step was emphasized early on by Donald Farrar, the economist who directed the Securities and Exchange Commission's *Institutional Investor Study*. The great majority of the financial and regulatory problems experienced by the market during the 1960s could be traced, Farrar testified before Congress,

> in whole or in part to attempts by the major exchanges and some types of institutional investors to protect noncompetitively determined fixed minimum commission rates and by other markets and institutional types to exploit competitive opportunities to avoid such rates.[8]

Accepting Farrar's assessment, Congress in the Reform Act barred stock exchanges from imposing any new fixed commission rate schedule and empowered the Securities and Exchange Commission to repeal any existing exchange rule that imposed a fixed rate schedule. While the commission was also authorized to approve fixed rates in the future, it could only do so after a lengthy process of public hearings to determine the necessity for such an action. The language and intention of the act were extraordinarily direct,

---

7 Norman S. Poser, "Restructuring the Stock Market: A Critical Look at the SEC's National Market System," *New York University Law Review*, 56 (November – December, 1981), 902.

8 Quoted in U. S. Congress, Senate, Subcommittee on Securities, Committee on Banking, Housing, and Urban Affairs, *Securities Industry Study* (Washington, D. C.: Government Printing Office, 1973), p. 49.

indicating the degree and strength of consensus Congress had reached on this issue.[9]

This action came somewhat late. Three years before the Reform Act was passed, the Securities and Exchange Commission (for reasons we shall notice later on) had already ordered exchanges to eliminate fixed commissions on large orders (over $500,000). It then proceeded steadily, on its own authority, to lower the threshold for competitive rates and finally to abolish fixed rates altogether effective May 1, 1975 over one month before the Reform Act was passed. But the commission's action was subject to judicial review. Congressional action strongly endorsed the commission's policies and put an end to any hope exchange leaders might have harbored that the commission's rulings could be overturned by court decree. And this was not the end to Congressional commitment to competition.

In addition to eliminating fixed commission rates restoring price competition among brokers belonging to the same exchange, Congress sought to reduce barriers to competition among brokers and dealers belonging to different exchanges or trading in the third market. To accomplish this, Congress established the major goal of the Reform Act: to create a "national market system."[10] This new market system was to be an exemplar of a competitive capital market. According to the terms of the Reform Act, the national market system was to assure "economically efficient execution of securities transactions," to promote "fair competition among brokers and dealers, among exchange markets, and between exchange markets and markets other than exchange markets [e.g., the third market]," and to supply a practical means for brokers to execute investors' orders "in the best available market."[11] The precise configuration of the market system was deliberately left vague on the belief that the most stable and effective configuration would evolve "through the interplay of competitive forces as unnecessary regulatory restrictions are removed."[12] But that is not to say that Congress had no idea what the configuration should be like.

The legislators assumed that a national market system was possible to create because of the demonstrated capabilities of automated market processes.

9 *Securities Exchange Act*, sect. 6(e). The opening sentence of this section reads: "On and after the date of enactment of the Securities Acts Amendments of 1975, no national securities exchange may impose any schedule or fix rates of commissions, allowances, discounts, or other fees to be charged by its members."

10 See Walter Werner, "Adventure in the Social Control of Finance: The National Market System for Securities," *Columbia Law Review*, 75 (November, 1975), 1270 – 1272 for a critical review of the background of this announcement.

11 *Securities Exchange Act*, sect. 11 A(a) (1).

12 *Report of the Senate-House Conference Committee* (House Report No. 92 – 229) as cited in *Securities Reform Act of 1975* (New York: Commerce Clearing House, 1975), p. 245.

At a minimum, available automated communications technology was to be employed to supply brokers, dealers, and investors with current data about prices for and transactions in stocks in various markets. They also assumed competition would supply sufficient incentives for private parties to create such a system only after restraints on competition were removed. Yet, as events of the 1960s had made clear, competition by itself could not be counted on to assure their removal. Some external stimulus was required. To this end, the act charged the Securities and Exchange Commission with an explicit obligation *to eliminate all present and future competitive restraints embodied in exchange rules or its own rules,* unless those rules were plainly justified by the puposes of the Reform Act — to include presumably establishment of a national market system.[13]

As a practical matter, this provision meant that the commission was supposed not only to abolish fixed commission rates. It was also supposed to eliminate off-board trading restrictions, which were the chief impediment to competition between markets and market makers. Congress directed the commission "to review any and all rules of national securities exchanges which limit ... the ability of members to effect transactions in securities otherwise than on such exchanges" and, within ninety days after the Reform Act was passed, "to amend any such rule imposing a burden on competition" that was not required to establish a national market system.[14] As the conference report made plain, this language referred primarily to the New York Stock Exchange's rules prohibiting its members from trading listed securities in the third market.[15] By freeing brokers and dealers to execute trades for any security in the market of their choice, an incentive would be created for various market centers to organize themselves to permit execution with the lowest possible transaction costs and to advertise their capacity through a consolidated price quotation and transaction reporting system. As a result of this competition, the national market system would take on a definite form.

The second part of the reform program was to increase the regulatory powers of the Securities and Exchange Commission. The original Securities Exchange Act required exchanges (and market associations) to register with the commission. Successful registration could be had if the commission approved the market organization's rules. After registration, exchanges and market associations could alter their rules or add new rules on their own initiative without prior approval. While the commission retained powers of

13 *Securities Exchange Act*, sect. 19(c).
14 *Securities Exchange Act*, sect. 11 A(c) (4).
15 *Report of the Senate-House Conference Committee* as cited in *Securities Reform Act of 1975*, p. 248; see also *Securities Exchange Act*, sect. 11 A(c) (3).

review over market rules, its power to initiate rule changes was by no means legally certain. This uncertainty had proved in the 1960s to be a hindrance. It prevented the commission from acting aggressively to alter exchange rules regulating the financial condition of brokerage firms or to eliminate anticompetitive practices which it knew to be causing problems for the market. Left unattended, this uncertainty would surely become a reason for delay in implementing the market reforms contemplated by Congress in the Reform Act. If the commission attempted to facilitate creation of a national market system by altering or eliminating market rules, its powers to do so would have been made the subject of a legal suit.

To dispel uncertainty, Congress modified the relation which existed between the commission, the exchanges, and the National Association of Securities Dealers. Reversing prior practice, exchanges and the National Association of Securities Dealers — which the act lumped together under the term "self-regulatory organizations," as I shall too — would have to submit proposed rules and proposed rule changes to the commission before they went into effect. Self-regulatory organizations would be required to justify their proposals and the commission would be required to give interested parties time and opportunity to comment. Echoing the *Silver* decision,[16] the act prescribed that before the rule could go into effect, the commission would have to make a positive determination that the rule was consistent with the requirements of the Securities Exchange Act.[17] In addition, Congress gave the commission plenary power to amend or to revoke the rules of any self-regulatory organization whenever necessary to achieve the purposes of the Securities Exchange Act as amended.[18] The only limit Congress placed on the commission's authority was to subject its decisions to judicial review.

By these means, Congress hoped so to strengthen the commission's control over market regulation as to avoid any repetition of that weakness and hesitancy to act which characterized it during the 1960s. The hope also was to encourage the commission to act boldly to eliminate anticompetitive practices, which was the first step toward establishing a national market system. That was the plan. What was the result? How was the market transformed by the Reform Act?

16 See chapter 5, footnote 6.
17 *Securities Exchange Act*, sect. 19(b).
18 *Securities Exchange Act*, sect. 19(c); *Report of the Senate Committee on Banking, Housing and Urban Affairs* (Senate Report No. 94–75) as cited in *Securities Reform Act of 1975*, p. 254.

A Limited Reform

The outlook for implementing changes outlined by the statute appeared to be favorable in 1975. Lobbying by conflicting interest groups within the financial community, which had delayed passage of the act, was never so intense as to endanger the reform movement in Congress and now was finally overcome.[19] The course of market reform was clearly charted: Eliminate anticompetitive practices which weakened the market in the past. Strengthen the Securities and Exchange Commission's authority to assure that such practices are not reestablished. And trust competition, newly unleashed, to prod leaders of self-regulatory organizations to adjust market rules in the best way to fit whatever circumstances the market might encounter in the future. The Securities and Exchange Commission appeared to be more than ready to fulfill its new and expanded role. It had already abolished fixed commission rates. It had studies on file to document the anticompetitive consequences of off-board trading rules. And it had lobbied hard to gain its new powers to regulate and control self-regulatory agencies.[20]

Nevertheless, achievements over the decade after passage of the act fell short of statutory expectations. The commission did move swiftly to eliminate off-board trading restrictions which blocked members of exchanges from trading in the third market as agents for their customers. It did not follow through by removing restrictions which prevented member firms from trading in the third market as principals for their own account.[21] The significance of this failure for the subsequent development of a national market system cannot be overestimated. The largest and financially most secure broker-dealers usually belong to the New York and American Stock Exchanges. To prevent their participation as dealers in the third market was artificially to protect the major stock exchanges from the pressures of competition. No market could be a serious rival to them until the largest and best capitalized firms were freed to trade in them, even to make markets in listed securities, if they chose, to attract customers from the exchange whenever they found it profitable to do so. Without competitive pressure of this kind, there was no economic incentive for self-regulatory organizations to modify their rules in

19 Rowen, "The Securities Acts Amendments of 1975;" Roberta Karmel, *Regulation by Persecution* (New York: Simon and Schuster, 1982), p. 115; Joel Seligman, *The Transformation of Wall Street* (Boston: Houghton Mifflin, 1982), pp. 473 – 476.

20 Karmel, *Regulation by Persecution*, p. 115.

21 Poser, "Restructuring the Stock Market," pp. 931 – 941; Seligman, *The Transformation of Wall Street*, pp. 509 – 520.

the directions contemplated by the Reform Act. By failing to use its new authority to abolish market rules restricting competition, the commission virtually assured that self-regulatory organizations would not voluntarily adjust market rules to adapt to changing competitive circumstances and that whatever evolution there was toward a national market system would be halting, rather a reluctant response to the push of political maneuver than an eager response to the pull of opportunities for profit.

This is not to imply that no movements in market regulation were made in the direction set by Congress. Fixed commissions were eliminated and their elimination brought about substantial improvements in market processing. It ended subterfuges to avoid paying overly high commission charges. It reduced artificially high profit margins which third-market dealers enjoyed when they undercut the transaction costs of exchanges to attract business – but undercut them just a little. And, by lowering transaction costs, it supplied a powerful incentive to increase trading volumes. These are not insignificant achievements. Some claim that this step alone might have exhausted the need for governmental action to alter market structure.[22]

The commission also pushed self-regulatory organizations to automate market processing. Under its aegis, a "composite tape" was created to report current price and transaction information for securities trading in multiple markets. It also favored development of an "intermarket trading system," designed by the New York Stock Exchange, to link the trading floors of the major and regional stock exchanges by an automated communication system so that brokers might direct their trades to the market offering the best price. In addition, the New York Stock Exchange strove mightily and with success to improve its trade settlement system enabling brokers to handle large trading volumes without recreating the "back office" crisis of 1967–1969.

Still, in the absence of competitive pressure among markets – impossible to exert so long as large member firms of the New York Stock Exchange were not free to act as third market dealers – the principal effect of these accomplishments has been to increase the concentration of trading in listed securities on the New York Stock Exchange.[23] We may doubt whether this result was what Congress had in mind when it directed the Securities and Exchange Commission to facilitate establishing a national market system.

22 See, e. g., Karmel, *Regulation by Persecution*, p. 109; and Werner, "Adventure in the Social Control of Finance."
23 Securities and Exchange Commission, *Fiftieth Annual Report, 1984* (Washington, D. C.: Government Printing Office, 1984), p. 109.

Within two years after the Reform Act was passed, two House subcommittees were both very critical of the commission and the securities industry for moving too slowly to establish a national market system. They called, but in vain, for the commission vigorously to exercise its new authority under the Reform Act.[24] Three years later, in 1980, Congress still found development of a national market system to be in its formative stages. Once again, the commission was roundly criticized for taking a passive role in the process; to be passive represented a misreading of the legislative history of the Reform Act.[25] Congress reiterated its argument that securities markets would fail to modernize themselves to maintain their status as the "finest" markets in the world unless they were subjected to the discipline of competition, and it reminded the commission of the broad powers it was given to assure an end to anticompetitive practices.

Referring specifically to the persistence of off-board trading restrictions, the House Subcommittee on Oversight and Investigations wrote:

> The Commission has clearly lost sight of its responsibility to eliminate anticompetitive rules and practices that cannot be justified in light of the purposes of the [Reform] Act. And it has lost sight of the relationship between the nurturing of competition among market makers and the development of a national market system.[26]

So far as Congress was concerned, "the Commission ... failed to fulfill its obligations with respect to anticompetitive rules and practices."[27] Not only had it failed to eliminate off-board trading restrictions, but it favored development of the "intermarket trading system," even though it was not fully automated and did not link all traders in a single competitive market system.[28]

---

24 Congressman John Moss observed: "The testimony we have received over the last 2 days troubles me greatly. With respect to the national market system, early drafts of the bill that became the Securities Acts Amendments of 1975 [the Securities Reform Act] contained detailed descriptions of that system. At the SEC's urging we replaced those detailed provisions with a broad policy statement and a charge to the agency to use its new powers vigorously to move this system forward. The SEC simply has not done this." U. S. Congress, House of Representatives, Subcommittee on Oversight and Investigations and Subcommittee on Consumer Protection and Finance, Committee on Interstate and Foreign Commerce, *Hearings* (Washington, D. C.: Government Printing Office, 1978), p. 511.

25 U. S. Congress, House of Representatives, Committe on Interstate and Foreign Commerce, *National Market System: Five Year Status Report*, 96th Congress, 2nd Session (Washington, D. C.: Government Printing Office, 1980), p. 2.

26 *Ibid.*, p. 15.

27 *Ibid.*, p. 17.

28 *Ibid.*, pp. 23 – 26.

And it ignored, or at least failed to encourage the use of, an alternative operational and fully automated trading system specifically designed to achieve the goals of the Reform Act.[29]

Once again, the commission was urged to act to facilitate creation of a national market system as called for by the Reform Act.

> It would be far better for the Commission to take appropriate action in light of these goals now than to wait until another crisis in the marketplace serves as a harsh reminder that it has left undone some things which must be done.[30]

But, once again, the advice went unheeded. The commission continued to play a passive role in the development of a national market system. It failed to abolish off-board trading restrictions, except for securities listed after April 26, 1979. As though to bring an end to the controversy, it announced in December 1983 that the existing market system was for all intents and purposes a close approximation to what the Reform Act proposed to achieve.[31]

Commission-Focused Explanations of the Failure

Why did the Securities and Exchange Commission fail to follow Congress's program for market reform through to conclusion? Why was it reluctant, after abolishing fixed commission rates in 1975, to pursue an aggressive policy to end anticompetitive practices?

Three different explanations of the commission's reticence to act have been offered. First, some say, the commission is not competent to deal with problems of market structure, to assume a "developmental" role building national market institutions as opposed to its traditional "regulatory" role controlling market fraud. So the commission decided wisely not to attempt what it was not competent to do well.[32] A second argument sometimes made is that the Reform Act itself was defective because it did not specify clearly what it wanted to be done.[33] If Congress wanted off-board trading restrictions to be removed, why did it not abolish them in the statute as it did with fixed

29 Ibid., pp. 30–31.
30 Ibid., p. 51.
31 Securities and Exchange Commission, Forty-Ninth Annual Report 1983 (Washington, D. C.: Government Printing Office, 1983, p. 22.
32 Poser, "Restructuring the Stock Market," pp. 946–947, 949; Seligman, The Transformation of Wall Street, p. 376.
33 Poser, "Restructuring the Stock Market," p. 950; Werner, "Adventure in the Social Control of Finance," pp. 1272–1275.

commission rates? The argument here is familiar to any who know the minimum demand of a rule of law, that it issue a clear, non-contradictory command. The third defense contends that there was never any need to do everything the law required. After fixed commission rates were abolished, need for any further reform was superfluous. Benefits of a national market system, after all, were only assumed, never demonstrated. Because our stock markets were already the "best in the world," it was prudent of the commission not to rush headlong to substitute a national market system which might not work as well.[34]

Superficially plausible, these arguments are not strong. The Securities and Exchange Commission has always had responsibility for market structure and has periodically exercised its authority to fulfill its responsibility: It determined that broker and dealer functions could be combined in a single firm, supported legislation to organize dealers in the over-the-counter market under the umbrella of the National Association of Securities Dealers, reorganized the government of the New York Stock Exchange, and (a generation later) of the American Stock Exchange, and it would not allow the New York Stock Exchange to prevent trading of its listed securities over regional exchanges. Each of these actions affected market structure, and all were supposed at the time they were taken (and now, too,) to have fallen legitimately within the domain of the commission. Whether the commission was staffed adequately to oversee market structure is, of course, a separate question. But even here, it was reasonable to suppose the commission did possess the necessary competence. Many of the expectations of the Reform Act were based on recommendations from the commission and backed by such impressive commission-sponsored studies as the *Institutional Investor Study*.

Perhaps the law was defective for not stating clearly what was to be done. Not only did Congress fail to remove off-board trading restrictions, but it also issued contradictory directions to the commission. The statute directs the commission to facilitate development of the national market system, but Congressional reports cautioned that the commission should not behave as an economic czar, dictating what private industry should do.[35] Was this a prescription for activism? The difficulty is real, but only so long as we ignore that Congress expected the exact design of the national market system to emerge from the cauldrons of competition, and not once, for all time, but continuously, changing as necessary precisely because no self-regulatory or-

---

34 Karmel, *Regulation by Persecution*, p. 109; Poser, "Restructuring the Stock Market," pp. 906 – 912; U. S. Congress, *National Market System* (Minority Report), pp. 89 – 94.
35 Poser, "Restructuring the Stock Market," p. 949.

ganization could rely on government regulation to fix market design by granting monopolies. The commission was to be active in ending anticompetitive practices, but not a czar deciding what the market should be like. Competition would reign. Why then did Congress not abolish off-board trading restrictions? The House version of the statute did. But the House version was replaced in conference by language allowing discretion to the commission. This was done at the commission's request. The request was acceded to because no one believed the commission would fail to exercise its powers.[36]

The third argument claims there was no need for the commission to act, that abolishing fixed commission rates removed the worst strains on market structure and enabled the market to sustain substantial further growth. But this argument ignores half the problem Congress tried to solve. While abolishing fixed commission rates alleviated structural strains, it provided no incentive for self-regulatory organizations to adjust market rules when changing circumstances create a new situation of structural strain. A major goal of the national market system was to rely on competition as the appropriate spur to make regulation self-adjusting. This goal could not be realized, and certainly its worthiness could not be demonstrated empirically until anticompetitive practices were abolished as contemplated by the statute. True, abolition meant facing uncertainty about the effects of competition on the viability of market structures. For this reason, Congress authorized the commission to retreat should too much competition begin to undermine market performance. But before a retreat, there must be some advance.

If these defenses of the commission are inadequate, how can we explain the failure of the commission to implement the Reform Act?

The question poses in particular terms what has been a perennial problem for students of public administration, namely, how to hold independent regulatory agencies accountable to Congress for their actions and policies.[37] The answer, in this case, however, is not to be found by looking at the relation between Congress and the commission. It lies rather in the structural

36 See above, note 26.
37 The classic formulations of this problem are found in Carl Joachim Friedrich, "Public Policy and the Nature of Public Administrative Responsibility," in *Public Policy*, ed. C. J. Friedrich and Edward S. Mason (Cambridge, Mass.: Harvard University Press, 1940), pp. 3 – 24 and Louis L. Jaffe, "The Effective Limits of the Administrative Process," *Harvard Law Review*, 67 (May, 1954), 1105 – 1135. See also, William L. Cary, *Politics and Regulatory Agencies* (New York: McGraw-Hill, 1967) and James O. Freedman, *Crisis and Legitimacy: The Adiministrative Process and American Government* (Cambridge: Cambridge University Press, 1978).

relations between the commission and the leaders of the self-regulatory organizations the commission is meant to regulate, a structure created by the
original federal securities acts passed in the 1930s. These acts did not create,
but sustained a system of fragmented market leadership having diverse and
conflicting interests. They did create a rule-making structure which encouraged
market leaders to pursue their organizational interests by political means. But
they failed to create a strong administrative agency in the Securities and
Exchange Commission able effectively to command market leaders to follow
a policy which they opposed.

Opposing Reform within a Fragmented Regulatory Structure

The stock market consists of various organizational entities of unequal stature.
The New York Stock Exchange stands alone as the most prominent market,
followed by the American Stock Exchange. But there are also several regional
exchanges dispersed throughout the country — declining in number throughout the century — and a loosely organized, though increasingly important,
over-the-counter market. These divisions among markets are not the creation
of federal securities law.[38] The divisions arose naturally over a century and a
half in response to the uneven demands of economic development. They were
no model of functional differentiation. Many markets performed overlapping
functions. Each market had its own administrative structure, its own rules,
its own leaders, and, most important, its own interests to defend. Conceivably,
the Securities Exchange Act might have rationalized this market structure,
but it was not so ambitious. The act created the Securities and Exchange
Commission (in part) to oversee administration of these markets. The markets
had to register with the commission and the commission had to approve their

---

38 The over-the-counter market is an exception. The National Association of Securities
Dealers, which governs this market, was created in 1939 in response to the Maloney
Act, an amendment to the Securities Exchange Act (sect. 15 A) passed in June 1938. The
enabling legislation to create this association was sought by industry leaders, and so in
the *Manual* of the association we find the strong statement: "The NASD is not an
organization which was imposed upon the investment banking and securities business
by the Congress or by the Securities and Exchange Commission. The privilege of self-
regulation was actively sought by the securities business ..." (Washington, D. C.:
National Association of Securities Dealers, 1967), p. 110.

operating rules. But the act did not create a hierarchical system of market administration with the commission at its head.

The aim was to create a cooperative regulatory regime between business and government, a system of "dual control," with exchange leaders taking the initiative to police their own members and their organization so as to prevent the need for government intervention. The commission's role was largely supportive. In private, it was to encourage market leaders to act in what it believed to be the public interest. In public, it was to maintain the coercive power to intervene whenever private leadership failed.[39] Borrowing terms from Mayer Zald, federal securities law, in the 1930s, was meant to regulate "output norms," not norms of market "auspices and ownership;" to assure the quality of stocks and stock prices, not to challenge private ownership of the market itself.[40] The result was to legitimate a system of fragmented, private administration in which no market leader was accountable to any interests except those of his own market organization. From the perspective of the stock market as a whole, it was a regime of institutional anarchy. There were few, if any, bases on which market leaders could come together and act in concert to achieve a common goal. Consider, for example, the major cleavages which divided market leaders about maintaining fixed commission rates, keeping off-board trading restrictions, and blocking exchange memberships for institutional investors.

The New York Stock Exchange very much favored retaining all three practices. In its view, these were essential to keep up if their auction markets were to hold the dominant position in the nation's stock trading. This is not to say that all three practices were supported equally. Because exchange memberships for institutional investors broke down the principle of mediated exchange on which all brokerage business was based, preventing this practice was an objective of first importance and not to be compromised. Similarly, it was important to retain off-board trading restrictions to prevent customer orders from being executed elsewhere than on the exchange. Fixed commission rates, though defended as an essential selective incentive to encourage brokers to belong to the exchange and to prevent small firms from going bankrupt, were a matter that might be compromised if the other two positions could be protected as a result.

39 William O. Douglas, *Democracy and Finance* (New Haven, Conn.: Yale University Press, 1940), pp. 82–83.
40 Mayer N. Zald, "On the Social Control of Industries," *Social Forces*, 57 (September, 1978), 89–90.

In contrast, regional exchanges strongly suported keeping off-board trading restrictions, which helped to preserve their order flow at the expense of the third market, but supported fixed commissions rates far less strongly and bluntly opposed barring institutional investors as exchange members. They objected to the fixed commission rate system when it meant their members had to pay the same commission as public customers when they traded with member firms of the New York Stock Exchange; under such a system, they could earn no profit on their trades.[41] And they wanted institutional investors as members of their exchanges, as they had been since the mid-1960s, because their membership greatly expanded the volume of business which they handled.

In the same way, leaders of the over-the-counter market favored direct dealing with institutional investors; third market trading was predicated and throve on such direct dealing. But in opposition to major and regional exchanges, they strongly opposed off-board trading restrictions because these limited their capacity to compete directly for business in exchange-listed securities. About fixed commissions they were indifferent. Their dealers charged no commissions, but negotiated trades in competition with other market makers.

In sum, there was no issue in which all three major market segments took the same position. The differences separating them were not random. They reflected the varying material – ownership – interests of each market organization. The Reform Act threatened everyone's interests. Unlike the securities legislation of the 1930s, it proposed to abolish the benefits of private market ownership, subordinating them to a broad public interest in a competitive national market system. Whether any one of the established market entities could retain their relative control over order flows under such a system was subject to doubt. Even the New York Stock Exchange was threatened, especially if off-board trading restrictions were abolished. Under these circumstances, market leaders worked vigorously (though obviously not in tandem) to staunch implementation of the reform. And not without success.

Yet how could they succeed? While it is obvious that anarchic leadership will prove difficult to coordinate to achieve a common goal, it is not obvious

41 Forced to do so by a ruling of the Securities and Exchange Commission, the New York Stock Exchange did allow nonmember firms a forty percent reduction in the usual commission fee, but only when they were trading for customers, not for their own account. There would be no reduction, no benefits of exchange membership, for nonmember firms, especially for nonmember firms dealing in the third market. See Thomas A. Russo and William K. S. Wang, "The Structure of the Securities Market – Past and Future," Fordham Law Review, 41 (1972), 5–6.

how a divided leadership could mount sufficiently potent resistance to prevent implementation of the law. Here we must consider the second effect of the federal securities laws, that they encouraged market leaders to pursue their organizational interests by political (rather than economic) means.

An objection sometimes raised against government regulation of markets is that it will reduce incentives for entrepreneurs to act innovatively. It would be more correct to claim that regulation redirects the creative energies of market leaders away from economic toward political uses. Rather than work to adjust their organizations to adapt to the new conditions posed by institutional investment or to abandon anticompetitive practices as prescribed by the Reform Act, market leaders bargained with the Securities and Exchange Commission to try to secure by political means what could not be achieved through competition (or from Congress). This tactic worked in part because, until 1975, the Securities and Exchange Commission did not have plenary power to alter market rules, but was forced to bargain privately with market leaders or to hold public hearings to try to prod change on an issue by issue basis. Although the Securities Reform Act gave the commission new powers to initiate rule changes, it did not and could not end the resort to political bargaining. Regulatory agencies are required by law to announce their proposals, invite comments, and hold public hearings before adopting a new rule.[42] Norms of due process make it impossible to do otherwise. Nevertheless, compliance with these norms put the commission at a disadvantage when trying to exercise its power.

Whenever the commission attempted to overturn anticompetitive practices, there was always time for opposition to mount. What form opposition would take varied depending on the particular proposal. When the commission attempted through private negotiation to persuade market leaders to abandon anticompetitive practices — as it did in the late 1960s and after, trying to persuade the New York Stock Exchange to loosen its off-board trading restrictions — it often received promises that rules would be liberalized. If enough pressure was applied, rules in fact would be revised. But then, after winning commission approval, the exchange would interpret the new liberal rule in such a way as to make practice as anticompetitive, if not more anticompetitive, than before.[43] When the commission acted bluntly on a particular issue, then the "injured" market interests might sue to have the decision reversed, as the Philadelphia-Baltimore-Washington Stock Exchange did (unsuccessfully) over the commission's refusal in the mid-1970s any longer

42 *Securities Reform Act of 1975*, p. 34.
43 Seligman, *The Transformation of Wall Street*, pp. 394–395.

to permit institutional investors to belong to stock exchanges and trade solely for their own account.[44] Alternatively, market leaders might simply refuse to cooperate, denying the commission's authority to act in a particular way. For three years, from 1972 until the Reform Act was passed, the New York Stock Exchange refused to comply with a commission rule requiring every exchange to make quotes available for a composite quote service. Even after 1975, after the Reform Act made clear the commission's authority to impose such a rule, the exchange threatened litigation, forcing the commission to attempt to settle the matter through private negotiation and compromise.[45]

Perhaps the most important form opposition took was to obfuscate the issue. When the commission asked for public comment on a proposed rule change to implement the aims of the Securities Reform Act, market leaders opposed to the change responded with objections which distracted attention from the main issue. This was at no time more evident than when the commission moved to eliminate off-board trading restrictions for principal transactions — that is, for transactions in which member firms might act as third-market dealers in direct competition with specialists on the exchange. The New York Stock Exchange argued that such an action would transform the stock market from an agency, auction market mediated by brokers into a dealer market, something the Reform Act urged the commission to avoid doing. In addition, it would fragment trading, reducing market liquidity and making the market less efficient. The argument was, as James Lorie observed, "absurd."[46] The market was already partly a dealer and partly an auction market, and what the exchange called "market fragmentation" was simply the effect of competition among markets which the Reform Act sought to encourage. Nevertheless, the argument effectively turned the commission's attention away from off-board trading restrictions toward devising an automated trading system which could admit competition as required by the Reform Act while also preserving features of an auction market and reducing the "risk" of fragmenting order flows. The commission accepted the exchanges' premise: Do not remove off-board trading restrictions before you have something better to put in their place.[47]

---

44 *Ibid.*, p. 470; Russo and Wang, "The Structure of the Securities Market," pp. 10 – 12.

45 Seligman, *The Transformation of Wall Street*, pp. 500 – 507.

46 James H. Lorie, "Conjectures on the Securities Industry," in *Impending Changes for Securities Markets*, ed. Ernest Bloch and Robert A. Schwartz (Greenwich, Conn.: JAI Press, 1979), p. 35.

47 James W. Davant, "Davant on the Davant Report: The NYSE Looks at the Central Market System," in *Impending Changes for Securities Markets*, pp. 80 – 81.

Here was a substantial reversal of the aims of the Reform Act. The act presupposed that competition would force market leaders to devise a market structure efficiently adapted (and continuously adapting) to the requirements of the capital market. The exchange's obfuscation of the issue on technical grounds substituted political bargaining for competition as the means to determine what the market's structure should be.[48] Once confined to the realm of politics, protected from competition, market leaders were freed to haggle over what superficially seemed to be a wide range of technological issues — e. g., order-routing switches, price protection for orders, time priority for orders, etc.[49] Yet their purpose throughout, perhaps more obvious in hindsight, was to design a system which preserved their control over the flow of orders.[50] From the point of view of the New York Stock Exchange, the purpose evidently has been achieved.

The commission did remove off-board trading restrictions for principal transactions, but only for securities listed after April 26, 1979, and this with little or no effect on trading.[51] Meanwhile, the New York Stock Exchange gained commission approval for its "intermarket trading system," a trading system which met few if any of the Reform Act's primary objectives to create a truly competitive, self-adjusting national market. The chief virtue of the "intermarket trading system," so far as the New York Stock Exchange was concerned, was that it removed the threat of "market fragmentation." Trading volumes in its listed securities were concentrated on its trading floor.[52] The competitive threat from regional exchanges and from third-market dealers was defeated.

It would be wrong to conclude at this point that the commission was an agency "captured" by industry leaders. To argue this way oversimplifies problems of regulatory leadership and it ignores the evidence. If market leadership was fragmented and the interests leaders pursued were often

---

48 On this tactic and its limits, see David P. McCaffrey, "Corporate Resources and Regulatory Pressures: Toward Explaining a Discrepancy," *Administrative Science Quarterly*, 27 (1982), 398 – 419, esp. 405 – 406.

49 I say superficially because technological problems were not difficult to resolve. A fully automated trading system, meeting all criteria for a national market system, was completely operational by the late 1970s, but was largely unused. To use it would probably have driven our traditional exchanges, including the New York Stock Exchange, out of business. See U. S. Congress, *National Market System*, pp. 28 – 31.

50 Davant, "Davant on the Davant Report," pp. 81 – 82.

51 Securities and Exchange Commission, *Forty-Ninth Annual Report*, p. 22 and *Fiftieth Annual Report*, p. 2.

52 U. S. Congress, *National Market System*, pp. 20 – 27.

competing, then any action taken by the commission could serve one while at the same time opposing another particular private interest: To support off-board trading restrictions, as the commission did, aided the exchanges but hurt over-the-counter third-market dealers. Far from compelling evidence that the commission does the bidding of industry interests, the evidence points instead to the relative autonomy of the commission. With arguments on every side of an issue to draw upon, commissioners were relatively free to choose the policy they preferred. It is here, in this relative freedom, not in deterministic explanations, that the answer to our question lies.

The Securities Exchange Act, typical of legislation creating independent regulatory agencies, delegates broad powers of discretion to commissioners on the Securities and Exchange Commission. The law is not a set of commands to regulators. Commissioners are not simply agents of Congress nor of the executive branch. It was for this reason that Felix Frankfurter argued the commission would be no more effective than the people who led it.[53] While reliance on the rule of law is an effective means to assure continuity of policy, reliance on the will of people is not. The orientation of regulators toward their object of regulation is not a constant, but varies, especially with turnover in office. Relatively long terms of office for commissioners (five years) and a system of overlapping terms are organizational devices meant to assure policy continuity over reasonable periods of time. But these devices were frequently undone because commissioners failed to serve their full terms of office, or often enough even half their terms. As a result, transient policy commitment is the norm. Policy changes, even startling policy reversals, must be expected. They occurred during the 1970s.

Both the commission's activism early in the decade and, later on, its lassitude about ending anticompetitive practices are explained in large part by the regulatory orientation of those who served as commissioners. Scandals surrounding the Watergate crisis caused President Nixon to make politically neutral and noncontroversial rather than patronage appointments of people to serve on the commission. To do this, he appointed leading staff members of the commission, people who, in James Q. Wilson's terms were "careerists," rather than "professionals" or "politicians."[54] As Wilson points out, careerists identify their careers with the agency. They may be risk averse, but they are not timid in defending the agency against any crisis or scandal, particularly

53 This in a letter to President Franklin D. Roosevelt, dated May 23, 1934. See *Roosevelt and Frankfurter: Their Correspondence, 1928–1945*, ed. Max Freedman (Boston: Little, Brown, 1967), pp. 220–221.

54 James Q. Wilson, "The Politics of Regulation," in *The Politics of Regulation*, ed. James Q. Wilson (New York: Basic Books, 1980), pp. 372–382.

against any actual or perceived failure of regulation. And it was just such a failure that threatened them in the early 1970s.

They had spent the 1960s trying, without success, to bring about needed market reforms through private negotiations with market leaders, and their lack of success sowed the seeds for the markets collapse. Now they were ready to act directly to achieve their goals. And they did all they could, within the limits of their powers. They abolished fixed commission rates even before the Reform Act was passed. They continued to support further reforms during the first two years after the act was passed. They abolished off-board trading restrictions for agency transactions in 1976 and proposed to do so for principal transactions in June 1977, to be effective in January 1978. They were prepared to create the "national market system" which Congress had proposed.[55]

But they did not remain in power. In 1977, President Carter appointed outsiders — Roberta Karmel and Harold Williams — who did not share the institutional history of the careerists, to serve respectively as a commissioner and as chair of the commission. Their appointment brought the reform movement to be halt. Neither believed it was necessary to end off-board trading restrictions for principal transactions, nor did they believe that government should take the lead in telling business leaders how their markets should be organized.[56] Williams was further concerned that the commission not do anything by acting precipitously which might unwittingly harm the nation's capital markets. He, of course, was able to act on his beliefs in part because he exercised the powers of chairman; he was well-placed to do so. But he could also count on the voting support of Karmel and of Philip Loomis, a long-time commissioner who shared their views on these issues, but who had heretofore been in the minority. Together they constituted a majority vote among the commissioners. Consequently, their policy commitments sooner or later would supplant those of the commission of the early 1970s.

The critical event occurred in 1980. Having kept the proposal to abolish off-board trading restrictions from going into effect, Williams proposed a less radical measure, namely the rule to end off-board trading restrictions on stocks listed on an exchange after April 26, 1979. But in return for his support of this weaker rule, he insisted that the commissioners withdraw their earlier, stronger proposal.[57] The commission did so, and the weaker rule was passed. It marked an end to Congressional hopes that competition would soon be

55 Poser, "Restructuring the Stock Market," pp. 934 – 935.
56 Karmel, *Regulation by Persecution*, p. 137; Seligman, *The Transformation of Wall Street*, pp. 501 – 502.
57 *Ibid.*, pp. 518 – 520; Poser, "Restructuring the Stock Market," pp. 934 – 936.

relied on to cause market leaders to adjust their rules to adapt their markets efficiently and without delay to changing economic circumstances.

Compliance with the Congressional movement to rely on competition as a tool of stock market regulation was limited, in sum, by the interaction of a variety of factors frequently noted in the literature on the social control of business. As Zald argues, the targets of regulatory control are not passive, but resist compliance when they disagree with the norms and purposes of the regulation and have the power to resist.[58] In this case, the costs and benefits of compliance were heavily concentrated. To work to create a competitive national market system most likely meant the sacrifice of traditional forms of private market organization and the establishment of a single market system, virtually a public monopoly, to gain all the material benefits stemming from control over order flow. In such a situation, Wilson teaches us to expect interest group politics, as conflicting groups lobby actively in defense of their own position.[59] One of the more effective tactics corporate interests will use to forestall regulatory change, McCaffrey suggests, is obfuscation of the issue through "technical lobbying," which was the tactic the New York Stock Exchange employed successfully over the issue of off-board trading restrictions.[60] And, as both Wilson and McCaffrey argue, compliance depends on the willingness of appointed officials to interpret and enforce regulatory laws as elected officials intended.[61] In agencies like the Securities and Exchange Commission where turnover among commissioners is high, that support is likely to be problematic as each new commissioner brings his or her own understanding of the agency's proper purpose to bear. The result, from the agency's point of view, is a history of transient policy commitments rather than consistent implementation of a particular reform program.

We must recognize, however, that these factors did not simply inhere in the situation. These factors are important, not others, and in combination because of the way federal securities laws passed in the 1930s organized market leadership and the relation between market leaders and the Securities and Exchange Commission. The laws created a regulatory structure through which market leaders were unlikely to limit their pursuit of self-interest by any regard for a broader collective value or goal, at least so far as institutional development is concerned. Authority within the institution was fragmented; political bargaining over rules was employed to shield private interests from

58 Zald, "On the Social Control of Industries," p. 98.
59 Wilson, "The Politics of Regulation," pp. 364–372.
60 McCaffrey, "Corporate Resources and Regulatory Pressure," pp. 405–406.
61 Wilson, "The Politics of Regulation," pp. 372–382; McCaffrey, "Corporate Resources and Regulatory Pressure," pp. 407–408.

competitive pressures within the marketplace; and transient policy commitments rendered impotent the sole enforcement agency in a position to steer
an alternative course.

Was the result an unmitigated disaster? Scarcely that. The market in the
1980s gives every appearance of being an efficient, well-managed enterprise.
The worst structural strains which plagued the market through the 1960s and
early 1970s are clearly part of the past. There are, as Harold Williams hoped
there would be, some signs of a gradual, but perceptible evolution toward
the kind of competitive market system which Congress envisioned in 1975.
Much depends on the direction and rate of economic growth. Firms whose
stocks are traded over-the-counter are typically smaller than those whose
stocks are listed on the New York Stock Exchange. In the past, as firms grew
they would eventually list their shares first on the American and then on the
New York Stock Exchange. But with the rule permitting off-board principal
transactions in newly listed securities, there are fewer advantages and many
costs to firms following this traditional path, and fewer firms are doing so.[62]
The over-the-counter market, now automated, is an able competitor of the
New York Stock Exchange, and when another generation of business enterprise matures, it may be the leading stock market in the country.

From the point of view of social control, however, this result is not totally
comforting. The problems which drove the market to the brink of collapse
were ameliorated in the end by government intervention. The drastic step
taken to improve the situation, to eliminate fixed commission rates, was
externally imposed on market leaders. The imposition was a legitimate act of
government authority, but it was an imposition nevertheless. Is this the only
way market institutions can be adapted to changing economic and technological circumstances? Must we expect other similar market dislocations to recur
in the future? Or can we by regulation create an authority structure in which
leaders might take initiative to limit the pursuit of self-interest, to modify
their market rules, and to adjust the operation of their particular organizations
to serve the minimal collective interest of institutional survival? These are the
unanswered questions of social control which rise as dark clouds over the
stock market's horizon.

---

62 David Pauly with Connie Leslie, "Can the Big Board Compete?" *Newsweek*, July 15,
1985, 59.

Part IV

Conclusions

Chapter 7

A Normative Assessment of Stock Market Regulation

The aim of this study has been to indicate the effects of federal securities regulation on the moral order and subsequent institutional development of the stock market. The origins of federal securities law were traced through a complex political process which prevented the law from embodying any clear intention of the purposes it would serve. Regulation, in other words, was not a certain technology for linking the pursuit of private market interests to the achievement of socially defined, extra-market ends. Although it constrained the behavior of market participants, more significantly, it altered the distribution of resources and opportunities within the market. Market participants, as they could, coopted these resources and took advantage of the new opportunities in pursuit of their own interests. The result was to reconstruct the normative order of the market, especially to alter beliefs about how one ought to trade and about who ought to trade. The new moral order which emerged was largely unintended, but that did not diminish its importance. It established new confidence in the safety of stock investment, facilitated the rise of institutional stock investing, and so spurred a huge growth in market transactions and competition among market participants.

The new competitiveness in turn undermined traditional regulatory principles which had limited conflicts of interest within the market. The resulting lack of restraint brought the market to the brink of financial ruin and regulatory collapse. There was no effective structure to accommodate competing market interests to assure the institutional viability of the market. Federal regulation did not guarantee effective regulatory control. Congressional rescue of the market was followed by a plan of reform which would turn over regulatory control to "free market" principles. But the plan was never fully implemented. The fragmented regulatory structure, though unable to control competition in a rapidly changing market, was able by political means to resist its own destruction.

Now the question remains how shall we evaluate the effects of federal securities regulation? In the end, it is not a summary of the argument that is wanted but an assessment — normative and theoretical — of the quality of the regulatory effort. Put in simple terms, we want to know whether federal regulation of the stock market has been any good. An answer to the question cannot be presupposed from what has been said so far. Adequate assessment requires clear specification of the criteria by which the "goodness" of regulation might be judged. Such criteria are not lacking. Two criteria have been implicit in the analysis. These should be made explicit and forced to do their evaluative work in the open. The first one is: That regulation is good which can accomplish what it intends and avoid unintended, undesirable consequences. The second one is: That regulation is good which can link the pursuit of private interest with some public good. Of course, there is no end to the difficulties associated with any idea of the "good." I make no pretense here of offering a comprehensive philosophical argument to justify these criteria. Yet there are two comments I wish to make in their defense.

It is in my view perfectly reasonable to assert that regulation must do what it intends and, if it does more, not do any harm, if we are to say it is good, just as it is reasonable to say that regulation is good when it helps us to articulate the pursuit of private and public interests. But it is good only on two assumptions which must be noted. I assume, first, a social context in which certain, what we might call universal, values are upheld, like truth-telling and honesty, or some notion of ownership and of justice, etc.[1] Without this assumption, someone could easily object to my first criterion of good regulation by making the following claim: The criterion would lead us to call "good" regulation which destroyed the value of truth-telling in markets — say, by encouraging market fraud — so long as that was what the regulation intended to do. Obviously, it fits into no one's scheme of the good to hold such a view. Even someone who would practice market fraud depends on other market participants to act truthfully. My second assumption is, simply, that regulation should not undermine the democratic political organization of our society. It is the social control of markets, not revolution, which we are interested in. Both assumptions are important and necessary to hold.

It may be objected also that these are not two criteria, but really only one. The grounds for saying so would be that regulation always intends to link the pursuit of private interest to achievement of a public good. The claim recalls, from chapter 1, the strong form of the structuralist argument about regulation as a means of control. To notice that, however, is already to provide reasons for defeating the objection. First, empirically, it has been shown by others that regulation often intends to serve a special interest. Second, this

1 Alasdair MacIntyre, *A Short History of Ethics* (New York: Macmillan, 1966), p. 95.

study has shown that it is possible to link private and public interests without necessarily intending to do so. Securities regulation, after all, facilitated the rise of institutional stock investing. The fact has tied the stock market, the state, and society closely together into a single community of fate. Most households in this country now have an important stake in how well the stock market does. They are beneficial owners of stock through the pension funds, insurance trusts, and mutual funds which financial institutions control. The fact is full of significance for policy analysis.[2] For present purposes, however, it is enough that it establishes the independence of the two criteria I offer for evaluating the quality federal securities regulation.

Can either of these standards be met? Is it necessarily the case that, in a democratic society, we would want them to be met? My conclusion will be that they cannot be met easily if they can be met at all and that failure to meet them may be one cost of democratic government we have to bear. Let us turn now to the task of evaluation, to consider why the consequences of market regulation are often unintended, when market regulation weakens social control, and what the role of regulatory authority in a democratic society might be.

Why Consequences of Market Regulation Are Unintended

There can be no doubt that the effects of federal securities regulation upon the stock market's moral order and institutional development were largely unintended and unforeseen by the lawmakers originally responsible for creating it. The laws they wrote were responsive primarily to the immediate pressures of political struggles, both national and local, and secondarily to moral concerns about particular abuses of trust by highly visible financiers. It is far flung to suppose that legislators looked beyond these matters to foresee and plan for the shift from materialist to pragmatic beliefs about how to trade stocks or the shift in beliefs about the safety of stock trading which permitted eliminating barriers to institutional stock investment. These outcomes were the work of market participants.

It is equally far flung to suppose that the market participants who brought about these changes in the market's moral order intended what the conse-

2 See, e. g., Peter F. Drucker, *The Unseen Revolution. How Pension Fund Socialism Came to America* (New York: Harper & Row, 1976) and Jeremy Rifkin and Randy Barber, *The North Will Rise Again* (Boston: Beacon Press, 1978).

quences would be: the unraveling of regulatory control, the near collapse of the market, and the weakened regulatory authority that resulted from the fragmentation of market interests. These consequences were arguably harmful to market participants. They entailed the financial ruin of many broker-dealer firms and might have led to a worse result had Congress failed to intervene.

Nevertheless, we are not free to leave matters at this. It is hardly surprising when a sociologist finds unintended consequences in social action. The finding has been a staple of sociological research extending back at least to the work of the Scottish moralists.[3] The unintendedness of social action is only partially explained by reference to physical limits on human thought, say, to our bounded rationality. It is a social outcome, not a natural law, that these consequences should occur. And so we must explore the social conditions under which the production of the unintended consequences of regulation are curbed or promoted.

In our case, two conditions worked especially to promote unintended outcomes of securities regulation. First, the original regulatory law did not embody or enact an externally given normative code about how the market should be conducted. It could not. Political motives precluded any such thing. But even if they had not, the law might not have been much more clear. High finance is sometimes referred to as a "game". But if the reference means to suggest some certainty about the objective which is sought and about what rules should be followed in the seeking, then the reference is misleading. Precisely because the stock market is not a game-like social situation, legislators could not specify in law what goal or purpose should control all market conduct. And they could not devise rules to follow which would lead toward accomplishing that goal. When such matters can be specified, as they can be in real games like baseball or contract bridge, then the unintended consequences of social action are limited.

Second, reconstruction of the market's moral order was an emergent consequence of market participants engaged in a prudential pursuit of their own group interests. Statisticians, disgraced by their involvements in fraudulent stock promotions in the 1920s, could in the 1930s rely on their analytic skills to put themselves forward as "professional securities analysts" able to interpret the new financial data corporations disclosed as required by the federal law. In so doing, they institutionalized new beliefs about how one ought to trade.

3 See Louis Schneider, ed., *The Scottish Moralists: On Human Nature and Society* (Chicago: University of Chicago Press, 1967), pp. 99 – 119. See also Robert K. Merton, "The Unanticipated Consequences of Purposive Social Action," *American Sociological Review*, 1 (1936), 894 – 904 and, more recently, Raymond Boudon, *The Unintended Consequences of Social Action* (New York: St. Martin's Press, 1982).

And financial institutions, stymied in their investment programs by the dele-terious consequences of the Great Depression, found in these new beliefs, and in regulatory limitations on manipulative stock trading, grounds for justifying destruction of the legal barriers which had prevented them from investing in stocks. In this way, they altered beliefs about who properly should trade stocks. But when the ends of action − what one ought to do − are in such a state of flux, contingently determined by the self-interested responses of institutional participants to opportunities opened up by regulation, it is unlikely that the outcome of actions can be accurately prefigured.

From these observations we are forced to conclude that federal securities regulation has not been effective; it has not been good, as judged by the standards of our first criterion. It had no clear intentions and it supported outcomes which were both unintended and undesirable. How might matters have been otherwise? Drawing on the lessons of this case, it would appear that regulatory law can avoid unintended, undesirable outcomes if and only if it can do two things. First, it must specify the ends or goals of social action as well as the means to achieve them. The object of regulation, in other words, must be made to resemble a game. Second, it must limit the pursuits of market participants which, by redefining moral beliefs about what one ought to do, cause the ends of action to change, making it harder to calculate what the consequences of action will be. These are necessary conditions to be met. But it is clear that federal securities regulation did not meet them (nor does it meet them now) with results we know well. And it is equally clear that we would not necessarily have wanted it to meet them. If the second condition could be met and market participants could be kept from redefining the market's moral order, it would not necessarily benefit a democratic society.

When Market Regulation Weakens Social Control

We may take as given that no regulatory authority sets out to weaken rather than strengthen social control. As Morris Janowitz observes, the purpose of regulation is to increase "the capacity of constituent groups in a society to behave in accordance with their acknowledged moral and collective goals."[4] Regulation is meant, in other words, to resolve difficulties of vertical integra-tion. Yet, as our study makes clear, that is not what always occurs.

4 *The Last Half-Century* (Chicago: University of Chicago Press, 1978), p. 29.

Especially given uncertainties posed by the unintended, undesirable consequences of the pursuit of private interests, market regulators who would succeed in their task must monitor market conduct with an eye out for developments which may adversely affect the market as a whole. The point here is not that unintended consequences can be avoided. It is that they should be noticed as early as possible and dealt with rather than ignored. This certainly was not done within the stock market during the 1960s when the market's regulatory structure was unsettled by the growth of institutional stock trading. The competition which developed at that point was from the market's point of view predatory and unhealthy. Brokers were unwilling to abide by the letter of market rules because the rewards for noncompliance were so huge. Nevertheless, despite gaining excess profits, they failed to build their capital base or an operating capacity sufficient to support the large volume of business they were doing. Market leaders meanwhile paid no attention to the breakdown of institutional control. Exchange leaders did not wish to endanger the large monopoly profits which the status quo seemed to assure and tried (in the end, without success) to affirm the rightness of all that they were doing. The Securities and Exchange Commission went along with them, doubting that it had sufficient power to do otherwise. There was, in other words, a short-term capitulation by market regulators to the pursuit of private interest with no larger public good in view.

Such a situation makes us curious to know when regulation will weaken social control, when regulation will not measure up to the second evaluative criterion we have set, that it should link the pursuit of private interests to the achievement of some public good. The events of this case study point to at least two factors which are of critical importance.

First, the regulatory structure of the stock market was fragmented by law. The justifications for the fragmentation were political. A system of "dual control" was created to preserve a series of relatively small regional markets and the monopolistic interests of larger exchanges. But it served no technically useful purpose. On the contrary, regulatory leaders represented interests which were only narrow and partial. The stock exchanges favored keeping fixed commissions which institutional investors opposed. They favored keeping off-board trading restrictions which the over-the-counter market and institutional investors opposed. And the smaller exchanges let institutional investors buy seats in their market, an action which the larger exchanges opposed. There was no simple ordering of these opposing interests, no organization of accountability to promote their aggregation to achieve a common good. As a consequence, there was no structural basis on which to reach agreement about how to respond to the market's crisis in the 1970s.

We must be careful not to suggest a too simple model of the human beings who fill regulatory roles. Of course, some market leaders were able to see that the narrow pursuit of fractional interests within the market of the 1960s was leading toward an institutional disaster, and many were able to propose alternative regulatory strategies to reform the market in the 1970s. But people try to act responsibly in the roles they fill, which means they respond to the demands their roles impose. They may perceive inconsistencies between the demands of their role, to pursue narrow interests, and a personal evaluation of the situation which suggests that some broader pursuit may better serve the institution as a whole. Yet they will not necessarily try to resolve them. They may doubt the appropriateness of using institutional resources to realize their personal conception of what is needed rather than to use them to represent the interests of their constituency. Or, they may fear the consequences for their career of attempting to do so. Typically, to resurrect a phrase from Chester Barnard, there is a large "zone of indifference" which encompasses even inconsistent policies; choices are not usually black and white, to pursue a private or a public interest.[5] And some may attempt to pursue alternative courses of action even when they suspect they are inconsistent on the hope that the situation might change in such a way to eliminate the inconsistency. It is always hard to serve only one master. A fragmented regulatory structure only makes it harder still.

Second, even if the regulatory structure had been more conductive to pursuing collective goals, there was no consensus within the stock market about what these goals were or should be. To press the metaphor of the game back into use, regulators had no external set of rules or understanding of the object of the game which they (and everyone) could draw on to decide what was right and wrong to do. They could not act, like an umpire or referee, making politically impartial or disinterested decisions to promote continuation of the game. In the end, of course, they made choices. But, in the context of a fragmented regulatory structure and without plainly acknowledged moral and collective goals to which every one subscribed, there was no way to know whether the choices they made would (or were intended to) promote what was good for the market as a whole. How are we to judge the turnaround in action by the Securities and Exchange Commission which in the early 1970s

5 Not without reason. Robert W. Haack, president of the New York Stock Exchange from 1967 to 1972, was forced to renounce any intention of seeking renewal of his five year contract after he spoke out publicly against the regime of fixed commission rates. See Leonard Sloane, *The Anatomy of the Floor* (Garden City, N. Y.: Doubleday, 1980), pp. 105 – 107. On the "zone of indifference," see Chester Barnard's *The Function of the Executive* (Cambridge, Mass.: Harvard University Press, 1938), pp. 167 – 169.

argued for a fully automated national market system, but by the late 1970s acted rather to adopt a far more conservative approach which advanced the interests of the New York Stock Exchange? The decision was based more on the personal beliefs and preferences of the commissioners, who changed over time, than on the logic of any collective agreement.

What we can see, in sum, is that federal securities regulation weakened social control. It was not an effective means for linking the pursuit of private interests to a public goal. The reasons why not are clear. Put positively, linking the pursuit of private and public interests requires a regulatory structure which supplies inducements to market leaders to act on behalf of the market as a whole rather than as committed representatives of partial market interests. It requires also that there be some consensus among market participants about what goals or purposes they want the market to achieve. These, then, are the critical requirements for regulation to meet if it would be judged "good" or "effective" under the second criterion. Federal securities regulation met neither one. The final task before us is to reflect on the prospects for market regulation in a democratic society.

Prospects for Market Regulation in a Democratic Society

As social scientists have begun in recent years more seriously to study the social organization of markets, they have found complex institutions which are not well-described by ideal typical formulations of perfect competition. Markets are not spheres defined by a set of relations among independent actors freely engaged in economic exchange for the pursuit of their own profit. Markets like all institutions are dual creations.[6] They are created in large part by the exercise of authority, by the enactment of rules which define what can be exchanged within the market, how, and on what terms. One therefore can never speak about an unregulated market. Markets are always rule-governed,

---

6 The idea that institutions possess a dual character of the kind I describe was expressed thirty years before by Philip Selznick in his book on *Leadership in Administration* (New York: Harper & Row, 1957). The duality of social structures in its broader meaning of both a creation of and constraint on social action is a concept thoroughly explored by Anthony Giddens, *The Constitution of Society* (Berkeley and Los Angeles: University of California Press, 1986).

moral orders.[7] But they are also institutions created and transformed from within as market participants jockey for advantage and their own self-advancement, often by challenging and attempting to redefine the normative order within which they operate. Regulation establishes the conditions for action in markets which market participants subsequently adapt and transform through the turbulent processes of economic and political exchange.[8]

This understanding of the way regulation constitutes markets has implications for the kinds of claims we can make about the effects of interventions by government to regulate markets. It suggests that attempts to assess the effects of regulation in terms of its consequences for rates of misconduct within the market may be misguided. I do not wish to be misunderstood. Important work has been done in this area. Susan Shapiro, for example, has shown that the apprehension of misconduct in the market depends very much on how illict activities are organized and on what techniques of intelligence the Securities and Exchange Commission employs to detect their occurrence.[9] Others have marshalled impressive evidence to criticize the commission on the grounds that the expense of its intelligence gathering activities, for example, in support of corporate disclosure requirements, exceeds the benefits gained from curbing misconduct.[10] Nevertheless, there is a tendency in this research to overemphasize regulatory technique and organizational efficiency.

The critical effects of stock market regulation are most pronounced in the ways — indirect, subtle, and yet clearly traceable — that it has altered the course of institutional development. Accurate assessment of the consequences of market regulation should be focused on the changes it has wrought for the

7 Mitchel Y. Abolafia, Market Crisis and Organizational Intervention. Paper presented at the annual meetings of the American Sociological Association, Washington, D. C., August, 1985; Huseyin Leblebici and Gerald R. Salancik, "Stability in Interorganizational Exchanges: Rulemaking Processes of the Chicago Board of Trade," *Administrative Science Quarterly*, 27 (1982), 227 – 242; Amitai Etizioni, "Encapsulated Competition," *Journal of Post-Keynesian Economics*, 7 (Spring, 1985), 287 – 302.

8 Harrison C. White, "Where Do Markets Come From?" *American Journal of Sociology*, 87 (November, 1981), 517 – 547; Wayne E. Baker, "Floor Trading and Crowd Dynamics," *The Social Dynamics of Financial Markets*, ed. Patricia A. Adler and Peter Adler (Greenwich, Conn.: JAI Prss, 1984), pp. 107 – 128; Wayne E. Baker, "The Social Structure of a National Securities Market," *American Journal of Sociology*, 89 (January, 1984), 775 – 784.

9 Susan P. Shapiro, *Wayward Capitalists* (New Haven: Yale University Press, 1984).

10 Susan M. Phillips and J. Richard Zecher, *The SEC and the Public Interest* (Cambridge, Mass.: MIT Press, 1981), pp. 27 – 51; William H. Beaver, "The Nature of Mandated Disclosure," in *Economics of Corporation Law and Securities Regulation*, ed. R. A. Posner and Kenneth Scott (Boston: Little, Brown, 1980), pp. 317 – 331.

market as a social institution. Doing so not only helps to organize our understanding of the market's past history. It provides us with some capacity to forecast future prospects which market regulation has to meet. Trends in the development of the stock market which federal securities law has fostered over the last fifty years have not been exhausted but continue to operate, transforming beliefs about how one ought to trade, who ought to trade, and the structure of market authority.

By the late 1960s, economists at the nation's leading business schools began to cast doubt on the basic tenet of the pragmatic growth stock theory that it was possible by studying the past history of corporate earnings to determine which stocks would rise and fall in price faster than the market.[11] Stock prices, their research showed, were not a consequence of past trends in corporate earnings growth, but were a leading indicator of future earnings growth. The movement of stock prices was highly correlated with what corporate earnings would be and not with what earnings used to be. The difference was important, because while in aggregate the market by merging many judgments could be expected to create the best estimate of what future corporate earnings would be, no one investor, no matter how expert, could be expected consistently to forecast accurately what future earnings growth would be. If not, then expert investment advice was of dubious worth. One might do as well picking stocks at random as by relying on the advice of security analysts. And one could do better by simply investing in a portfolio which mirrored one of the major stock indices — the Dow Jones Industrials or Standard & Poor's 500 — for, over the long run, expert investment advisers were unable "to beat" the market.[12]

The consequences of these new beliefs for the organization of stock trading were not immediately clear. Advice to invest in a market index, while it contained a certain logic, was not really practical. A few "index" mutual funds were created in the 1970s.[13] But if all or even most investors large and small gave up securities analysis for passive index investing, then it is doubtful

---

11 See James H. Lorie and Mary Hamilton, *The Stock Market: Theories and Evidence* (Homewood, Ill.: Richard D. Irwin, 1973); Burton G. Malkiel, *A Random Walk Down Wall Street* (New York: W. W. Norton, 1975); Vincent J. Tarascio, "Economic Theories of the Market: Random or Non-Random Walk," *The Social Dynamics of Financial Markets*, ed. Patricia A. Adler and Peter Adler (Greenwich, Conn.: JAI Press, 1984), pp. 41–55.

12 John H. Langbein and Richard A. Posner, "Market Funds and Trust Investment Law, Part I," *American Bar Foundation Research Journal*, I (1977), 1–43.

13 Fischer Black and Myron Scholes, "From Theory to a New Financial Product," *Journal of Finance*, 29 (May, 1974), 399–412.

after a time that the index of stock prices would move. Who would cause the movement? And if it did move, what would the movement mean? In any case, the lure of large rewards to be gained if an investment analyst was only sometimes right made most investors reluctant to depart from past practices. Nevertheless, departures were made, though not in obvious ways.

If the economists were right about the nature of stock selection, then stock investing was not very different from investing in commodities where the final price of a product is often determined by future weather conditions which no one yet knows how to predict. Uncertainty in commodities trading is controlled by hedging investments: A trader offsets the risk of buying or selling by selling or buying (in the opposite direction) a futures contract for an equivalent amount of the commodity to settle at a later date.[14] A similar principle can be (and has been) applied to stock trading. During the 1970s, futures markets in stocks were created in Chicago and New York, trading in stock options and in futures contracts which estimate the value of stock indices. Relying on these vehicles, large institutional investors − large enough to afford the sophisticated machinery to track price movements in multiple markets and to act quickly to take advantage of trading opportunities which such tracking supplies − are able to follow the advice of their securities analysts, but also to hedge their commitment, limiting their loss if the analysts are wrong.

One problem facing market regulators today is to monitor trading activity in this increasingly differentiated system of markets. Stock market regulation, thought of in narrow terms as an effort to prevent market fraud (or at least to apprehend and punish fraudulent investors), cannot remain focused on activities in a single market, but must widen its surveillance to include activities in futures markets as well. More broadly, programmed (hedging) investment by institutional investors has increased the apparent volatility of stock price change. Individual investors, who cannot afford to protect their investments through hedging, are nonetheless subjected to the vagaries of these sharp price swings. Regulators must think about the consequences of these developments for the "fairness" of the market. Left as it is, the likely consequence will be to promote withdrawal from the market of individual investors who will seek protection for their funds by investing them through financial intermediaries, spurring the rise of institutional stock investing.

The rise of institutional stock investing has tied the stock market, the state, and society closely together into a single community of fate. Most households

14 This definition of hedging is paraphrased from Cedric B. Cowing, *Populists, Plungers, and Progressives* (Princeton: Princeton University Press, 1965), p. 8.

in this country have an important stake in how well the stock market does. They are the beneficial owners of the pension funds, insurance trusts, and mutual funds over which financial institutions exercise control. We may doubt how many people consciously perceive of themselves as investing in the market. Still it is possible to think of the rise of institutional stock investing as a kind of socialization of investment capital.[15]

As investments are concentrated under the control of large financial institutions, the question, how shall these funds be invested, becomes increasingly a matter for public debate. Pressure put on university endowment funds and on public employee retirements funds to rid themselves of investments in companies doing business in South Africa is an obvious example of the way social values other than profit-seeking may influence the disposition of collective investment funds. But other examples may be cited.[16] Jeremy Rifkin and Randy Barber argue that the assets of pension funds alone constitute a substantial pool of capital that might be used to reindustrialize the country.[17] Samuel Bowles, David Gordon, and Thomas Weisskopf wish to see these funds and others put under "democratic control," by which they mean the funds should be invested by elected representatives of the people to whom the investments ultimately belong.[18]

These analyses emphasize incipient possibilities which do not yet dominate the objective situation. They tend to underemphasize the paradoxical conflict which greater social and economic integration represent. Institutional investors are controlled by a fiduciary's duty to seek out the best investment return, consistent with safety, for the clients whose money they invest. There is in this duty a mixing together of economic and social logics which are not always compatible. Pension fund monies invested in multinational corporations may earn the highest return and be relatively low in economic risk, but they may also facilitate creation of competing factories and jobs in other places and thereby reduce the pension fund contributor's own job security. Yet to invest money defensively, in ways that will promote or at least not threaten the worker's job security, may entail investments which fail to produce returns large enough to fund retirement benefits. The conflict was evident when New York City employees were forced to use their retirement funds to purchase "Big Mac"

15 Peter F. Drucker, *The Unseen Revolution: How Pension Fund Socialism Came to America* (New York: Harper & Row, 1976).
16 Samuel Bowles, David M. Gordon, and Thomas E. Weisskopf, *Beyond the Waste Land* (Garden City, N. Y.: Anchor Books, 1984), pp. 332–333; Richie P. Lowry, "Doing Good While Doing Well," *The Social Report*, 3 (1982), 2–3.
17 *The North Will Rise Again* (Boston: Beacon Press, 1978).
18 *Beyond the Waste Land*, pp. 329–337.

bonds of questionable value to help prevent the city from slipping into bank-ruptcy.[19]

For government the problem is not only to sort out these conflicting concerns, which no doubt will be done only over time through a variety of court cases. It is more generally to devise some way to maintain the store of value stock investments represent. No government today could permit a stock market crash as terrible as the one of 1929–1932. To do so would not only mean the liquidation of so many "paper profits." It would not only adversely affect the wealthy. It would seriously undermine the fiscal security, especially the retirement funds, of well over half the population.

My aim is not to focus on the likelihood of such a stock market crash. Though the dramatic collapse of stock prices in the fall of 1987 invites comparisons, the conditions of 1929–1932 may have been unique. Our very reliance on institutional investment helps to assure a continuing flow of new money into the market which does in fact help maintain stock prices even when economic times are bad. Nonetheless, we are not necessarily safe from all dangers. Withdrawal of foreign investment from the market owing to our inability to curb either the federal deficit or the trade deficit could, when coupled with volatile programmed trading, set off a steep and prolonged price decline. The close integration of market, society, and the state today makes such an event a matter for regulatory concern. The matter is serious because it is probably impossible for government to regulate the course of stock prices, especially to staunch a prolonged crash should one begin. The only obvious alternative would be to close the market and attempt to maintain belief in corporate values by administrative fiat. It is by no means clear whether that alternative would be viable.

The capacity of stock market regulation to respond proactively to changing economic circumstances is still quite limited. When institutional investors entered the market on a large scale in the 1950s and 1960s, they upset the regulatory status quo and demanded concerted action to reform traditional market rules. Conflicting interests among leaders of different markets coupled with a relatively weak Securities and Exchange Commission prevented any reform from being attempted until the market was driven to the brink of collapse in 1969–1970. And it curtailed implementation of reforms which Congress sought in the 1970s. Intra-industry conflicts of interest and the weakness of the commission were structural products of political compromises embedded in the federal securities law and are unlikely to be altered in the foreseeable future. Political consensus

---

19 See Judith W. Marees, *The Use of Pension Fund Capital: Its Social and Economic Implications – Some Background Issues* (Washington, D. C.: Government Printing Office, 1979).

for stock market regulation continues to require a system of dual control, mixing private and public leadership. So long as conflicts of interest among various market segments are relatively contained, as they have been by and large through the 1980s, then dual control should cause no difficulty. But it is too rigid a system for effective regulation conceived of, ideally perhaps, in purely instrumental terms. Given a new period of market turbulence which challenges the current regulatory status quo, there is no reason to expect market leaders will be any more quick to adjust market rules to the new situation than they were in the 1960s. Yet failure to adjust market rules, as we know, easily leads to institutional decline.

The lesson is important to remember, given the increasingly international character of capital markets. National markets, of course, have never been completely isolated from international affairs. What is different today is the extent to which national markets are integrated into a single global network. Development of communications technologies over the last ten years now permits trading in many stocks to follow the sun from London to New York to Tokyo. Moreover, the growth of multinational enterprise has stimulated the demand for efficient mobilization of capital on a global scale. Market regulation, therefore, is not only a national concern. Should market regulators in this country try to respond to the challenges we have already mentioned by pursuing social values which are somehow perceived as uneconomic, investors in today's market are increasingly free to evade regulation by trading their shares abroad. As Harold S. Bloomenthal suggests,

> to the extent that there is a worldwide network of securities laws, there is likely to be a race to the bottom in terms of clever or fraudulent operators seeking the jurisdiction with lax regulation.[20]

Fear of the prospect of "capital flight" may drive national governments to seek international agreements about how to organize and operate their stock markets. The effort, however, must reconcile a greater number and diversity of interests than Congress sought to do when it passed the securities reform act in 1975. Success will not be easy to define, much less to achieve. The final challenge facing market regulators which I shall notice, and perhaps the most important one to meet, is to devise a governance structure that promotes rapid adaptation of market rules to the new peculiar circumstances of competition in an international market.

Much further than this in prognosis we cannot go. Institutional analysis can identify where challenges for market regulation lie. It cannot specify how these

---

20 "Introduction," *International Capital Markets and Securities Regulation*, ed. Harold S. Bloomenthal (New York: Clark, Boardman, 1982), p. 1 – 147.

challenges ought to be met. The reason why has nothing to do with a lack of nerve or normative conviction on the analyst's part. It follows from the theory.

We have argued from the start that market regulation has significant consequences for the institutional development of markets. But its origins are not technocratically rational and its consequences are difficult to foresee. In origin, regulatory law is a product of political struggles the outcome of which is not simply determined to meet "functional needs" for market stability. And, in effect, it does not operate as a "big cause," exogenous to markets, determining mechanistically the institutional form markets will assume. The substance and effects of regulatory law are mediated through the relatively free actions of political actors and market participants as they figure out ways to use the law in the pursuit of their own interests. They act with relatively clear intentions, but their purposes are narrowly framed within limited institutional contexts. Their understanding of the ramified consequences of their actions for other market regions and over time is therefore highly bounded and no real restraint on what they do. And precisely because the stock market in America is a highly partitioned institution — partly by institutional accident, but since the 1930s increasingly by political defense — there is limited consensus on what purposes the market ought to serve. The result is to heighten uncertainty about the course market regulation and market development will take.

In democratic societies, in sum, where people are free to choose the purposes they would pursue, the moral order of the institutions they create is always under revision with consequences for institutional development which are not very predictable and which sometimes thwart reasoned efforts at social control. In such a society, every attempt at market regulation is bound to be, as federal securities regulation has been, ungainly, far less than perfect. It is hard to know how it could be otherwise without resorting to an authoritarian structure of market control incompatible with democratic polity.

Yet I do not mean to glorify an outcome which occurs "inevitably" within the American social context. The extent of regulatory imperfection is a variable the magnitude of which we should try to minimize. Exactly how this might be done poses an important problem beyond the scope of this study to solve. But what needs to be done in broad strokes at least has been clearly indicated. The regulatory task is carefully to monitor the consequences of a dynamic moral order for unintended and undesirable effects on institutional development and squarely to face and to act upon the problems which such monitoring brings to light. Only when this task is well done will markets maintain a normative climate of trust sufficiently strong to sustain our willingness to part with our money, with our power to satisfy present wants, on nothing more than the promise of future prosperity.

Appendices

Appendix A

Descriptive Statistics

Table A.1: Stocks Listed on New York Stock Exchange, 1885 – 1985

Year	Number of Stock Issues	Number of Companies
1885	310	—
1890	354	—
1895	370	—
1900	377	—
1905	374	—
1910	426	—
1915	511	—
1920	691	—
1925	927	—
1930	1,293	—
1935	1,187	800
1940	1,233	—
1945	1,269	912
1950	1,472	1,057
1955	1,508	1,087
1960	1,528	1,147
1965	1,623	1,273
1970	1,840	1,351
1975	2,111	1.557
1980	2,228	1,565
1985	2,298	1,541

Sources: New York Stock Exchange, *Year-Book – 1940* (New York, 1940), p. 49; New York Stock Exchange, *Fact-Book – 1982* (New York, 1982), p. 71; New York Stock Exchange, *Fact Book – 1987* (New York, 1987), p. 77.

Table A.2: Share Volume of Stock Trading 1900 – 1985 (in millions of shares)

Year	NYSE	Exchange AMEX	Other	Total
1900	139.1	–	–	–
1905	260,6	–	–	–
1910	163.7	–	–	–
1915	172.5	–	–	–
1920	227.6	–	–	–
1925	459.7	–	–	–
1930	810.6	–	–	–
1935	513.6	84.7	63.6	661.9
1940	282.7	47.9	41.4	372.0
1945	496.0	152.4	96.1	744.5
1950	655.3	114.9	86.9	857.1
1955	820.5	243.9	148.0	1,212.4
1960	985.3	300.6	129.6	1,415.5
1965	1,809.4	582.2	195.3	2,586.9
1970	3,213.1	878.5	444.1	4,535.7
1975	5,164.0	571.9	640.2	6,376.1
1980	12,460.2	1,680.3	1,446.5	15,587.0
1985	30,315.4	2,149.4	4,722.9	37,187.7

Sources: New York Stock Exchange, *Year-Book – 1940* (New York, 1940), p. 72; New York Stock Exchange, *Fact-Book – 1982* (New York, 1982), p. 67; Securities and Exchange Commission, *52 nd Annual Report – 1986* (Washington, D. C.: Government Printing Office, 19), p. 134.

Table A.3: Dollar Volume of Stock Trading, 1935 – 1985 (in millions of $)

Year	NYSE	Exchange (in $) AMEX	Other	Total
1935	13,335	1,205	736	15,226
1940	7,166	643	595	8,404
1945	13,462	1,728	1,036	16,226
1950	18,725	1,481	1,571	21,777
1955	32,745	2,593	2,530	37,868
1960	37,960	4,176	3,083	45,219
1965	73,200	8,612	7,402	89,214
1970	103,063	14,266	13,579	130,908
1975	133,983	5,771	17,503	157,257
1980	398,021	34,927	43,553	476,501
1985	1,023,041	26,764	150,384	1,200,189

Sources: New York Stock Exchange, *Fact-Book – 1982* New York, 1982), p. 67; Securities and Exchange Communities, *52nd Annual Report – 1986* (Washington, D.C.: Government Printing Office, p. 134.

Table A.4: Public Volume of Stock Trading by Type of Investor, Selected Years, 1952 – 1980 (in percent)

Year	Type of Investors Individuals	Institutions
1952	69.2 %	30.8 %
1953	75.0 %	25.0 %
1954	75.5 %	24.5 %
1955	75.5 %	24.5 %
1956	75.0 %	25.0 %
1957	71.1 %	28.9 %
1958	71.4 %	28.6 %
1959	70.6 %	29.4 %
1960	68.6 %	31.4 %
1961	66.7 %	33.3 %
1963	69.1 %	30.9 %
1965	60.7 %	39.3 %
1966	57.0 %	43.0 %
1969	44.1 %	55.9 %
1971	40.3 %	59.7 %
1974	41.1 %	58.9 %
1976	42.7 %	57.3 %
1980	35.1 %	64.9 %

Source: New York Stock Exchange, Fact-Book – 1982 (New York, 1982), p. 52.

Table A.5: Large Block Transactions, New York Stock Exchange, 1965 – 1985

Year	Number	Shares Traded (in thous.)	% of Reported Volume
1965	2,171	48,262	3,1
1966	3,642	85,298	4.5
1967	6,685	169,365	6.7
1968	11,254	292,681	10.0
1969	15,132	402,064	14.1
1970	17,217	450,908	15.4
1971	26,941	692,536	17.8
1972	31,207	766,406	18.5
1973	29,233	721,356	17.8
1974	23,200	549,387	15.6
1975	34,420	778,540	16.6
1976	47,632	1,001,254	18.7
1977	54,275	1,183,924	22.4
1978	75,036	1,646,905	22.9
1979	97,509	2,164,726	26.5
1980	133,597	3,311,132	29.2
1981	145,564	3,271,442	31.8
1982	254,707	6,742,481	41.0
1983	363,415	9,842,080	45.6
1984	433,427	11,492,091	49.8
1985	539,039	14,222,272	51.7

Sources: New York Stock Exchange, *Fact-Book* – *1982* (New York, 1982), p. 64; New York Stock Exchange, *Fact-Book* – *1987* (New York, 1987), p. 71.

Table A.6: Corporate Stocks Held by Type of Investors, 1900–1977 (in billions of $)

Year	Households	Nonfinancial Corporations	Banks	Type of Investor Investment Companies	Insurance Companies	Pension Funds	Other	Total
1900	10.7	2.8	.1	—	.2	—	.1	13.9
1912	30.1	7.1	.3	—	.3	—	.1	37.9
1922	55.5	19.2	.6	.1	.4	—	.3	76.1
1929	138.3	42.3	1.3	2.2	1.9	.1	.6	186.7
1933	57.1	40.5	1.1	1.0	1.5	.1	.4	101.7
1939	73.2	22.0	.7	1.2	2.0	.2	.7	100.0
1945	111.6	27.7	.4	2.9	3.4	.3	.3	146.6
1949	109.8	27.7	.3	3.5	4.8	.8	.4	147.3
1953	161.4	39.0	.6	6.9	7.1	2.6	.3	217.9
1958	343.0	79.0	1.0	18.1	12.6	11.3	.5	465.5
1962	435.5	—	1.0	18.3	17.4	22.7	.4	495.3
1966	593.9	—	—	39.3	22.6	40.6	.6	697.0
1970	747.7	—	2.5	39.3	31.4	71.8	.8	893.5
1973	761.5	—	4.6	44.6	42.6	109.2	—	962.5
1975	618.7	—	5.2	36.4	46.6	116.1	—	823.0
1977	777.0	—	6.0	31.7	50.0	131.9	3.1	999.7

Sources: Raymond W. Goldsmith, Robert E. Lipsey, and Morris Mendelson, Studies in the National Balance Sheet of the United States, vol. 2 (Princeton; Princeton University Press, 1963), pp. A71.15 – A71.21; U. S. Census Bureau, Statistical Abstract of the United States – 1974 (Washington, D. C.: Government Printing Office, 1974), pp. 446, 448; U. S. Census Bureau, Historical Statistics of the United States, Colonial Times to 1970 (Washington, D. C.: Government Printing Office, 1976), pp. 477, 479; Board of Governors, Federal Reserve Annual Statistical Digest, 1973–1977 (Washington, D. C.: Federal Reserve System, 1978), pp. 184–185.

Table A.7: Corporate Stocks as a Percent of Total Financial Assets Held by Type of Investor, 1900–1977

Year	Households	Nonfinancial Corporations	Banks	Type of Investor Investment Companies	Insurance Companies	Pension Funds	Other	Total
1900	70.8	98.3	5.5	–	18.4	–	50.5	62.3
1912	72.7	98.6	6.0	–	12.2	–	50.2	65.3
1922	63.6	83.1	4.4	97.2	8.4	22.0	47.0	57.1
1929	79.0	90.7	7.8	93.2	19.4	22.2	70.7	72.4
1933	58.3	92.0	5.6	90.4	14.0	22.2	38.3	55.8
1939	68.1	90.6	2.6	89.0	10.0	22.2	17.6	50.2
1945	73.6	91.4	0.3	86.6	8.5	12.3	9.6	42.5
1949	77.3	94.5	0.4	90.0	9.5	17.0	32.2	42.1
1953	82.0	92.0	1.0	92.0	11.8	25.0	23.0	48.3
1958	87.7	93.5	1.3	91.4	15.7	42.6	27.5	60.3
1962	87.0	–	1.0	88.8	17.7	35.1	12.1	56.4
1966	87.3	–	–	90.1	19.5	41.6	17.6	59.2
1970	85.9	–	0.8	87.5	22.1	50.0	13.6	57.8
1973	78.6	–	2.1	77.6	23.1	54.6	–	54.3
1975	70.9	–	1.9	69.1	21.6	48.8	–	44.6
1977	72.2	–	1.9	77.5	17.5	45.8	28.4	44.0

Sources: See Table A.6.

Table A.8: Number of Member Firms, New York Stock Exchange, 1899 – 1985

Year	Partnerships	Member Firms Corporations	Total
1899	521	0	521
1909	581	0	581
1919	563	0	563
1930	649	0	649
1940	591	0	591
1950	620	0	620
1960	589	78	667
1970	353	219	572
1975	236	258	494
1980	207	363	570
1985	164	435	599

Source: New York Stock Exchange, *Fact-Book — 1987* (New York, 1987), p. 80.

Table A.9: Major Federal Securities Laws, 1933 – 1975

Year Passed	Law	Major Provisions
1933	Securities Act	Required federal registration of securities offerings and public disclosure of material financial information about issuer
1933	Glass-Steagall Act	Required investment bankers to be either commercial banks of deposit or securities underwriters
1934	Securities Exchange Act	Created SEC, required exchanges to submit rules for SEC approval and barred manipulative trading
1935	Public Utility Holding Company Act	Authorized SEC to regulate and oversee reorganization of capital structure of public utility holding companies
1938	Maloney Act	Authorized formation of National Securities Dealers Association to be registered with SEC and to oversee ethical conduct of broker-dealers in over-the-counter market
1939	Trust Indenture Act	Required obligers of bonds to register with SEC and empowers SEC to oversee investment company operations
1940	Investment Company Act	Required investment companies to register with SEC and empowers SEC to oversee investment company operations

Year Passed	Law	Major Provisions
1964	Securities Act Amendments	Required registration with SEC of all widely held securities in large securities and raised requirements for entry into brokerage business
1970	Investment Company Act Amendments	Limited number of interested persons who could serve as directors on investment company boards and assigned fiduciary duty to investment advisers with respect to receipt of compensation
1970	Securities Investor Protection Act	Created Securities Investor protection Corporation to insure customer deposits with brokerage firms
1974	Employee Retirement Income Security Act	Created Employee Benefit Guaranty Corporation to insure plan beneficiaries against loss due to plan termination and broadened scope of fiduciary responsibility to include all who serve the plan in some professional capacity.
1975	Securities Reform Act	Empowered SEC to establish a national market system, strengthened the SEC's regulatory authority over exchanges

Sources: Commerce Clearing House, *Securities Reform Act* (New York, 1975); Louis Loss, *Securities Regulation* 2nd ed. (Boston: Little, Brown, 1961); David L. Ratner, *Securities Regulation* (St. Paul, Minn.: West Publishing, 1978).

Appendix B

Diffusion of Individual Stockholding

Although the dominant trend in stockholding statistics since 1950 highlights the growth of institutional stock investing, when looked at since the turn of the century there has also been an impressive growth of stockholding by individual investors. The proportion of the population owning stock rose from less than 5 % in 1927 to over 20 % by 1985 (see Table B.1). This secondary trend poses two questions. First, to what degree has direct own-

Table B.1: Estimated Number of Individual Shareholders, 1927–1980 (in millions)

Year	Number	Percent of Population
1927	4–6	3.4–5.0
1930	9–11	7.3–8.9
1932	10–12	8.0–9.6
1937	7–10	5.4–7.8
1947	5.4	3.7
1950	5.0	3.2
1952	6.5	4.1
1956	8.6	5.1
1959	12.5	7.0
1962	17.0	9.1
1965	20.1	10.3
1970	30.8	15.0
1975	25.3	11.9
1980	30.2	13.3
1985	47.0	20.2

Sources: A Berle and G. C. Means, *The Modern Corporation and Private Property* (New York: Harcourt, Brace, and Jovanovich, 1968), pp. 60, 331–334; N. R. Danielian, "Ownership of Securities in the United States," *The Securities Markets*, ed. A. Bernheim and M. G. Schneider (New York: Twentieth Century Fund, 1935), pp. 35–62; R. W. Goldsmith and R. C. Parmalee, *The Distribution of Ownership in the 200 Largest Nonfinancial Corporations* (Washington, D. C.: Government Printing Office, 1940), pp. 167–168; L. Kimmel, *Share Ownership in the United States* (Washington, D. C.: Brookings Institution, 1952), p. 139; New York Stock Exchange, *Fact Book* (various years).

ership of corporate stocks affected the portfolio composition of ordinary households? And, second, how well are individual investors able to fare when investing in the stock market?

Individual Stockholding and Economic Inequality

Individual stockholders are customarily characterized by their place within an economic hierarchy of wealth-holders or of income earners. The fundamental assumption, of course, is that stockholding is concentrated in the hands of the wealthy few. But growth in the number of stockholders as a proportion of the population suggests that stockholding has dispersed down the economic hierarchy. The problem for most students of stockholding has been to measure how far it has dispersed. To what degree (if any) is stockholding less concentrated than it used to be?

Adolf Berle and Gardiner C. Means were the first to attempt systematically to measure the diffusion of stockholding through economic hierarchies.[1] To do this, they had first of all to find some way of estimating accurately who owned how much stock. Relying heavily on analyses of income tax statistics, they concluded that there were between four and six million stockholders in 1927. Estimates for earlier years were provided by H. T. Warshow based on the number of *book* stockholders from 1900 to 1923.[2] But these data are not suitable as a basis for comparison with numbers of shareholders. Counts of book shareholders include everyone who owns more than one stock or several shares of the same stock registered in different names each time they appear on a corporate stockholder roll. The result is to overestimate the number of stockholders. While Seymour Cromwell, formerly president of the New York Stock Exchange, estimated in 1926 that there were only a few hundred thousand stockholders before World War I, Warshow's estimates indicate that there were 4.4 million shareholder accounts by 1900.[3]

Despite lack of good comparative data about the number of individual stockowners for earlier years, Berle and Means were persuaded that the number of investors had increased substantially from the turn of the century to the 1930s and that there had been a dramatic diffusion of stock ownership. They based their conclusion on an analysis of the distribution of dividends paid to income earners from 1916 to 1927. In 1916, 57.2 % of all dividend income (reported on tax returns) was paid to recipients of the country's 25,000 largest incomes. By 1927, the percentage of dividends paid to this group had fallen to 35.2 %. In contrast, those whose incomes were not among the 100,000 largest and who received only 22 % of the dividend income reported in 1916, got 45.8 % of the dividends reported in 1927. The greatest part of this redistribution occured before 1920. On the basis of these data, Berle and Means concluded that there was "a major shift in the ownership of industry from people of large income to those of moderate means."[4]

Berle and Means were correct to suppose a large number of stockholders was an important factor explaining this redistribution of income. But we cannot accept their conclusion about a "major shift in ownership." Because they use absolute numbers to define boundaries between their rough categories of income earners, their comparisons fail to control for exogenous effects due,

1 *The Modern Corporation and Private Property*, rev ed. (New York: Harcourt, Brace, and Jovanovich, 1968), pp. 47 – 65.
2 "The Distribution of Corporate Ownership in the United States," *Quarterly Journal of Economics*, 39 (November, 1924), 15 – 38.
3 Seymour Cromwell, "The Small Investor," *Outlook*, 146 (February 17, 1926), 250 – 252.
4 *The Modern Corporation and Private Property*, p. 59.

for example, to changes in general price or population levels. And adding such controls appears to make a difference. Inspection of Table B.2 shows that, far from there being a major shift of stock ownership, the share of the personal sector's holdings of stock held by the top one percent of adult wealth-holders increased from 1922 to 1929. Stockholding, in other words, became rather more concentrated in the hands of top wealth-holders than less as Berle and Means supposed.

It is difficult to say with certainty whether the increased concentration was due to the rapid rise of stock prices in the boom of the late 1920s, or, perhaps, to acquisitions of more stock. Robert Lampman favors the view that price appreciation was the main factor at work in the 1920s.[5] A cautionary note must be sounded here: Lampman's wealth-holding data, based on estate tax returns, are not strictly comparable to stockholding data based on the analysis of income tax returns, primarily because top wealth-holders may have comparatively small taxable incomes. Problems of comparability, however, are probably not so large as to affect the conclusions reached here one way or the other.[6]

Greater concentration of stockholding does not preclude a simultaneous and substantial increase in the number of moderate income earners who owned stock. Yet it does arouse skepticism about the belief that moderate income earners took a great share in the ownership of industry away from top income earners.[7] It is certainly the case that no significant diffusion of ownership occured in the twenty years between 1932 and 1952. There hardly could have been. As shown in Table B.1, the number of individual shareholders declined without interruption over these years. Meanwhile, increases in the share of personal sector stock held by top wealth-holders were interrupted only during the war years, 1939 to 1945. In fact, concentration of the personal sector's holding of corporate stock reached its peak in 1953 when top wealth-holders owned 76 % of all personal sector stockholdings (see Table B.2).

Since then, it is arguable that stockholding has diffused more widely. The incidence of direct stockholding as proportion of the population rose rapidly

---

5 *The Share of Top Wealth-Holders in the National Wealth, 1922 – 1956* (Princeton: Princeton University Press, 1962), pp. 220 – 229, esp. 228.

6 Marshall Blume and Irwin Friend, *The Changing Role of the Individual Investor* (New York: Wiley, 1978), p. 29.

7 One plausible alternative to the "major shift in ownership" hypothesis is that dividend income was less attractive to income earners who in the 1910s were still adjusting to the new federal income tax but by 1920 had shifted their investments to lower or non-dividend paying stocks.

Table B. 2: Share of Personal Sector's Corporate Stock Held by Top One Percent of Adult Wealth-Holders, 1922 – 1972

Year	Percent Held
1922	61.5
1929	65.6
1939	69.0
1945	61.7
1949	64.9
1953	76.0
1958	75.4
1962	62.0
1969	57.9
1972	62.7
1976	46.0

Sources: R. J. Lampman, *The Share of Top Wealth-Holders in the National Wealth, 1922 – 1956* (Princeton: Princeton University Press, 1962), p. 209; U. S. Census Bureau, *Statistical Abstract – 1985* (Washington D. C.: Government Printing Office, 1985), p. 463.

from the 1950s through the 1960s and then, after slumping somewhat in the 1970s, rose again in the 1980s. And the most recent data available on the share of stockholding by the top wealth-holders show a decline in the percentage held from the peak of 76 % in 1953 to a low of 46 % in 1976. Nevertheless, we cannot leap to conclude that there has been a great levelling of economic inequality in terms of direct stock ownership. Rather it is apparent that the diffusion of direct ownership has been confined to the upper income classes.

As of 1984, the average worth of stocks held by those whose net worth equalled or exceeded $ 1 million was over $ 90,000. In contrast, the average worth of stocks held by those whose net worth was between one-half and $ 1 million was less than $ 20,000. By way of comparison, the median value of stock and mutual fund shares owned by all households equalled only $ 3,892.[8] While these figures are not directly comparable, they suggest that substantial holdings by individuals of corporate stock remain highly concentrated in the hands of a few.

8 U. S. Census Bureau, *Statistical Abstract of the United States, 1987* (Washington, D. C.: Government Printing Office, 1987), p. 448.

Management of Individual Portfolios

When we consider return on their investments, individual stockholders have usually been compared unfavorably with the professional portfolio managers who advise institutional investment funds. In fact, the opinion of "professional" investment advisors has been that nine of ten individual investors *lost* money on their investments.[9] If their opinion was exaggerated, it was not baseless. In 1939, when asked by Elmo Roper, only 27.5 % of individuals owning stock said that they had profited from their investment; 44.4% admitted that they had lost money. The findings could be of limited generality since the rate of return on common stock investment at the time of Roper's survey was − 5.2 % per year.[10]

Nevertheless, the survey responses are confirmed by a painstaking analysis done by Paul Francis Wendt.[11] Wendt thoroughly examined the financial experience of several hundred accounts maintained at the brokerage house of Goodbody & Company from 1933 to 1938 when the rate of return on stocks averaged + 6.9 % per year.[12] Despite the generally favorable market, about 40 % of the accounts showed a loss before unrealized gains or losses were counted. After they were counted, 75 % of the accounts showed a loss. In dollars, before unrealized gains and losses, the median profit for all accounts was $ 159, but when counting unrealized gains and losses, accounts showed a median *loss* of $ 428. Beside demonstrating that people find it easier to take gains, however small, than losses, these data reconstruct experiences ostensibly shared by many. They help to explain the report that, in the late 1940s, five times as many people thought common stocks "not safe" and "a gamble" as thought them "safe" and "not a gamble."[13]

There is some evidence, however, that the position of individual investors may be improving. Marshall E. Blume and Irwin Friend, in their extensive study of individual shareholders, have shown that the financial returns investors can expect are significantly improved when they hold diversified port-

---

9 Martin Mayer, *Wall Street: Men & Money* (New York: Harper & Brothers, 1955), p. 212.

10 Roger G. Ibbotson and Rex A. Sinquefield, *Stocks, Bonds, Bills, and Inflation: Historical Returns, 1926−1978* (Charlottesville, Va.: Financial Analysts Research Foundation, 1979), p. 44; Elmo Roper, *American' Attitudes Toward Investing* (New York: New York Stock Exchange, 1940), p. 75.

11 The Classification and Financial Experience of the Customers of a Typical New York Stock Exchange Firm from 1933 to 1938, Ph. D. dissertation, Columbia University, 1944.

12 Ibbotson and Sinquefield, *Stocks, Bonds, Bills, and Inflation*, p. 44.

13 *Federal Reserve Bulletin* (1948), p. 777.

folios.[14] The distribution of returns realized by individuals who held New York Stock Exchange stocks between July 1971 and June 1972 varied inversely with levels of diversification: 65.6 % of portfolios of one stock and 62.7 % of those of only two showed losses. In contrast, only 44.7 % of those holding three to nine issues and about 30 % of those with ten or more issues showed losses.[15] In short, greater diversification of individual portfolios means fewer losses.

Their finding is significant in light of the evidence, summarized in Table B.3, which shows that individual shareholders are increasingly likely to hold diversified portfolios.[16] While roughly one in five individual shareholders owned portfolios with more than five stocks in 1952, over 46 % owned portfolios with over five stocks in 1975. If this trend continues, individuals may eventually refashion opinions about their investment performance, even when compared to "professional" investment advisors.

In sum, those who own stock today are not unlike those who did so at the beginning of the century. Despite increases in the number of individual investors, substantial diffusion of stock ownership has not been a significant factor affecting the wealth characteristics or income of those outside the upper income brackets. Yet there have been changes in the way individuals manage their stock portfolios. The poorest performing portfolios have been held by

Table B.3: Relative Diversification of Shareholder Portfolios

Number of Stock Issues in Portfolio	Percentage of Individual Shareholders		
	1952	1971	1975
1 – 2	62.0	50.9	36.4
3 – 4	17.7	38.8	17.2
5 – 9	12.0	6.8	21.1
10 or more	8.3	3.9	25.3

Sources: L. H. Kimmel, Share Ownership in the United States (Washington, D. C.: Brookings Institution, 1952, p. 110; M. E. Blume and I. Friend, The Changing Role of the Individual Investor (New York: Wiley, 1978), pp. 47, 119.

14 The Changing Role of the Individual Investor, p. 48.
15 Ibid., pp. 50 – 58, esp. 53.
16 What is unclear from their data is the extent to which this trend in diversification may be due to an increase in the average income earned by stock investors. Diversification is positively associated with income earned. And we have good reason to suppose, if owing only to the growth of mutual funds, that the ranks of the lower income investors have thinned since the Second World War.

the less well-to-do owners who are less able to reduce the risk of investment by diversifying their stockholdings. Still, losing money in the market apparently has not been the exceptional experience, even when stock prices have, generally speaking, been on the rise. Happily for stock owners, the trend toward greater diversification in recent years promises investment returns that more closely approximate returns to the market.

Appendix C

Early Securities Regulation

Because state governments took the lead in exercising their (originally colonial) right to charter corporations, the first attempts at securities regulation in America are found in state laws rather than national laws. The attempts are rooted in the effort by states to promote economic development by making it easier to adopt the corporate business form. As shown in Table C.1, states increasingly adopted general incorporation laws to replace the old system of chartering each corporation by specific legislative enactment.[1] The movement to permit corporate charters to any applicants who met the qualifications

Table C.1: Growth of State Reliance on General Incorporation Laws

| Decade | Number of States Allowing Incorporation Under General Laws | | |
	Total in Decade	Cumulative Total	Percentage of all States
1830 – 1839	1	1	4.0
1840 – 1849	6	7	24.1
1850 – 1859	7	14	43.8
1860 – 1869	8	22	61.6
1870 – 1879	7	29	78.4
1880 – 1889	4	33	78.6
1890 – 1899	7	40	88.9
1900 – 1909	3	43	93.5
1910 – 1919	3	46	95.8

Source: George Heberton Evans, *Business Incorporations in the United Stated, 1800 – 1943* (New York: National Bureau of Economic Research, 1948), pp. 11, 98 – 99, 124 – 125.

1 George Heberton Evans, *Business Incorporation in the United States, 1800 – 1943* (New York: National Bureau of Economic Research, 1948), pp. 10 – 30.

under general law represented a significant delegation of the state's authority to its citizens. Yet the delegation was conditional. The states had no desire completely to rescind their traditional responsibility for corporate oversight.

Almost immediately after states passed general incorporation laws, they also imposed requirements, for example, on the amount of capital that had to be "paid in" before corporate operations could begin or which, to cite another example, made authority to issue stock contingent on approval by a specifically designated state commission. Through these laws, states managed to retain some of their former control over ventures incorporated within their boundaries. A listing of the major securities laws passed during this period is provided in Table C.2. The main point to observe in the table is that the object of securities law in the nineteenth century was almost exclusively to regulate the activities of corporations chartered by the state. (Federal securities law, in contrast, aims to regulate securities transactions.)

Such a provincial outlook toward securities regulation could not last. For several reasons — e. g., competition among states to issue corporate charters, then as now a profitable business, and the growing national economy after the Civil War — it was unlikely that ventures incorporated in one state intended to do business only in the state.[2] Given the large amounts of capital necessary to carry on interstate enterprises, it was equally unlikely that sales of corporate stock could be conducted within any one state. The rapid growth of multi-state enterprise (with the competition among states for corporate charters and among entrepeneurs for investors' dollars which it entailed) caused some to wonder whether state laws provided the most appropriate means for securities regulation and corporate control. The central question — sufficiently well-known and controversial at the end of the century to be a required debate topic for high schoolers — asked whether a national incorporation act might not be better than continuing efforts at regulation on the state level.[3] Supporters of proposals for a federal incorporation law, among whom many businessman and politicians could be counted, had two aims. First, they hoped to eliminate the tangle of conflicting state laws. They also wanted to use centralized, uniform, and mandatory federal reporting requirements to make it easier to discover those who tried to defraud the public through sales of false securities.[4]

2 Thomas C. Cochran, *200 Years of American Business*, (New York: Delta Books, 1977), pp. 76—77.

3 Louis Loss, *Securities Regulation* (Boston: Little Brown, 1961), p. 107.

4 *Ibid.*, pp. 107—110; Michael E. Parrish, *Securities Regulation and the New Deal* (New Haven: Yale University Press, 1970), p. 17; Cedric B. Cowing, *Populists, Plungers, and Progressives* (Princeton: Princeton University Press, 1965), p. 59.

Table C.2: Major Actions by Various States to Regulate Securities Business, 1852 – 1921

Year	State	Action
1852	Massachusetts	Required railroads to file statement that at least 20 % of par value of stock issued was actually paid in before construction could begin
1869	Massachusetts	Established railroad commission to secure compliance with regulations concerning railroad securities
1873	Pennsylvania	Corporations could issue stock only on tangible assets and must confine themselves to business specified in charter
1879	California	Voided sales of stock on margin sales
1893	Texas	Stock and bond law established railroad commission to register and approve all issues of railroad securities
1894	Massachusetts	Required railroads to obtain approval of railroad commission before issuing shares
1903	Connecticut	Required mining and oil corporations to file certificate specifying details of their physical operations before offering shares
1909	Nevada	Required mining companies to file statements about their finances and operations twice annually
1910	Rhode Island	Required corporations to file statement of financial condition and operation. If found insolvent, bank commissioner could petition courts to have a receiver appointed
1911	Kansas	First state to enact comprehensive licensing system providing for registration of securities salesmen
1921	New York	Martin Act empowered state attorney general to investigate fraudulent securities practices, to subpoena and seek injunctions against suspected individuals

Sources: Louis Loss, *Securities Regulation* (Boston: Little, Brown, 1961), pp. 120 – 121; Louis Loss and Edward Cowett, *Blue Sky Law* (Boston: Little, Brown, 1958), pp. 3 – 10; Gerald D. Nash, "Government and Business: A Case Study of State Regulation of Corporate Securities, 1850 – 1933," *Business History Review*, 38 (Summer, 1964), 146 – 154.

The highwater mark of this first push for federal securities control was reached in the early 1900s. The Industrial Commission, created by Congress in 1898, recommended once in 1900 and again in 1902 that promoters and organizers of corporations be required to disclose information necessary for investors to make a safe and intelligent decision about their offerings and that larger corporations be required to publish annual statements of their financial condition.[5] Failure to comply with these requirements, the Commissioners argued, should be labelled "fraud" with the responsible promoters and company directors being held liable for any damages.[6] Except as a last resort, however, even the Industrial Commission failed to support proposals for a federal incorporation statute.[7]

The most significant and innovative act to result from the impetus to reform securities law in the early decades of this century succeeded on the state level. It shifted the object of regulation from the corporation per se to the securities transaction. Written by J. N. Dolley, a Democrat, but "progressive" bank commissioner in Kansas, the so-called "blue-sky" law was enacted in 1911. It required that all securities within the state had to be licensed by the state. The objective was to curb fraudulent securities transactions by refusing licenses for "worthless" securities and to the swindlers willing to peddle them. No means were to be spared in accomplishing this objective either. As legal scholars Louis Loss and Edward Cowett observed, "the statute introduced standards for denial of permits which must have seemed strikingly broad."[8]

To cite the most controversial provisions: If the bank commissioner found the corporate organization in any way "unfair, unjust, inequitable or oppressive to any class of contributors," then he could withold permission to allow its securities to be sold in Kansas. Even more broadly, he could deny a permit if in his judgment the security failed to promise a "fair return" to investors.[9] Thus the law provided wide latitude for discretionary action by the bank

---

5 Leon Stein, *Big Business* (New York: Arno Press, 1978), p. 25.

6 Loss, *Securities Regulation*, pp. 107 – 108.

7 To date, there is still no federal incorporation statute. Whether there should be one remains a controversial question among lawyers. For arguments in favor, see William L. Cary, "Federalism and Corporate Law: Reflections Upon Delaware," *Yale Law Journal*, 83 (March, 1974), 663 – 705. For arguments against, see David A. Drexler, "Federalism and Corporate Law: A Misguided Missile," *Securities Regulation Law Journal*, 3 (Winter, 1976), 374 – 386. A middle ground is sought by Joel F. Henning, "Federalism and Corporate Law: The Chaos Inherent in the Cary Proposal," *Securities Regulation Law Journal*, 3 (Winter, 1976), 362 – 373.

8 *Blue Sky Law* (Boston: Little, Brown, 1958), p. 8.

9 *Ibid.*

commissioner first to define and then to realize the legislative hope to stop securities swindles.

Although the Kansas act represented a radical departure from previous securities regulation and however "shocking" its broad standards, other states watched the Kansas experiment carefully. Not modest about his achievement, Dolley advertised the benefits of blue sky legislation throughout the country during the two years following passage of the act, he urged other states to pass similar measures, and he was an effective salesman. By 1913, twenty-three states, mainly from the West, adopted blue sky statutes of their own. All but six of these closely followed the Kansas act in form and substance. By 1933 every state except Nevada had adopted some form of blue sky regulation.[10] The states had been content to regulate securities issued by the corporations they chartered. But by the 1910s they were evidently anxious to join Kansas in regulating securities transactions. They hoped to protect their citizens against the possibility of fraud even when those citizens bought securities issued by corporations chartered by other states.

Consensus about the object of securities regulation, however, did not lead to a similar consensus about the appropriate means by which to afford investor protection. In general, as Cedric Cowing has shown, geographical regions which traditionally opposed stock speculation, usually in the West, adopted measures that were most paternalistic and sought to keep any investor from ever losing money as the result of fraudulent stock promotions.[11] Financiers vehemently opposed such preventive measures on the grounds that they imposed requirements on the trustworthy as well as the fraudulent securities promoter.[12] They formed the Investment Bankers Association (IBA) in 1912 in part to bolster the public image of security underwriters, but in larger part to prevent the spread of blue sky statutes among states on the eastern seaboard where stock investing was most heavily concentrated.[13]

Because the "blue sky" bills passed so rapidly through so many state legislatures, the Investment Bankers Association's first tactic was to have the existing blue sky statutes struck down by the courts or substantially modified. They had substantial reason to hope they could succeed in this task. The federal courts treated this new form of securities control with little respect.

---

10 *Ibid.*, pp. 16 – 17.
11 *Populists, Plungers, and Progressives.*
12 Robert R. Reed, "Regulation of the Business of the Investment Banker," *Investment Bankers of America Bulletin*, 11 (July 15, 1914), 9 – 17.
13 Parrish, *Securities Regulation and the New Deal*, pp. 5 – 20.

Judges declared the acts of five states to be unconstitutional.[14] The courts were concerned, in part, by the states' paternalistic attitude toward investors. The consequence of that attitude, as was argued in one decision, was unreasonably to constrain the investment banker's private business of selling securities, a business no more "affected by the public interest" than the buying and selling of groceries.[15] The courts were also negatively impressed by the broad and vague language of the law because it subjected every issue or general sale of securities in the state to "the practically uncontrolled discretion of the Commission."[16]

Nevertheless, the early success of the financiers' direct assault against the blue sky laws was short-lived. For the courts, the fundamental question was whether a state could "enact a comprehensive licensing system if its legislature believed that such a system would protect its citizens from fraud." And about this legal question there were not many doubts. By 1917, the U. S. Supreme Court affirmed blue sky legislation generally when it decided "that the prevention of deception (was) within the competence of government."[17] In the end, it was an indirect assault which proved more effective in watering down this attempt at state securities regulation.

However legal it was, the competence of state governments to prevent deceptive practices in securities transactions was in practice quite limited. States had no means to enforce compliance with their statutes by out-of-state financiers. Thwarted in its attempts to block blue sky legislation by overt means, the Investment Banker Association's legal counsel advised members quietly to ignore the laws. "Just stay out of the state whose law you want to evade," was the substance of his advice to them, "and you will not be subject to extradition."[18]

Second, and more serious, the states generally failed to construct an effective administrative apparatus to accomplish the review of a security's quality which the law contemplated. Although the number of new securities issues increased in the decade following World War I, there was no complementary increase in the moral fervor which had originally inspired passage of the blue sky laws. Consequently, the public was unwilling to pay any increased expense for regulatory administration. According to Michael Parrish, in the early 1930s only eight states had separate commissions "devoted full-time to the labor of

14 Loss and Cowett, Blue Sky Law, p. 10.
15 Quoted in Reed, "Regulation of the Business of the Investment Banker," p. 10.
16 Quoted ibid., p. 12.
17 Loss and Cowett, Blue Sky Law, p. 13.
18 Loss, Securities Regulation, p. 105.

security analysis, regulation and investigation."[19] The rest put the responsibility upon bank superintendents, state auditors, or other short-term political appointees who were "inexpert in their task." Nor was this administrative failing subject to improvement with experience. Twenty years later, Louis Loss found that in seventeen states, less than one full-time staff member was charged with administration of the blue sky statutes.[20] Rather than an expense collectively born to protect citizens from securities fraud administering securities control is a money making venture. In thirty-one states, the fees charged for securities registration exceed the costs of administration. For twenty-three of these thirty-one states, the margin of revenues over costs exceeded 25 %, a rate of profit sufficiently high perhaps to arouse the admiration of financiers who believed that securities regulation was somehow opposed to the market ethos.[21]

Practically speaking, therefore, as early as the 1920s, expedients proved necessary to effect the states' new objective in securities control, namely, to protect their citizens against deceptive securities transactions. One expedient was recommended by the Investment Bankers Association and endorsed by the New York Stock Exchange. It was to exempt securities from state registration requirements if they were listed (say) on the New York, Chicago (now the Midwest), or Boston stock exchanges or on the Board of Trade or New York Curb (now the American Stock) Exchange.[22] The data in Table C.3 show how many states continue to rely on this expedient. (They also provide evidence for the degree of confidence states have in the quality of securities listed on the various exchanges.)

Another expedient recommended by the Investment Bankers Association was to simplify registration requirements or else (and "better") to abandon the practice of registration altogether. This expedient was urged particularly upon the eastern states where most securities dealers had their principal offices. The financial community pointed to New York's Martin Act of 1921 as a model statute. Rather than establish any registraion requirements, the act empowered New York's attorney general to stop such fraudulent practices as he could discover.[23] Adopting these expedients eased the administrative burden of securities regulation on the states without doubt. Such resources as were at their disposal could be focused on protecting the investor by

19 Parrish, *Securities Regulation and New Deal*, pp. 28 – 29.
20 Loss, *Securities Regulation*, p. 106.
21 Loss and Cowett, Blue Sky Law, p. 62.
22 Parrish, *Securities Regulation and the New Deal*, p. 26.
23 *Ibid.*, pp. 21 – 22; Loss, *Securities Regulation*, pp. 120 – 122.

Table C.3: States Exempt Stocks Listed on Certain Stock Exchanges from Registration under the "Blue Sky" Acts

Exchange Exempted	Number of States Exempting
New York Stock Exchange	38
American Stock Exchange	36
Midwest Stock Exchange	33
Boston Stock Exchange	20
Chicago Board of Trade	15
Cincinnati Stock Exchange	8
Philadelphia Stock Exchange	6
Detroit Stock Exchange	3
New Orleans Stock Exchange	3
Richmond Stock Exchange	2

Source: Louis Loss, Commentary on the Uniform Securities Act (Boston: Little, Brown, 1976), p. 115.

apprehending those believed actually to be defrauding the public through securities sales. In doing so, however, they debased the original promise of the Kansas act which was to prevent fraud from being committed in the first place.

Appendix D

A Note on Sources

Historical researchers emphasize the distinction between primary and secondary sources and make a virtue of their own reliance on primary sources. I appreciate their point. Sociologists also prefer direct observation and contact with their subject matter whenever possible. Nevertheless, it would have been impossible to complete this study without relying on materials already available as a result of the scholarly toil of others in the fields of economics, history, and law. One aim of this appendix is to acknowledge my substantial intellectual debt to others through a brief bibliographic essay of the secondary sources I found most helpful. A second aim, of course, is to describe the primary sources I used to inform my research. Where pertinent, I will indicate voids that future efforts at data collection might fill with profit to forward research about the social organization of financial institutions.

Major Secondary Sources

A major objective was to obtain quantitative materials which described how many participants in the market engaged in how much of a particular kind of activity and for how long a period they did so. Such data help define what social actions need to be explained and set limits on the number and range of alternative explanations. Most useful in accomplishing this task was work done by Raymond W. Goldsmith. His *Financial Intermediaries in the American Economy Since 1900, Studies in the National Balance Sheet of the United States,* and *Institutional Investors and Corporate Stock* provided essential raw data without which it would have been impossible to trace changing patterns of stock ownership. Fortunately for this study, Goldsmith's work has been institutionalized, principally in the Federal Reserve Board's ongoing flow-of-funds analysis, so that analyses based on Goldsmith's work can be brought up to date.

Other valuable sources of quantitative data are the yearbooks published regularly by trade associations. The yearbook of the New York Stock Exchange, which has gone under various titles over the years and is currently called a *Fact Book,* is an indispensable (though unevenly useful) resource. Also helpful are the yearbooks published by the Investment Company Institute, the American Stock Exchange, and, of course, the annual reports of the Securities and Exchange Commission. When these sources failed, historical statistics published by the U. S. Census Bureau were often available to fill in the gaps. Despite numerous sources of quantitative data, it is nonetheless true that data available after 1935 — when the Securities and Exchange Commission began publishing its records — are far superior in detail and quantity than data available before then. As for information about shareholders, no accurate descriptive data preceded the census undertaken by the New York Stock Exchange in 1952 which has been periodically updated ever since. A useful review of these surveys is found in Marshall E. Blume and Irwin Friend's *The Changing Role of the Individual Investor.*

A wealth of evidence about the internal structure and activities within the financial community between 1900 and 1980 is available in four important standard works by Vincent Carosso, Joel Seligman, Michael Parrish, and Cedric Cowing. Carosso's *Investment Banking in America* is the most encompassing of the four. Based to an unusual extent on company records, Carosso's work provides a fine-grained portrait of the attitudes and actions of leading banking firms. Seligman's *The Transformation of Wall Street* is the standard history of the Securities and Exchange Commission. It provides invaluable information about the relations between Wall Street and Washington since 1935 and the issues which often divided them. Next in importance was Michael Parrish's book on *Securities Regulation and the New Deal* which describes the political controversies prevailing within Roosevelt's administration about the most significant pieces of federal securities regulation passed during the 1930s. Though narrower in scope than Carosso's or Seligman's work, Parrish's study equals Carosso's work for being exceptionally well-grounded in primary sources. Finally, Cedric Cowing's *Populists, Plungers, and Progressives* is an interesting study of public opinion about speculation and the speculative markets and the impact of that opinion on attempts at public securities regulation through the New Deal. Cowing's work is based primarily on an exhaustive search of the periodical literature between 1880 and 1930.

Less scholarly, but still interesting popular histories of the period are to be found in Fredrick Lewis Allen's *The Lords of Creation*, John Kenneth Galbraith's *The Great Crash*, and John Brook's *Once in Golconda*.

There are no institutional histories of the financial community for the period following the Second World War which are comparable in scope and scholarly quality to those by Carosso, Seligman, Parrish, and Cowing. (Carosso's book contains a short epilogue on the period, but no more than that, and while Seligman's work deals in detail with the post-war period, his focus is on the Securities and Exchange Commission more than it is on the institutions of Wall Street.) Rather we are left with the works of popular historians and journalists. Some of these works contain sound and reliable accounts of the main events of the period. I have in mind Martin Mayer's work on *Wall Street: Men and Money*, John Brook's *The Go-Go Years*, and Chris Welles's *The Last Days of the Club*. More polemical, but also helpful if used with care, is Hurd Baruch's *Wall Street: Security Risk*. Serious researchers can safely ignore Leonard Sloane's *The Anatomy of the Floor* and Alan Lechner's *Street Games*. Neither work does more than glide quickly over the surface of events.

It is worth emphasizing the lack of a scholarly history of the stock market. Robert Sobel comes closest to having written one. His series of books, *NYSE, The Curbstone Brokers, AMEX, Inside Wall Street*, and *Panic on Wall Street*, deal comprehensively with the events, persons, and institutions of Wall Street. What is missing, but necessary for a definitive study, is access to the archives of the major stock exchanges to gain the kind of information reported, for example, by H. G. S. Noble in his *The New York Stock Exchange in the Crisis of 1914* and then to subject that information to a critical analysis. The New York Stock Exchange has maintained orderly archives, open to scholarly researchers since 1980, but no one yet has seen fit to exploit this resource to do a full-blown institutional history of the stock market. (Hopefully, this condition will not continue indefinitely.) Because the archives are most complete for the period before the 1930s and begin to tail off afterwards, their usefulness for the present study was limited.

The legal history of securities regulation is more complete, and I have relied extensively on the work of legal historians and scholars for evidence about the institutionalization of particular value positions within the market. It is possible to criticize the work of Louis Loss on the grounds that his work is too technical and lacks historical and political depth. Still, I found Loss's books on *Blue Sky Law* and *Securities Regulation* to be good sources concerning the object and controversies surrounding securities law in this area; his work is full of facts and leads for further research which I would have been hard pressed to do without. A condensed, but good summary of the statutes and major court decisions which is more up to date than Loss's work is found in David Ratner's *Securities Regulation*. Also, there are many good articles available to those who search through legal journals and even such quasi-legals journals as *Trust and Estates*. These were especially helpful in tracing changes in the laws regarding prudent investment by trustees. Lastly, an interesting collection of articles on the *Economics of Corporation Law and Securities Regulation* has been edited by Richard A. Posner and Kenneth E. Scott. The connection between economics and law is always close, but not often dealt with explicitly even in the area of securities regulation where the connection would appear to be most evident.

In addition to special studies about the financial community, I also depended on more general histories of the time to put my own research in context. Most useful were works by Richard Hofstadter, e. g., the *Age of Reform*, *Social Darwinism in America*, and *Amerian Political Tradition*, Margaret Myers's *A Financial History of the United States*, E. Digby Baltzell's *The Protestant Establishment*, and a quite good intellectual history by Edward Purcell on *The Crisis of Democratic Theory*.

Primary Sources

The distinction between primary and secondary sources is not always so clear as it might at first appear. A crucial source of primary data from my point of view was the scholarly and professional writing of economics, business school teachers, and financial journalists about why stock prices change and about how one might invest profitably. There is a large body of such writings, most of it derivative or worse. I did not attempt to select from it by any scientific means of sample selection. It would have been difficult or impossible empirically to define the population from which such a sample might be drawn. In any case, I wished to avoid the substantive assumptions involved in supposing that all entries in the field were of equivalent rank or influence within the financial community. My purpose was to trace the leading, influential theories about stock price change and stock investment. To do so I turned to writings by prominent figures in the field: John Moody, Edgar Lawrence Smith, Benjamin Graham, John Burr Williams, William Baumol, Eugene Fama, and James Lorie. The test of whether their ideas actually exerted influence over the financial community came from an analysis of the content of law and of evidence about the growth of institutional mechanisms for carrying out their ideas. Perhaps a more direct way to test the influence of their ideas would be through systematic analysis of portfolio changes over time and of the minute books of investment advisory committees recommending one change or another. But this test cannot be carried out on any grand scale. The largest source of such data is kept in the archives of trust departments. These are confidential records. They are not likely to be available for use by scholars in the foreseeable future.

The Oral History Collection at Columbia University contains four transcripts of interviews with important figures within the financial community. Least useful were the reminiscences of George Whitney, a long-time partner of J. P. Morgan. Whitney remained taciturn throughout most of the interview, refusing to talk about some things and suggesting other things (e. g., a personal animosity borne toward Franklin Roosevelt) only to deny them later on. There are some interesting parts, as when he asserts that Albert Wiggin was one of the finest bankers of the time, but too few to reward the more general research in hand. More helpful were the reminiscences of Walter Sachs, partner in the firm of Goldman, Sachs, and of James Landis. Both were central figures in the market, one on the side of the brokers and the other on the side of government, during the critical period of transition between 1925 and 1935. Sach's interview in particular provides much useful information to help one understand the failure of the Goldman Sachs Trading Corporation after the crash in 1929. Also available for inspection are the reminiscences of Ferdinand Pecora. These are extraordinarily rich in detail about the period of the 1930s. Fortunately, the most relevant parts of the transcript, dealing with Pecora's role as counsel to the Senate's investigation of stock exchange practices, have already been disclosed by Carosso in *Investment Banking in America* (Carosso did the interview of Pecora) or by Pecora himself in his book *Wall Street Under Oath*. Nevertheless, reading the transcript was most helpful to me as I attempted to make use of these alternative sources.

The Columbia University Library also contains the papers of Frank A. Vanderlip, once head of National City Bank and protégé of James Stillman.

Vanderlip's papers are a vast resource. I made limited use of the files on the National City Bank and of Vanderlip's correspondence with Stillman. The correspondence was especially rich because at the time the letters were written Stillman was head of the bank, but lived in Europe, while Vanderlip was second in command and lived in New York City. During this period, from about 1905 to 1914, financiers traveled often from New York to Europe and back, so both Vanderlip and Stillman had current news to report. Reading their correspondence was slow going, however, because many of the messages between them were written in code. Luckily for me, some messages were decoded and, since they did not appear to alter their code, I was able to decipher most of every message. Once done, the letters provided a fair record describing the daily routines of senior bank management. Also described is their uncertainty about how to respond to "political" attacks against Wall Street bankers and financiers. I suspect that much could be learned about high finance in America if only some enterprising researchers could find and systematically analyze transatlantic correspondence between financiers at the turn of the century.

Published memoirs are a handier source of similar information. The memoirs of Richard Wyckoff, *Wall Street Adventures through Forty Years*, and Alexander Dana Noyes, *The Market Place*, were most helpful in describing practices in the stock market between 1900 and 1930, as was Edward Lefevre's *Reminiscences of a Stock Operator*, a thinly "fictionalized" account of Jesse Livermore's career through the 1920s. One excellent source, Henry Clew's *Fifty Years in Wall Street*, concentrates and is most useful when describing events which occurred before 1900. William Douglas's *Go East Young Man* was a disappointment. Full of puffery, it contains little information about Douglas and the Securities and Exchange Commission which is not better gotten from *Democracy and Finance*. For the post-World War II era, Donald Reagan's *A View from the Street* stands alone as a useful "insider's" account of Wall Street and this despite the unhidden bias favoring Merrill Lynch. Though not a memoir, Cary Reich's *Financier: The Biography of Andre Meyer* supplies a thorough account of the market machinations underlying the conglomerate business of the 1960s and 1970s.

The most exhaustive collection of primary source materials about the market's history is kept in government archives. Collections of testimony before Congress, from the "money trust" investigation to the investigation of stock exchange practices and finally up to the several hearings held before passage of the Securities Reform Act of 1975, provide an overwhelming volume of materials to be surveyed, most of which is not very helpful. More useful to me were special reports done by the Securities and Exchange Commission sometimes at the request of Congress. I mean especially the *Special Study of the Securities Markets* done in 1964 and the *Institutional Investor Study* done in 1970. The Securities and Exchange Commission maintains an excellent library in which submissions by interested parties about current issues, on which the commission has invited comment, are kept on file; these files are readily accessible for use by researchers. I relied most heavily on the files concerning the development of an automated national market system. No issue was more prominent than this one throughout the 1970s. The files revealed the wide range of opinion about the virtue of establishing an "electronic" market. Useful background information was available also in the Minutes of the National Market Advisory Board.

The difficulty with official files, of course, is that people are not always so candid on as off the record. (Vanderlip's papers dealing with preparations to testify before the "money trust" investigation provide ample evidence of the fact, if any is needed.) To help correct that bias on current developments in the market, I arranged to spend several days on the floor of the New York Stock Exchange observing the conduct of "trading in the crowd" as well as the use of the automated Intermarket Trading System. I also conducted informal interviews with eight members of the exchange (four specialists, two floor brokers, one registered competitive market maker, and one floor trader working for a public firm) in order to get their opinions about the importance of maintaining a market *place*. Further insight into the attitude of market participants concerning proposed changes in the market's organization are available in articles written by members of the financial community, broadly defined, for a useful book *Impending Changes in the Securities Markets* which is edited by Ernest Bloch and Robert A. Schwartz.

Lastly, like anyone who attempts a historical analysis of some aspect of American life in the twentieth century, I am indebted to the record left by the press, the *New York Times*, to be sure, but also the *Wall Street Journal* and the *Commercial and Financial Chronicle*. Unlike some researchers, however, I also owe a special debt to the experience of having worked in a medium-sized bank trust department from 1969 to 1976. During that term of employment, I was actively engaged, trying to understand the traditions then current on Wall Street, to improve the performance of my employer. I have long since given up profit-seeking endeavors, but I cannot begin to estimate how helpful it was to have once participated in the life of the institution I have studied.

Selected Bibliography

Abolafia, Mitchel Y. 1985. Market Crisis and Organizational Intervention. Paper presented at the annual meetings of the American Sociological Association, Washington, D. C. August.

Allen, Frederick Lewis, (1935) 1966. *The Lords of Creation*. Chicago: Quadrangle Books.

Allswang, John A. 1978. *The New Deal and American Politics*. New York: John Wiley & Sons.

Angell, Robert Coley. 1965. *Free Society and Moral Crisis*. Ann Arbor, Mich.: University of Michigan Press.

Baker, Wayne E. 1984. "The Social Structure of a National Securities Market." *American Journal of Sociology*, 89 (January), 775 – 811.

——. 1984. "Floor Trading and Crowd Dynamics." In *The Social Dynamics of Financial Markets*. Ed. Patricia A. and Peter Adler. Greenwich, Conn.: JAI Press.

Baltzell, E. Digby. 1966. *The Protestant Establishment: Aristocracy and Caste in America*. New York: Vintage Books.

Barnard, Chester I. 1938. *The Function of the Executive*. Cambridge, Mass.: Harvard University Press.

Barnes, Leo. 1965. "What Difference Does Knowledge Make to Investors?" *Financial Analysts Journal*, 21 (September), 60 – 68.

Baruch, Hurd. 1971. *Wall Street: Security Risk*. Baltimore: Penguin Books.

Beaver, William H. 1980. "The Nature of Mandated Disclosure." Pp. 317 – 331 in *Economics of Corporation Law and Securities Regulation*. Ed. Richard A. Posner and Kenneth Scott. Boston: Little, Brown.

Bender, Ann K. 1942. "Prudent Investor Rule in the Investment of Trust Funds." *Temple University Law Quarterly*, 16, 216 – 221.

Bentson, George J. 1973. "Required Disclosure and the Stock Market." *American Economic Review*, 63, 132 – 155.

Bentson, George J. 1980. "Required Disclosure and the Stock Market: An Evaluation of the Securities Exchange Act of 1934." Pp. 363 – 374 in *Economics of Corporation Law and Securities Regulation*. Ed. Richard A. Posner and Kenneth Scott. Boston: Little, Brown.

Berle, Aldoph and Gardiner C. Means. (1932) 1968. *The Modern Corporation and Private Property*. Rev. ed. New York: Harcourt, Brace, and Jovanovich.

Bernheim, Alfred and Margaret G. Schneider, eds. 1935. *The Securities Markets*. New York: Twentieth Century Fund.

Black, Fischer and Myron Scholes. 1974. "From Theory to a New Financial Product." *Journal of Finance*, 29 (May), 399 – 412.

Bloch, Ernest. 1979. "Securities Markets under Stress: 1967 – 1976." Pp. 3 – 38 in *Impending Changes for Securities Markets*. Ed. Ernest Bloch and Robert A. Schwartz. Greenwich, Conn.: JAI Press.

Bloch, Ernest and Arnold V. Sametz. 1973. *A Modest Proposal for a National Securities Market System and Its Governance*. New York: Graduate School of Business Administration, New York University.

Block, Fred. 1977. "The Ruling Class Does Not Rule: Notes on the Marxist Theory of the State." *Socialist Revolution*, 7, 6 – 28.

——. 1986. "Political Choice and the Multiple 'Logics' of Capital." *Theory and Society*, 15, 175 – 192.

Bloomenthal, Harold S. 1982. "Introduction." In *International Capital Markets and Securities Regulation*. Ed. Harold S. Bloomenthal. New York: Clark, Boardman.

Blume, Marshall E. and Irwin Friend. 1978. *The Changing Role of the Individual Investor*. New York: Wiley.

Board of Governors. 1978. *Federal Reserve Annual Statistical Digest, 1973 – 1977*. Washington, D. C.: Federal Reserve System.

Bosland, Chelcie C. 1937. *The Common Stock Theory of Investment*. New York: Ronald Press.

Bossard, James H. 1931. "University Education for Business: A Survey." *Journal of Business*, 4 (July), 64 – 77.

Boudon, Raymond. 1982. *The Unintended Consequences of Social Action*. New York: St. Martin's Press.

Bowles, Samuel, David M. Gordon, and Thomas E. Weisskopf. 1984. *Beyond the Waste Land: A Democratic Alternative to Economic Decline*. Garden City, N. Y.: Anchor Books.

Brandeis, Louis D. (1914) 1932. *Other People's Money and How Bankers Use It*. New York: Frederick A. Stokes.

Brimmer, Andrew. 1962. *Life Insurance Companies in the Capital Market*. East Lansing, Mich.: Bureau of Business and Economic Research, Michigan State University.

Brooks, John. 1969. *Once in Golconda*. New York: Harper & Row.

——. 1973. *The Go-Go Years*. Dublin: Gill and Macmillian.

Buchanan, Allen. 1985. *Ethics, Efficiency, and the Market*. Totowa, N. J.: Rowman & Allanheld.

Burns, Helen M. 1974. *The American Banking Community and New Deal Banking Reform*. Westport, Conn.: Greenwood Press.

Carosso, Vincent P. 1970. *Investment Banking in America*. Cambridge, Mass.: Harvard University Press.

Cary, William L. 1974. "Federalism and Corporate Law: Reflections Upon Delaware." *Yale Law Journal*, 83 (March), 663 – 705.

Chandler, Lester V. 1970. *American's Greatest Depression, 1929 – 1941*. New York: Harper & Row.

Chapman, R. P. 1944. "Investing Trust Funds under the Prudent Man Rule." *Trust Bulletin*, 23, 2.

Cochran, Thomas C. 1977. *200 Years of American Business*. New York: Delta Books.

"Code of Ethics." 1945. *The Analysts Journal*, 1 (January), 49.

Commerce Clearing House. 1975. *Securities Reform Act*. New York. Commerce Clearing House.

Cowing, Cedric B. 1965. *Populists, Plungers, and Progressives*. Princeton: Princeton University Press.

Cowles, Alfred. 1933. "Can Stock Market Forecasters Forecast?" *Econometrica*, 1, 309 – 324.

——. 1939. *Common Stock Indexes*. Bloomington, Ind.: Principia Press.

Cromwell, Seymour. 1926. "The Small Investor." *Outlook*, 146 (February 17), 250 – 252.

Danielian, N. R. 1935. "Ownership of Securities in the United States." Pp. 35 – 62 in *The Securities Markets*. Ed. Alfred Bernheim and Margaret G. Schneider. New York: Twentieth Century Fund.

Davant, James W. 1979. "Davant on the Davant Report: The NYSE Looks at the Central Market System." Pp. 75 – 83 in *Impending Changes for Securities Markets*. Ed. Ernest Bloch and Robert A. Schwartz. Greenwich, Conn.: JAI Press.

Dean, Arthur H. 1933. "The Federal Securities Act," *Fortune*, (August), 50 – 52, 97 – 102, 104 – 106.

Dill, James B. 1900 a. "Industrials as Investments for Small Capital." *Annals of the American Academy of Political and Social Science*, XV (May), 109 – 119.

——. 1900 b. "Industrials as Investments." *The American Banker*, (June 6), 955 – 996.

Domhoff, G. William. 1978. *The Powers That Be*. New York: Vintage Press.

Douglas, William O. 1933. "Protecting the Investor." *Yale Review*, 23, 521 – 533.

——. 1940. *Democracy and Finance*. New Haven, Conn.: Yale University Press.

Drexler, David A. 1976. "Federalism and Corporate Law: A Misguided Missile." *Securities Regulation Law Journal*, 3 (Winter), 374 – 386.

Drucker, Peter F. 1976. *The Unseen Revolution: How Pension Fund Socialism Came to America*. New York: Harper & Row.

Emery, Henry Crosby. (1896) 1969. *Speculation on the Stock and Produce Exchanges of the United States*. Westport, Conn.: Greenwood Press.

Etzioni, Amitai. 1985. "Encapsulated Competition," *Journal of Post-Keynesian Economics*, 7 (Spring), 287 – 302.

Evans, George Heberton. 1948. *Business Incorporations in the United States, 1800 – 1943*. New York: National Bureau of Economic Research.

Federal Securities Laws. 1940. New York: Commerce Clearing House.

Filler, Louis. 1976. *The Muckrackers*. University Park, Pa.: Pennsylvania State University Press.

Fischer, Lawrence. 1965. "Outcome for 'Random' Investments in Common Stocks Listed on the New York Stock Exchange." *Journal of Business*, 38 (April), 149 – 161.

Fischer, Lawrence and James H. Lorie. 1964. "Rates of Return on Investments in Common Stocks." *Journal of Business*, 37 (January), 1 – 24.

Fletcher, William Franklin. 1982. *Supplement to Scott on Trusts*, 3rd ed. Boston: Little, Brown.

Forbes. 1969. "An Old Curmudgeon's New Era," (July 1), 62 – 63.

Frankfurter, Felix. 1933. "The Federal Securities Act." *Fortune*, 8 (August), 53 – 55, 106 – 111.

Freedman, James O. 1978. *Crisis and Legitimacy: The Administrative Process and American Government*. Cambridge: Cambridge University Press.

Freedman, Max (ed.). 1967. *Roosevelt and Frankfurter, Their Correspondence: 1928 – 1945*. Boston: Little, Brown.

Freidel, Frank. 1973. *Franklin D. Roosevelt: Launching the New Deal*. Boston: Little, Brown.

Friedman, Milton. 1953. *Essays in Positive Economics*. Chicago: University of Chicago Press.

Friedman, Milton and Anna Jacobson Schwartz. (1963) 1971. *A Monetary History of the United States, 1867 – 1960*. Princeton: Princeton University Press.

Friedrich, Carl Joachim. 1940. "Public Policy and the Nature of Public Administrative Responsibility." In *Public Policy*. Ed. C. J. Friedrich and Edward S. Mason. Cambridge, Mass.: Harvard University Press.

Friend, Irwin and Edward S. Herman. 1964. "The S. E. C. Through a Glass Darkly." *Journal of Business*, 37, 382 – 405.

Galbraith, John Kenneth. (1955) 1972. *The Great Crash: 1929*. Boston: Houghton Mifflin.

Gallup, George H. 1972. *The Gallup Poll: Public Opinion 1935 – 1971*. 3 vols. New York: Random House.

——. 1978. *The Gallup Poll: Public Opinion 1972 – 1977*. 2 vols. Wilmington, Del.: Scholarly Resources, Inc.

Giddens, Anthony. 1986. *The Constitution of Society*. Berkeley and Los Angeles: University of California Press.

Gillis, John G. 1974. "Responsibilities of Professionals Under Securities Law." *Financial Analysts Journal*, (March/April), 12, 88 – 90.

Goldsmith, Raymond W. 1958. *Financial Intermediaries in the American Economy Since 1900*. Princeton: Princeton University Press.

——. (ed.) 1973. *Institutional Investors and Corporate Stock*. New York: National Bureau of Economic Research.

Goldsmith, Raymond W. and Rexford C. Parmelee. 1940. *the Distribution of Ownership in the 200 Largest Nonfinancial Corporations*, Temporary National Economic Committee, Monograph No. 29. Washington, D. C.: Government Printing Office.

Goldsmith, Raymond W., Robert E. Lipsey, and Morris Mendelson. 1963. *Studies in the National Balance Sheet of the United States*. Vol. 2. Princeton: Princeton University Press.

Graham, Benjamin and David L. Dodd. (1934) 1940. *Security Analysis*. 2nd ed. New York: MacGraw-Hill.

Granovetter, Mark. 1985. "Economic Action and Social Structure: The Problem of Embeddedness." *American Journal of Sociology*, 91 (November), 481 – 510.

Guttman, Egon. 1976. "Broker-Dealer Bankruptcies." Appendix F in *Modern Securities Transfer*. Rev. ed. Boston: Warren Gorham & Lamont.

Hamilton, Gary G. 1978. "The Structural Sources of Adventurism: The Case of the California Gold Rush." *American Journal of Sociology*, 83 (May), 1466 – 1490.

Hamilton, William Peter. 1922. *The Stock Market Barometer*. New York: n. p.

Hawke, G. R. 1980. *Economics for Historians*. Cambridge: Cambridge University Press.

Hawkins, David F. 1963. "The Development of Modern Financial Reporting Practices Among American Manufacturing Corporations." *Business History Review*, 37 (Autumn), 135 – 168.

Hayek, Friedrich A. 1948. *Individualism and Economic Order*. Chicago: University of Chicago Press.

——. 1979. *Law, Legislation, and Liberty*. Vol. 3. Chicago: University of Chicago Press.

Hayes, Douglas A. 1967. "Potential for Professional Status." *Financial Analysts Journal*, (November), 29 – 31.

Headley, Louis S. 1949. "Trustees or 'Gentlemen Adventurers'?" *Trusts and Estates*, 88, 91.

Henning, Joel F. 1976. "Federalism and Corporate Law: The Chaos Inherent in the Cary Proposal." *Securities Regulation Law Journal*, 3 (Winter), 362 – 373.

Hicks, John. 1977. *Economic Perspectives*. Oxford: Clarendon Press.

Horwitz, Robert B. 1986. "Understanding Deregulation." *Theory and Society*, 15, 139 – 174.

Hughes Committee, *Report* (feell reference under Horace white; see below).

Ibbotson, Roger G. and Rex A. Sinquefield. 1979. *Stocks, Bonds, Bills, and Inflation: Historical Returns, 1926 – 1978*. Charlottesville, Va.: Financial Analysts Research Foundation.

Jaffe, Louis L. 1954. "The Effective Limits of the Administrative Process." *Harvard Law Review*, 67 (May), 1105 – 1135.

Janowitz, Morris. 1978. *The Last Half-Century*. Chicago: University of Chicago Press.

Jansson, Solveig. 1977. "The Shrinking Power of Institutional Analysts to Direct Business." *Institutional Investor*, 13 (December), 49 – 54.

Jensen, Michael. 1968. "The Performance of Mutual Funds in the Period 1945 – 1964." *Journal of Finance*, 23 (May), 389 – 416.

Johnson, Arthur W. 1968. *Winthrop W. Aldrich: Lawyer, Banker, Diplomat*. Cambridge, Mass.: Graduate School of Business Administration, Harvard University.

Keeton, George W. 1964. *The Investment and Taxation of Trust Funds*. London: Sir Isaac Pitman & Sons.

Keller, Morton. 1963. *The Life Insurance Enterprise, 1885 – 1910*. Cambridge, Mass.: Harvard University Press.

Kemmerer, Donald L. 1952. "The Marketing of Securities, 1930 – 1952." *Journal of Economic History*, 12 (Fall), 454 – 468.

Ketchum, Marshall D. 1967. "Is Financial Analysis a Profession?" *Financial Analysts Journal*, (November), 33 – 37.

Kimmel, Lewis H. 1952. *Share Ownership in the United States*. Washington, D. C.: Brookings Institution.

Kindleberger, Charles P. 1978. *Manias, Panics, and Crashes.* New York: Basic Books.

Kripke, Homer. 1980. "Can the SEC Make Disclosure Policy Meaningful?" Pp. 331 – 342 in *Economics of Corporation Law and Securities Regulation.* Ed. Richard A. Posner and Kenneth Scott. Boston: Little, Brown.

Lambourne, Richard W. 1978. "The Evolution of Financial Analysts' Professional Standards." Pp. 65 – 73 in *Professional Standards of Practice.* Ed. M. H. Earp and John G. Gillis. Charlottesville, Va.: Financial Analysts Research Foundation.

Lampman, Robert J. 1962. *The Share of Top Wealth-Holders in the National Wealth, 1922 – 1956.* Princeton: Princeton University Press.

Landis, James M. 1959. "The Legislative History of the Securities Act of 1933." *George Washington Law Review,* 28 (October), 29 – 49.

——. 1975. *Reminiscences of James M. Landis.* New York: Oral History Collection, Columbia University.

Langbein, John H. and Richard A. Posner. 1976. "Market Funds and Trust Investment Law, Part I." *American Bar Foundation Research Journal,* (January), 1 – 34.

——. 1977. "Markets Funds and Trust Investment Law, Part II." *American Bar Foundation Research Journal,* (January), 1 – 43.

Langevoort, Donald C. 1985. "Information Technology and the Structure of Securities Regulation." *Harvard Law Review,* 98 (February), 747 – 804.

Larson, Magali Sarfatti. 1977. *The Rise of Professionalism.* Berkeley and Los Angeles: University of California Press.

Lawson, Thomas. (1905) 1968. *Frenzied Finance.* Westport, Conn.: Greenwood Press.

Leblebici, Huseyin and Gerald R. Salancik. 1982. "Stability in Interorganizational Exchanges: Rulemaking Processes of the Chicago Board of Trade." *Administrative Science Quarterly,* 27, 227 – 242.

Lefevre, Edwin. 1903. "The American Gambling Spirit." *Harper's Weekly,* 47 (May), 704 – 705.

——. (1923) 1964. *Reminiscences of a Stock Operator.* Larchmont, N. Y.: American Research Council.

Lewis, Emerson. 1946. "The Prudent Man Investment Rule." *Illinois Bar Journal,* 35, 656 – 66.

Lilley, Theodore. 1977. "Why Broaden the Definition of Financial Analysis?" *Financial Analysis Journal,* (January), 79.

Link, Arthur S. 1963. *Woodrow Wilson and the Progressive Era.* New York: Harper Torchbooks.

Little, Ian M. D. and A. C. Rayner. 1966. *Higgledy, Piggledy Growth Again.* Oxford: Basil Blackwell.

Loomis, Carol J. 1978. "The Shakeout on Wall Street Isn't Over Yet." *Fortune,* (May 22), 59 – 66.

Lorie, James H. 1979. "Conjectures on the Securities Industry in 1983." Pp. 29 – 39 in *Impending Changes for Securities Markets.* Ed. by Ernest Bloch and Robert A. Schwartz. Greenwich, Conn.: JAI Press.

Lorie, James H. and Richard Brealey. 1972. "Introduction: A Startling Idea – Current Prices Reflect What Is Knowable." Pp. 101 – 108 in *Modern Developments in Investment Management.* Ed. James H. Lori and Richard Brealey. New York: Praeger.

Lorie, James H. and Lawrence Fischer. 1965. "Knowledge Makes a Difference." *Financial Analysts Journal,* 21 (November), 118 – 120.

Lorie, James H. and Mary Hamilton. 1973. *The Stock Market: Theories and Evidence.* Homewood, Ill.: Richard D. Irwin.

Loss, Louis. 1961. *Securities Regulation.* 3 vols. Boston: Little, Brown.

——. 1976. *Commentary on the Uniform Securities Act.* Boston: Little, Brown.

Lowi, Theodore J. 1979. *The End of Liberalism,* revised edition. New York: W. W. Norton.

Lowry, Richie P. 1982. "Doing Good While Doing Well." *The Social Report,* 3, 2 – 3.

Lybecker, Martin E. 1977 a. "Bank Sponsored Investment Management Services: A Legal History and Statutory Interpretative Analysis – Part I." *Securities Regulation Law Journal,* 5, 110 – 164.

Lybecker, Martin E. 1977 b. "Bank Sponsored Investment Services: A Legal History and Statutory Interpretative Analysis – Part II." *Securities Regulation Law Journal,* 5, 195 – 258.

MacCauley, Fred R. 1951. *Short-Selling on the New York Stock Exchange.* New York: Twentieth Century Fund.

MacIntyre, Alasdair. 1966. *A Short History of Ethics.* New York: Macmillian.

MacNeill, Earl S. 1950. "New York's Trust Investment Statute." *Banking,* 42, 54.

Malkiel, Burton G. 1975. *A Random Walk Down Wall Street.* New York: W. W. Norton.

Marees, Judith W. 1979. *The Use of Pension Fund Capital: Its Social and Economic Implications – Some Background Issues.* Washington, D. C.: Government Printing Office.

Martin, H. S. 1913. *The New York Stock Exchange and the "Money Trust."* New York: n. p.

Matherly, Walter J. 1931. "Present and Probable Future Needs for Collegiate Business Education." *Journal of Business*, 4 (July), 45 – 63.

Mayer, Martin. 1955. *Wall Street: Men and Money*. New York: Harper & Brothers.

——. 1969. *New Breed on Wall Street*. New York: Macmillian.

——. 1974. *The Bankers*. New York: Ballentine Books.

McCaffrey, David P. 1982. "Corporate Resources and Regulatory Pressure: Toward Explaining a Discrepancy." *Administrative Science Quarterly*, 27, 398 – 419.

McGeary, M. Nelson. (1940) 1966. *The Development of Congressional Investigative Power*. New York: Octagon Books.

Merton, Robert K. 1936. "The Unanticipated Consequences of Purposive Social Action." *American Sociological Review*, 1, 894 – 904.

Miliband, Ralph. 1969. *The State in Capitalist Society*. London: Weidenfeld & Nicholson.

Mintz, Ilse. 1951. *Deterioration in the Quality of Foreign Bonds Issued in the United States, 1920 – 1930*. New York: National Bureau of Economic Research.

Mizruchi, Mark S. 1982. *The American Corporate Network, 1904 – 1974*. Beverly Hills, Calif.: Sage.

Moley, Raymond. 1939. *After Seven Years*. New York: Harper & Brothers.

——. 1966. *The First New Deal*. New York: Harcourt, Brace & World.

Molodovsky, Nicholas. 1959. "Valuation of Common Stocks." *Financial Analysts Journal*, 15 (February), 23 – 27, 84 – 99.

Moody, John. 1906. *The Art of Wall Street Investing*. New York: Moody Corporation.

——. 1919. *The Masters of Capital*. New Haven, Conn.: Yale University Press.

Murray, Roger F. 1968. *Economic Aspects of Pensions*. New York: Columbia University Press.

Nash, Gerald D. 1964. "Government and Business: A Case Study of State Regulation of Corporate Securities, 1850 – 1933." *Business History Review*, 38 (Summer), 144 – 162.

National Association of Securities Dealers. 1967. *Reprint of the Manual*. Chicago: Commerce Clearing House.

Navin, Thomas R. and Marion V. Sears. 1955. "The Rise of a Market for Industrial Securities, 1887 – 1902." *Business History Review*, 29 (Summer), 105 – 138.

Nelson, S. A. 1902. *ABC of Stock Speculation*. New York: n. p.

New York Stock Exchange. 1940. *Year Book*. New York.

——. 1955. *Year Book*. New York.

———. 1964. *Institutional Share Ownership*. New York.

———. 1967. *N. Y. S. E. Constitution and Rules*. New York: Commerce Clearing House.

———. 1976. *Annual Report*. New York.

———. 1980 – 1987. *Fact Book*. New York.

———. 1981. *Public Transaction Study, Fourth Quarter 1980*. New York.

New York City Bar Association. 1977. "Report of the Special Committee on Lawyer's Role in Securities Transactions." *The Record of the Association of the Bar of the City of New York*, 32 (May/June), 345 – 364.

Noble, H. G. S. (1915) 1975. *The New York Stock Exchange in the Crisis of 1914*. New York: Arno Press.

Nordlinger, Eric A. 1981. *On the Autonomy of the Democratic State*. Cambridge, Mass.: Harvard University Press.

Noyes, Alexander Dana. (1938) 1969. *The Market Place*. New York: Greenwood Press.

Nozick, Robert. 1974. *Anarchy, State, and Utopia*. New York: Basic Books.

Oakeshott, Michael. 1983. *On History and Other Essays*. Totowa, N. J.: Barnes & Noble.

O'Connor, James. 1973. *The Fiscal Crisis of the State*. New York: St. Martin's Press.

O'Leary, James J. 1952. "Trends of Yields on the Investments of Financial Institutions." *Law and Contemporary Problems*, 17, 26 – 44.

Olmstead, Alan L. 1976. *New York City Mutual Savings Banks, 1819 – 1861*. Chapel Hill: University of North Carolina Press.

Olson. Mancur. 1965. *The Logic of Collective Action*. Cambridge, Mass.: Harvard University Press.

Parker, Carl. 1911. "Government Regulation of Speculation." *Annals of the American Academy of Political and Social Science*, XXXVIII, 444 – 472.

Parrish, Michael E. 1970. *Securities Regulation and the New Deal*. New Haven, Conn.: Yale University Press.

Parsons, Talcott. 1968. *The Structure of Social Action*. New York: Free Press (orig. 1937).

Patterson, Solon P. 1977. "Analysts – Stand Up and Speak Out!" *Financial Analysts Journal*, (July), 16.

Payne, Wilson Fels. 1930. The Analysis and Research Department in Certain Types of Fiduciary Companies. M. A. Thesis, University of Chicago.

Pecora, Ferdinand. 1939. *Wall Street Under Oath*. New York: Simon & Schuster.

Phillips, Susan M. and J. Richard Zecher. 1981. *The SEC and the Public Interest: An Economic Perspective*. Cambridge, Mass.: MIT Press.

Poser, Norman S. 1981. "Restructuring the Stock Market: A Critical Look at the SEC's National Market System." *New York University Law Review*, 56 (November-December), 883 – 958.

Posner, Richard A. and Kenneth Scott, eds. 1980. *Economics of Corporation Law and Securities Regulation*. Boston: Little, Brown.

Poulantzas, Nicos. 1973. *Political Power and Social Classes*, trans. Timothy O'Hagen. New York: New Left Books.

Ratner, David L. 1978. *Securities Regulation*. St. Paul, Minn.: West Publishing.

Reed, Robert R. 1914. "Regulation of the Business of the Investment Banker." *Investment Bankers of America Bulletin*, 11 (July 15), 9 – 17.

Regan, Donald T. 1972. *A View from the Street*. New York: New American Library.

Rhea, Robert. 1932. *The Dow Theory*. New York: Barron's.

Rifkin, Jeremy and Randy Barber. 1978. *The North Will Rise Again*. Boston: Beacon Press.

Ripley, William Z. 1927. *Main Street and Wall Street*. Boston: Little, Brown.

Ritchie, Donald A. 1980. "Reforming the Regulatory Process: Why James Landis Changed His Mind." *Business History Review*, 54 (Autumn), 283 – 302.

Rollins, Montgomery, 1905. *A Compilation of Laws Regulating the Investment of Bank Funds*. Boston: n. p.

Roper, Elmo. 1940. *Americans' Attitudes Toward Investing*. New York: New York Stock Exchange.

Roosevelt, Franklin D. 1967. "The Commonwealth Address." *The People Shall Judge*. Vol. 2. Chicago: University of Chicago Press.

Rosenman, Samuel (ed.). 1938. *The Public Papers and Addresses of Franklin D. Roosevelt*. Vol. 2. New York: Random House.

Rowen, Harvey A. 1976. "The Securities Acts Amendments of 1975: A Legislative History." *Securities Regulation Law Journal*, 3 (Winter), 329 – 346.

Rowland, Benjamin M. 1986. "Roll the Dice and Cross Your Fingers." *New York Times Book Review*, (December 14), 35.

Rueschemeyer, Dietrich and Peter B. Evans. 1985. "The State and Economic Transformations." In *Bringing the State Back In*. Ed. Peter B. Evans, Dietrich Rueschemeyer, and Theda Skocpol. Cambridge: Cambridge University Press.

Ruml, Francis. 1928. "The Formative Period of Higher Commercial Education in American Universities." *Journal of Business*, 1 (April), 238 – 263.

Russo, Thomas A. and William K. S. Wang. 1972. "The Structure of the Securities Market – Past and Future." *Fordham Law Review*, 41, 1 – 42.

Ruykeyser, Merryle Stanley. 1928. "Wall Street's Speculative Optimism." *The Nation*, (November 14), 514 – 516.

Sachs, Walter. 1972. *Reminiscences of Walter Sachs*. Oral History Collection, Columbia University.

Sayre, Frank G. 1950. "Prudent Man Rule for Trust Investments." *Trust and Estates*, 89, 706.

Schneider, Louis, ed. 1967. *The Scottish Moralists: On Human Nature and Society* Journal. Chicago: University of Chicago Press.

Schram, Emil. 1945. "A Message to the Society." *The Analysts Journal*, 1 (April), 11 – 14.

Schudson, Michael. 1978. *Discovering the News*. New York: Basic Books.

Schultze, Charles L. 1977. *The Public Use of Private Interest*. Washington, D. C.: Brookings Institution.

Scott, Austin Wakeman. 1956. *The Law of Trusts*, 2 nd ed., 5 vols. Boston: Little, Brown.

Scott, W. Richard. 1981. *Organizations: Rational, Natural, and Open Systems*. Englewood Cliffs, N. J.: Prentice Hall.

Scully, C. Allison. 1937. *The Purchase of Common Stocks as Trust Investments*. New York: Macmillian.

Securities and Exchange Commission. 1936. *Report on the Feasibility and Advisability of the Complete Segregation of the Functions of Dealer and Broker*. Washington, D. C.: Government Printing Office.

——. 1963. *Special Study of the Securities Markets*, Parts 4 and 5. Washington, D. C.: Government Printing Office.

——. 1965 – 1986. *Annual Report*. Washington, D. C.: Government Printing Office.

——. 1971 a. *Study of Unsafe and Unsound Practices of Brokers and Dealers*. Washington, D. C.: Government Printing Office.

——. 1971 b. *Institutional Investor Study*, 5 vols. Washington, D. C.: Government Printing Office.

——. 1971 c – 1972. *Annual Report*. Washington, D. C.: Government Printing Office.

——. 1973. Policy Statement on the Structure of a Central Market System. Washington, D. C.: xerox.

——. 1976. Analysis of Financial Data of Specialists' Operations. Washington, D. C.: xerox.

——. 1978. Report of the Special Study of the Options Markets, vol. 1. Washington, D. C.: xerox.

——. 1979. Development of a National Market System. Washington, D. C.: xerox.

Seligman, Joel. 1982. *The Transformation of Wall Street.* Boston: Houghton Mifflin.

Selznick, Philip. 1957. *Leadership in Administration.* New York: Harper & Row.

Shattuck, Mayo A. 1951. "The Development of the Prudent Man Rule for Fiduciary Investment in the United States in the Twentieth Century." *Ohio State Law Journal,* 12, 491 – 521.

Shattuck, Mayo A. and Louis S. Headley. 1950. "Whither Trusteeship?" *Trusts and Estates,* 89, 92 – 95, 120 – 125.

Sheppard, C. Stewart. 1967. "The Professionalization of the Financial Analysts." *Financial Analyst Journal,* (November), 39 – 41.

Silver v. the New York Stock Exchange, 373 *U.S.* 341 (1963).

Simmons, E. H. H. 1930. "The Principal Causes of the Stock Market Crisis of 1929." *Commercial and Financial Chronicle,* (March 22), 1941 – 1943.

Sirkin, Gerald. 1975. "The Stock Market of 1929 Revisited." *Business History Review,* (Summer), 223 – 231.

Skocpol, Theda. 1980. "Political Response to Capitalist Crisis: Neo-Marxist Theories of the State and the Case of the New Deal." *Politics and Society,* 10, 155 – 202.

———. 1984. "Emerging Agendas and Recurrent Strategies in Historical Sociology." Pp. 356 – 391 in *Vision and Method in Historical Sociology.* Ed. Theda Skocpol. Cambridge: Cambridge University Press.

Skocpol, Theda and Kenneth Finegold. 1982. "Economic Intervention and the New Deal." *Political Science Quarterly,* 97, 255 – 278.

Skocpol, Theda and John Ikenberry. 1983. "The Political Formation of the American Welfare State." *Comparative Soial Research,* 6, 114 – 116.

Skowronek, Stephen. 1982. *Building a New American State.* Cambridge: Cambridge University Press.

Sloane, Leonard. 1980. *The Anatomy of the Floor.* Garden City, N. Y.: Doubleday.

Smith, Adam. 1976 (1776). *The Wealth of Nations,* ed. Edwin Cannan. Chicago: University of Chicago Press.

Smith, Edgar Lawrence. 1923. *Common Stocks as Long-Term Investments.* New York: Macmillian.

———. 1925. "Speculation and Investment." *Atlantic Monthly,* (October), 542 – 547.

Smith, James G. 1928. *The Development of Trust Companies in the United States.* New York: Henry Holt.

Sobel, Robert. 1977. *Inside Wall Street.* New York: W. W. Norton.

Solodovsky, Robert M. 1971. *Institutional Holdings of Common Stock, 1900 – 2000*. Ann Arbor, Mich.: Bureau of Business Research, University of Michigan.

Sproull, Lee S. 1981. "Beliefs in Organizations." In *Handbook of Organizational Design*. Ed. Paul C. Nystrom and William H. Starbuck, vol. 2. New York: Oxford University Press.

Stein, Leon. 1978. *Big Business*. New York: Arno Press.

Stigler, George J. 1964. "Public Regulation of the Securities Market." *Journal of Business*, 37 (April), 117 – 147.

——. 1975. *The Citizen and the State*. Chicago: University of Chicago Press.

Stoll, Hans R. 1979. *Regulation of Securities Markets*. New York: New York University Press.

Strauss, Paul. 1977. "The Heyday is Over for Analysts' Compensation." *Institutional Investor*, (October), 121 – 122, 211.

Tarascio, Vincent J. 1984. "Economic Theories of the Market: Random or Non-Random Walk." In *The Social Dynamics of Financial Markets*. Ed. Patricia A. Adler and Peter Adler. Greenwich, Conn.: JAI Press.

Thomas, Patton. 1900. "The Bucket Shop in Speculation." *Munsey's*, (October), 68 – 70.

Thompson, James D. 1967. *Organizations in Action*. New York: McGraw-Hill.

Tolchin, Susan J. and Martin Tolchin. 1983. *Dismantling America: The Rush to Deregulate*. Boston: Houghton Mifflin.

Torrance, Bascom H. 1952. "Legal Background, Trends, and Recent Developments in the Investment of Trust Funds." *Law and Contemporary Problems*, 17, 128 – 161.

Trust Bulletin. 1935. "Widening the Field of Trust Investments." (December), 22 – 25.

U. S. Census Bureau. 1972 – 1987. *Statistical Abstract of the United States*. Washington, D. C.: Government Printing Office.

——. 1976. *Historical Statistics of the United States, Colonial Time to 1970*. Washington, D. C.: Government Printing Office.

U. S. Comptroller of the Currency. 1938. *Annual Report*. Washington, D. C.: Government Printing Office.

U. S. Congress, House, Subcommittee of the Committee on Banking and Currency. 1913. *Investigation of Financial and Monetary Conditions in the United States under House Resolutions Nos. 429 and 504*. Washington, D. C.: Government Printing Office.

U. S. Congress, Senate, Committee on Banking and Currency. 1914. *Regulation of the Stock Exchange*. Washington, D. C.: Government Printing Office.

——. 1932. *Stock Exchange Practices*. Washington, D. C.: Government Printing Office.

——. 1969. *Costs of Mutual Fund Investment*. Washington, D. C.: Government Printing Office.

U. S. Congress, Senate, Subcommittee on Securities of the Committee on Banking, Housing, and Urban Affairs. 1972. *Clearance and Settlement of Securities Transactions*. Washington, D. C.: Government Printing Office.

——. 1973 a. *Securities Industry Study*. Washington, D. C.: Government Printing Office.

——. 1973 b. *Regulation of Clearing Agencies and Transfer Agents*, Hearings on S. 2058, July 11 – 12, 1973. Washington, D. C.: Government Printing Office.

U. S. Congress, Senate, Subcommittee on Reports, Accounting, and Management of the Committee on Government Operations. 1977. *The Accounting Establishment*. Washington, D. C.: Government Printing Office.

Untermyer, Samuel. 1915. "Speculation on the Stock Exchanges and Public Regulation of the Exchanges." *American Economic Review*, 5 (March), 24 – 68.

Valentine, Jerome P. 1975. *Investment Analysis and Capital Market Theory*. Charlottesville, Va.: Financial Analysis Research Foundation.

Van Antwerp, W. C. 1913. *The Stock Exchange From Within*. Garden City, N. Y.: Doubleday, Page.

Vanderpool, Waid R. 1966. "Whither the Prudent Man?" *Barron's*, (April 18), 5.

Vernon, Raymond. 1941. *The Regulation of Stock Exchange Members*. New York: Columbia University Press.

Walker, R. S. 1939. "Investment of Trust Funds under the So-called 'Massachusetts Rule'." *Connecticut Bar Journal*, 13, 237 – 253.

Warshow, H. T. 1924. "The Distribution of Corporate Ownership in the United States." *Quarterly Journal of Economics*, 39 (November), 15 – 38.

Weber, Max. 1958. *The Protestant Ethic and the Spirit of Capitalism*, trans. Talcott Parsons. New York: Scribner's.

——. 1961. *General Economic History*. New York: Collier-Macmillian.

Weeden, Donald E. 1972. *A Stock Exchange Trading System for the Future*. New York: Weeden & Co.

Weissman, Rudolph L. (1939) 1975. *The New Wall Street*. New York: Harper Brothers.

Welles, Chris. 1975. *The Last Days of the Club*. New York: Dutton.

Wendt, Paul Francis. 1941. The Classification and Financial Experience of the Customers of a Typical New York Stock Exchange Firm from 1933 to 1938. Ph. D. dissertation, Columbia University.

Werner, Walter. 1975. "Adventure in the Social Control of Finance: The National Market System for Securities." *Columbia Law Review*, 75 (November), 1233 – 1298.

White, Harrison. 1981. "Where Do Markets Come Frome?" *American Journal of Sociology*, 87 (November), 517 – 547.

White, Horace. (1909) 1913. *Report of the Governor's Committee on Speculation in Securities and Commodities.* Pp. 415 – 446 in W. C. Van Antwerp's *The Stock Exchange From Within.* Garden City, N. Y.: Doubleday.

Whitely, Richard. 1986. "The Transformation of Business Finance into Financial Economics: The Role of Academic Expansion and Changes in U. S. Capital Markets." *Accounting, Organizations, and Society*, 11, 2, 171 – 192.

Whitesell, William E. and Janet F. Kelly. 1970. "Is the Glass-Steagall Act Obsolete?" *The Banking Law Journal*, 87 (May), 387 – 403.

Whitney, George. 1972. *Reminiscences of George Whitney.* New York: Oral History Collection, Columbia University.

Willis, H. Parker and Jules I. Bogen. 1929. *Investment Banking.* New York: Harper & Brothers.

Williams, John Burr. (1938) 1958. *The Theory of Investment Value.* Amsterdam: North-Holland Publishing.

Williamson, Oliver. 1975. *Markets and Hierarchies.* New York: Free Press.

Wilson, James Q. 1980. *The Politics of Regulation.* New York: Basic Books.

Wilson, Thomas. 1976. "Sympathy and Self-Interest." Pp. 73 – 99 in *The Market and the State.* Ed. Thomas Wilson and Andrew S. Skinner. Oxford: Clarendon Press.

Wolfe, Alan. 1977. *The Limits of Legitimacy.* New York: Free Press.

Wyckoff, Richard. (1930) 1968. *Wall Street Adventures through Forty Years.* Westport, Conn.: Greenwood Press.

Zald, Mayer. 1978. "On the Social Control of Industries." *Social Forces*, 57 (September), 79 – 102.

Zysman, John. 1983. *Governments, Markets, and Growth.* Ithaca: Cornell University Press.

Author Index

Subject Index

de Gruyter Studies on North America
Politics, Government, Society, Economy, and History

Series Editors
Willi Paul Adams, Helga Haftendorn, Carl-Ludwig Holtfrerich, Hans-Dieter Klingemann, and *Knud Krakau* (Freie Universität Berlin)

Advisory Board
David P. Calleo (School of Advanced International Studies of the Johns Hopkins University, Washington, D. C.), *Robert Dallek* (UCLA), *Robert J. Jackson* (Carleton University, Ottawa), *Roger Morgan* (London School of Economics), *Richard Sylla* (North Carolina State University, Raleigh), *Martin P. Wattenberg* (University of California, Irvine)

It is the aim of this new series to facilitate transatlantic scholarly communication in the areas of politics, government, society, economy, and history of the United States and Canada. The series is designed to foster North American research in English, and will include original works and English translations of authoritative North American Studies. Special consideration will be given to:
1. Studies on the relations between the United States or Canada and other, especially European, countries;
2. Studies comparing developments in the United States or Canada with those in European countries;
3. Analyses of historical or current socioeconomic and political phenomena in North America.

In preparation:

Vol. 1

The Reagan Administration: Toward a Reconstruction of American Strength
Edited by *Helga Haftendorn* and *Jakob Schissler*
1988. 15.5 x 23 cm. Approx. 320 pages. Cloth.
ISBN 3 11 011380 5; 0-89925-413-6 (U. S.)

Vol. 3

Economic and Strategic Issues in U. S. Foreign Policy
Edited by *Carl-Ludwig Holtfrerich*
1989. 15.5 x 23 cm. Approx. 288 pages. With 15 tables. Cloth.
ISBN 3 11 011793 2; 0-89925-535-3 (U. S.)

Walter de Gruyter · Berlin · New York

Technological Innovation and Human Resources

An international bi-annual book series

Edited by *Urs E. Gattiker* and *Laurie Larwood*

This new book series offers not only background research but also future implications for academics as well as practitioners about
- micro and macro effects of computerization
- organizational structure and innovation
- R & D issues
- new technologies for the workplace
- productivity and profitability
- human resource management in the age of technology
- career implications at various levels
- employee acceptance/resistance
- end-user considerations, and
- government and policy decisions.

The volumes contain conceptual articles, deal with practical application issues and attempt to be a guide as technology permeates the workplace more and more. A strong emphasis on multidisciplinary perspectives makes this series an essential reference work for the fields of industrial psychology, organizational behavior and theory, management, sociology, education and public policy. Each book covers specific subject areas.

Vol. 1

Managing Technological Development: Strategic and Human Resources Issues
Edited by *Urs E. Gattiker* and *Laurie G. Larwood*
1988. 15.5 x 23 cm. VIII, 232 pages. Cloth.
ISBN 3 11 011084 9; 0-89925-414-4 (U. S.)

In preparation:

Vol. 2

Computers and End-User Training

Walter de Gruyter · Berlin · New York